The Holy Odu

A Collection of verses from the 256 Ifa Odu with Commentary

Awo Fategbe Fatunmbi Fasola
Stuart B. Soto

2nd Printing

Copyright © 2014 Fategbe Fatunmbi Fasola
All rights reserved.
ISBN: 10: 1508633045
ISBN-13: 978-1508633044

Introduction: African Thought and Worldview 1

Chapter 1   Yoruba Theology 23

Chapter 2   Interpreting the verses of Ifa 81

Chapter 3 Sixteen Meji Odu 98

    Èji Ogbè 98

    Òyèkú Méji – 103

    Ìwòrì Méji – 106

    Òdí Méji – 110

    Ìrosùn Méji – 114

    Òbàrà Méji 124

    Òkànràn Méji 132

    Ògúndá Méji 139

    Òsá Méji 144

    Ìká Méji – 149

    Òtúrúpòn Méji 153

    Òtùrá Meji – 159

    Ìretè Meji 167

    Òsé Méji – 170

    Òfún Méji – 176

Book of Ogbe 180

    Ogbe Oyeku 180

    Oyeku Ogbe 181

    Ogbe Iwori – 182

Iwori Ogbe	183
Ogbe Odi	186
Odi Ogbe	187
Ogbe Irosun	189
Irosun Ogbe	190
Ogbe Owonrin	192
Owonrin Ogbe	197
Ogbe Obara	199
Obara Ogbe	200
Ogbe Okanran	202
Okanran Ogbe	204
Ogbe Ogunda – a.k.a. Ogbe Yonu	205
Ogunda Ogbe	208
Ogbe Osa	209
Osa Ogbe	211
Ogbe Ika	212
Ika Ogbe	214
Ogbe Oturupon	216
Oturupon Ogbe	217
Ogbe Otura	218
Otura Ogbe	219
Ogbe Irete	221
Irete Ogbe	222

- Ogbe Ose ... 224
- Ose Ogbe ... 226
- Ogbe Ofun ... 229
- Ofun Ogbe ... 230

Book of Oyeku ... 232
- Oyeku Iwori – ... 232
- Iwori Oyeku ... 233
- Oyeku Odi ... 234
- Odi Oyeku ... 235
- Oyeku Irosun ... 237
- Irosun Oyeku ... 239
- Oyeku Owonrin ... 240
- Owonrin Oyeku ... 242
- Oyeku Obara ... 242
- Obara Oyeku ... 244
- Oyeku Okanran ... 245
- Okanran Oyeku ... 246
- Oyeku Ogunda ... 246
- Ogunda Oyeku ... 248
- Oyeku Osa ... 250
- Osa Oyeku ... 252
- Oyeku Ika ... 254
- Ika Oyeku ... 256

Oyeku Oturupon	256
Oturupon Oyeku	258
Oyeku Otura	259
Otura Oyeku	261
Oyeku Irete	263
Irete Oyeku	264
Oyeku Ose	265
OSE OYEKU	267
Ofun Oyeku	269
Book of Iwori	273
Iwori Od	273
Odi Iwori	274
Iwori Irosun	275
Irosun Iwori	277
Iwori Owonrin	278
Owonrin Iwori	278
Iwori Obara	279
Obara Iwori	280
Iwori Okanran	281
Okanran Iwori	283
Iwori Ogunda	284
Iwori Osa	286
Osa Iwori –	287

Iwori Ika ... 288

Ika Iwori ... 289

Iwori Oturupon ... 290

Oturupon Iwori ... 291

Iwori Otura ... 291

Otura Iwori ... 292

Iwori Irete ... 295

Irete Iwori ... 296

Iwori Ose ... 297

Ose Iwori – ... 298

Iwori Ofun ... 300

Ofun Iwori ... 301

Book of Odi ... 303

Odi Irosun ... 303

Irosun Odi – ... 304

Odi Owonrin ... 306

Owonrin Odi ... 307

Odi Obara ... 308

Obara Odi ... 309

Odi Okanran ... 310

Okanran Odi ... 310

Odi Ogunda ... 311

Ogunda Odi ... 312

Odi Osa	313
Osa Odi	314
Odi Ika	315
Ika Odi	315
Odi Oturupon	316
Oturupon Odi	317
Odi Otura	318
Otura Odi	319
Odi Irete	321
Irete Odi	322
Odi Ose	323
Ose Odi	324
Odi Ofun	325
Ofun Odi	325
Book of Irosun	328
Irosun Owonrin	328
Owonrin Irosun	329
Irosun Obara	330
Obara Irosun	330
Irosun Okanran	331
Okanran Irosun	332
Irosun Ogunda	333
Ogunda Irosun	334

- Irosun Osa 335
- Osa Irosun 336
- Irosun Ika 337
- Ika Irosun 338
- Irosun Oturupon 338
- Oturupon Irosun 339
- Irosun Otura 340
- Otura Irosun 341
- Irosun Irete 343
- Irete Irosun 343
- Irosun Ose 344
- Ose Irosun 345
- Irosun Ofun 346
- Ofun Irosun 347

Book of Owonrin 349

- Owonrin Obara 349
- Obara Owonrin 350
- Owonrin Okanran 351
- Okanran Owonrin 352
- Owonrin Ogunda 353
- Ogunda Owonrin 354
- Owonrin Osa 356
- Osa Owonrin 357

- Owonrin Ika 358
- Ika Owonrin 359
- Owonrin Oturupon 360
- Oturupon Owonrin 361
- Owonrin Otura 362
- Otura Owonrin 362
- Owonrin Irete 363
- Irete Owonrin 364
- Owonrin Ose 365
- Ose Owonrin 366
- Owonrin Ofun 367
- Ofun Owonrin 368

Book of Obara 370
- Obara Okanran 370
- Okanran Obara 371
- Obara Ogunda 372
- Ogunda Obara 372
- Obara Osa 374
- Osa Obara 375
- Obara Ika 376
- Ika Obara 377
- Obara Oturupon 378
- Oturupon Obara 379

Obara Otura	380
Otura Obara	381
Obara Irete	382
Irete Obara	383
Obara Ose	384
Ose Obara	385
Obara Ofun	386
Ofun Obara	387

Book of Okanran 389

Okanran Ogunda	389
Ogunda Okanran	390
Okanran Osa	393
Osa Okanran	394
Okanran Ika	395
Ika Okanran	396
Okanran Oturupon	397
Oturupon Okanran	398
Okanran Otura	399
Otura Okanran	400
Okanran Irete	401
Irete Okanran	402
Okanran Ose	403
Ose Okanran	404

- OkAnrAn Ofun ... 405
- Ofun Okanran ... 406

Book of Ogunda ... 411
- Ogunda Osa ... 411
- Osa Ogunda ... 412
- Ogunda Ika ... 413
- Ika Ogunda ... 414
- Ogunda Oturupon ... 415
- Oturupon Ogunda ... 416
- Ogunda Otura ... 419
- Otura Ogunda ... 420
- Ogunda Irete ... 420
- Irete Ogunda ... 422
- Ogunda Ose ... 423
- Ose Ogunda ... 424
- Ogunda Ofun ... 425
- Ofun Ogunda ... 426

Book of osa ... 429
- Osa Ika ... 429
- Ika Osa ... 430
- Osa Oturupon ... 431
- Oturupon Osa ... 433
- Osa Otura ... 434

Otura Osa 435

Osa Irete 436

Irete Osa 437

Osa Ose 438

Ose Osa 440

Osa Ofun 441

Ofun Osa 442

Book of Ika 445

Ika Oturupon 445

Oturupon Ika 446

Ika Otura 447

Otura Ika 448

Ika Irete 449

Irete Ika 450

Ika Ose 451

Ose Ika 452

Ika Ofun 453

OFUN IKA 454

Book of Oturupon 456

Oturupon Otura 456

Otura Oturupon 457

Oturupon Irete 458

Irete Oturupon 459

Oturupon Ose	460
Ose Oturupon	462
Oturupon Ofun	463
Ofun Oturupon	465
Book of Otura	469
Otura Irete	469
Irete Otura	470
Otura Ose	471
Ose Otura	472
Otura ofun	473
Ofun Otura	474
Book of Irete	477
Irete Ose	477
Ose Irete	478
Irete Ofun -	480
Ofun Irete	481
Book of Ose	485
Ose Ofun	485
Ofun Ose	486

DEDICATION

I dedicate this book to my ancestors, who have lead me down this road, to them I give the highest praise. For my mother, who loved me like no other, and my father who showed me what character looks like. To my elder and good friend Baba Falokun I thank you for being my inspiration and for your great assistance. My good friend, Ayele Kumari, who pushes and prods and assists from her soft heart. To Fasola Faniyi Babatunde, whose support and teachings have been integral to my continued study. To all those who have supported my efforts over the years, I give thanks and praise. Ifa a gbe wa!

INTRODUCTION: AFRICAN THOUGHT AND WORLDVIEW

By Iyanifa Iyafunfun Fayele Faseguntunde
(Ayele Kumari, PhD.)

Indigenous faiths of Africa hold within them the roots of our past, the healing for our now, and the path to a future of peace. These traditions grew out of the wisdom of the first humans on the planet. The ancestors and the ancestral traditions are the crux of African thought and world view. Recognizing the continuity of life through the cycle of birth, life, death, and rebirth, the ancients understood that we are spiritual beings who who experience human life for a time only to return to the place we came from after life is over. There, we continue to exist in our original form until which time we choose to come back and experience another incarnation. The ancestral world is recognized as just as real as the one of gross matter. So real in fact, the idea of maintaining the connection pervades throughout the entire continent as the foundation for family and community.

The ancestors are recognized as those who are the first line of appeal and defense in our world. They are there, still loving and guiding us from the other side just as they did while living here. However, they are not viewed as "holy" or to be worshiped as a supernatural power. Instead, they are to be honored if they have lived an honorable life. They also are recognized as having greater access in ways we cannot have with our human bodies. They can see us but we cannot see them. That ability gives them insight into what others around us may be doing for or against our interest. In this way, they have the insight to warn us when something is amiss. They can see the bigger picture whereas we may only be able to see a very tiny view. It can be seen in terms of a multidimensional world in that we live in the 3rd dimension of gross matter, influenced by the senses, time and space and the ancestral world is where we transition to the 4th or 5th dimension amid a world comprised more of thought and mind. Mastery of telepathic thought allows them to be able to communicate with us even if we are not aware it is them speaking. Likewise, they are able to communicate and influence others through the same process when appealing on our behalf. In this way, it is helpful to have a relationship with one's ancestors for very practical reasons in addition to spiritual ones.

Feeding the ancestors allow us to meet between worlds. They don't need food to survive. Instead, the food carries a lower vibration that allows them to have a greater impact on this side. It gives them fuel to impact this world. Regular offerings of food and drink to the ancestors is a key component of traditional spiritual practice along with our prayers to them and for them. In other words, we support them to support us. They require our prayers to lift them up in their world.

Ancestors also offer teachings to us that can surpass our present knowledge. Through those who led exemplary lives or did important work on earth, they can teach us to do the same and assist us. So, Africans remember ancestors in thought and deed so that we may learn from their lives and use those lessons to support our own.

Communicating through dreams is a primary means through which knowledge is shared between the world of the living and the ancestral world. Dreams are often considered a sacred technology that is used to obtain information that is otherwise hard to find or verify. Dreams are an inherent part of indigenous knowledge systems in that they offer insight into ourselves, our past, our future, and the way messages are relayed from ancestors and divinities. The metaphors and sometimes direct messages help guide us in our waking life as an oracle. To that end, our ancestors took great measures to improve the means of communication between worlds in order to receive guidance. Everything from the metaphor of nature to bones, to contemplation of the cycles of the seasons, changing stars and night sky, the animal world, etc., was used to measure what was happening on earth as well as to fortell what might be coming down the line. Subtle messages were gained through quiet observation and inner reflection.

Through the sacred technology of indigenous knowledge systems, our ancestors brought forth binary oracles as a means to communicate with source, the ancestral world, and to reflect nature. It became our foundation in mathematics, physics, biology, ecology, psychology, chemisty, and community. It gave way to pyramids and complicated cosmological configurations of stone megaliths that mapped out the heavens. Understanding the dance of day and night, sun and moon, shadow and light, the binary configurations taught us how to map out everything on earth and heaven. All things that were, are, or will be are found in these binary codes. Reflecting the changes identified in the lunar phases from new moon to full moon from the vantage point outside the earth, sixteen phases or lunar days marks a complete cycle.

Our relationship with the earth and nature is guided by them as well. Throughout Africa each ethnic group mapped these codes and merged them with their ethnic history and tradition. Sangoma in South Africa call their system Hakata. Four wooden tablets thrown to produce sixteen codified answers. Those answers may be thrown on a four quadrant map of the world to produce a variety of answers. Bones and seeds may be added overtime to create a basket of bones known by Lembe as the *Mind of God* where all things can be seen. In Madagascar, the Skiddy oracles map out sixteen codes on to sixteen areas of life to give a full scope of a person's life, including the best occupations for him or her, things to watch out for, as well as solutions to forseen problems.

Four tablet Hakata

Ancient Egypt's binary oracles called the book of fate was uncovered during a raid of the tombs in the Valley of the Kings. Dated to at least 5000BC, these oracles were already in full use and had even been simplified by invaders to a system of 32 principles (16x2) by 32 categories. Also included in this ancient text is how to actually use the oracle itself. It is noted that the use is described the same way it is used in sand divination in which the binary codes are drawn in West Africa.

By marking random lines that produce odd or even numbers, the binary codes emerge from them. These oracles were documented by Babastis, a priest of Tehuti who gave instruction to its use and interpretations. Finally stolen out of the tombs by Napoleon, these same oracles were used by him to strategize his pursuits and renamed under his name. Babastis, however is a name depicting a praise name for Tehuti which was Baba. The name is related to the word baboon which was an animal totem symbolizing wisdom because the baboon was used to collect palm nuts high in the trees and also chanted the word of power "hu" (also hidden within Tehuti's name) when gazing at the moon. Tehuti's priesthood derived from Seshat, a predynastic goddess of wisdom whose praise name was Sa Fekh-t and who guided the mystery system in Ancient Egypt. She was also known as a side of Maat, a goddess of truth and justice. Seshat is identified by the palm leaf she wears on top of her head signifying her wisdom. As new priesthoods emerged in Kemet, she became joined with Tehuti in marriage and their priesthood became one. Some have suggested that the true Metu Neter (Word of God) is the mysterious coded language of the oracles which were the first use of the written word.

Tehuti and Seshat shown on Temple of Luxor (above) Seshat with Palm Leaf (below)

Awo Fategbe Fatunmbi Fasola

Metu Neter- Binary Language Code in the Egyptian Mysteries

1   THE BOOK   OF FATE.

As the glorious sun eclipseth the light of the stars, so will be accounted the partner of thy bed the fairest among women.	
She shall have sons and daughters.	
Thy friend is in good health; his thoughts are, at present, bent on thee.	
Thou hast no enemies, who can in any degree injure thee.	
Choose that for which thy genius is best adapted.	
Set not thy mind on searching after that which hath been hidden; but attend diligently to the duties of thy calling.	
Choose right trusty companions for thy intended journey, and no ill can befal thee.	
Despair not: thy love will meet its due return.	
Take not the advice of ignorant pretenders to the art of healing, but apply, at once, to the fountain head of knowledge.	
Thy husband will follow arms.	
Look for the approbation of the virtuous, and heed not the evil report of the wicked.	
O man! be prepared for any change of fortune which may happen.	
It signifieth a speedy marriage.	
Though fortune now turn her back upon thee; thine own exertions will soon enable thee to triumph over her capricious humour.	
Bestow careful culture on the sapling, and when the tree arriveth at maturity, it will produce good fruit.	
Let not busy and meddling persons, who call themselves friends, disturb the happiness of the married pair.	

Page from the Book of Fate reflecting Binary star

The relevance of this history is demonstrated by the use of the palm nuts in Ifa along with the name Baba as in Babalawo which means "Father of the Mysteries" in the Yoruba tradition. While there are conflicting viewpoints as to whether Ifa came out of Kemet or was cultivated on the land of West Africa, what is certain is that they are both extensions of African Indigenous Wisdom and offer a long historical view of its use on the continent.

West Africa finds the use of the sixteen mother principles in the traditions of Ifa/Afa/Fa which is practiced from Nigeria to Benin, Togo, Ghana, to Senegambia. Each ethnic group translates the 256 binary codes through their own ethnic history, culture, divinities, ancestral lineages, ecology, and proverbs.

Ifa, from the Yoruba stands out because of the massive oral tradition that contains thousands of verses and stories that make up the Ifa literary Corpus found within the 256 Odus. To scale that information into perspective, each odu is a book or chapter in itself. The Bible has 66 books and the Quran has 114 chapters or Suras. The Ifa literary corpus has 256 books or chapters, more than four times the content in the Bible and more than twice the content of the Quran! What is more fascinating is that its contents were all memorized (it is an oral corpus)! The Ifa literary Corpus is considered a living history; verses are still being added by its priests as history and evolution unfold across the globe.

To document all of it may very well be an impossible feat given its magnitude and extent. Much has probably already been lost to ancient Priests who carried the old ways. Islam's 800 year history in Africa and the influence of Christian missionaries surly made an impact on the tradition and some of the interpretations. While some have speculated as to if Islam brought Ifa to the contentment, it is morely that Ifa grew organically out of Africa due to its long history of use in Africa and Egypt for over 5000 years. This was long before the advent of Islam in 603AD and its migration into Africa 800 years ago.

African World Oracles reflecting Intercontinental African Thought

What we can find through these common African ethnicities are core principles that become guiding truths in relationship to how we relate to our source, ourselves, nature, and how we view our existence. These core themes transcend ethnic boundaries to link a wider process of evolutionary African thought. Some of those core principles lie in the following ideas and principles:

Everything is predicated on natural law and a vital force that permeates all. The oracles express the dance of natural law, vital force, and its expression in the outer world. In nature, there are two forces. One is potential which allows energy to be stored up and reserved and one is kinetic which allows for energy to be outwardly expressed. These forces can also be described as active and receptive, assertive and yielding or yin and yang. We can see this energy expressed further in the following page:

Kinetic	Potential
Sympathetic	Parasympathetic
day	night
heaven	earth
external	internal
hot	cold
dry	moist
masculine	feminine
Light	dark
Superficial	deep
Known	Unknown
Individual	Indivisible

All energy is contained within these two forces. These forces are expressed as assertive kinetic energy of the singular line or dot and the yielding energy of the double lines or dots.

The Igbo express this idea through its principle of the Mystical "O" as expressed by Dr. John Anenechukwu Umeh in *After God Is Dibia vol 2*.

He notes that this Mystical "O" is the source through which two complementary opposites emerge that lay the foundation from oneness to duality in this world and that there is a constant play between the two.

Dr. Umeh asserts further that this cosomogy reflects that :
1. The only certainty about life is change and nothing is permanent.
2. When a force reaches a climax or becomes old, it changes to its opposite because there can be no vacuum in Nature.

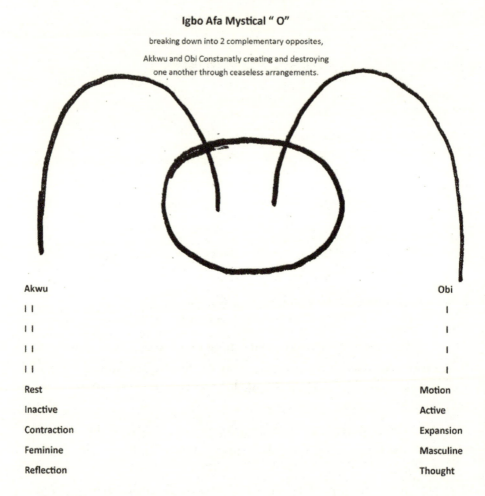

The law of the development of the universe is expressed through nature itself. Everything is first birthed out of darkness and this darkness is called the "womb of existence." This womb can be described as the black hole, the heavens, the sum total of noumenal and phenomenal worlds, primordial waters of space, etc. Within this primordial womb, this oneness, lay infinite possibilities for expression.

That womb is expressed as Olodumare in Yoruba, Mawu in Fon, Chineke in Igbo, Nut in ancient Kemet, Mumbi in Kikuyu and Ataa-Naa Nyonmo in GaDangme. This womb then gave birth to twins male and female or strong and yielding energy and these strong and yielding energies became the polarities expressed in the world as complementary opposites. Neither good or bad better or worse, but natural expressions of energy within all things.

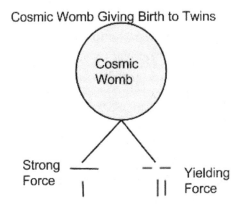

African Cosmology relates its symbolism to the natural elements around it and the most basic element is that of the family so these polarity twins when doubled to be strong can be expressed as Mother and Father of the family. While these are expressed as the core family it is important to keep in mind that this is simply a description of energy and is not to imply strict application to men and women. To do so will severely limit your understanding and application of the principles. Each are within us and in everything.

Mother and Father will then produce children which are a son and a daughter. These become the basis of the lines used in the signs. They reflect at their core level the basic family structure and core elements.

I (Father)   I I (Mother)   I (Son)   I I (Daughter)
I   I I   I I   I

The symbolism that is inherent within the signs further demonstrates the relationship in that the Father lines resemble the shape of a male body in straight lines and the mother resembles the body of a woman with two breasts and wide hips, creating either a rounded appearance or an hourglass. The son resembles a penis and testicles at the bottom and the daughter resembles two ovaries and a vaginal canal.

As we begin to contemplate the nature of the lines further, we will see that the ancients used the lines as metaphors or symbols to express its meaning. These forces can further be expressed within the natural cycle of life and the womb as it relates to the four elements that can be related to as seasons, elements, directions, body parts, the cycles of life, the passage of day and night, and the spiritual forces between heaven and earth. In the oracle itself, these four directions represent the four phases of the moon. The New moon, Waxing moon, Full moon, and Waning moon.

In addition it is replicated by the sun's relationship to the earth in the winter and summer solstices and the spring and fall equinoxes. The Kikongo and Kemetic further elaborate on this as the stages of the development of the earth and its people. In the book *The Cosmology of the Bantu Kongo* the colors red, black, yellow, and white reflect the process of the sun from sunrise, noon, afternoon, and sunset.

These four directions can be found on the opon Ifa (divining board) reflecting a similar cosmology.

These ideals in nature express how African indigenous thought is demonstrated through its oracular systems. These themes are not just found in one area but throughout the continent, and it demonstrates a profound understanding of order, how to extablish it out of chaos and how to manifest it.

The Personal Deity

Within that framework, all of nature is found, and, by extension, all beings are found. Africans recognize that everything is alive and has consciousness as the earth is alive and has consciousness. To that end, all things require respect and care from the water we bathe with and drink from to the forests, to the air we breath, the fire that warms, to the healing stones and metals.

These become the forces of nature and because our bodies are made up of these same elements we find oneness with them. Copper or iron outside is reflective of copper and iron inside. Water outside is also inside of us as is fire and air. We are made of organic elements drawn from eating plants and other life, incorporating them within us to be expressed as living manifestations of these natural combinations. Spiritually, we are said to come from the heavens to earth and therefore spiritually we are stars.

This synchronicity allows us to understand that the divinities within African systems are also not separate from us but part of us, nature, and often as our nature. Whatever is done to an outside representation is reflected inside as well. We also note that with nothing as separate, our ancestral spiritual world is not separate from our living world.

Within that framework, we have that which brings it all together within our conscious state, subconscious state, and super conscious state: Our own personal divinity. Throughout African Thought is the inherent understanding that God is in everyone and each person has to look no further than within to find the divine. However, this belief should not lead to an over-identification of the individual identity. Rather, this inner divinity is a direct extension of source found within us. This personal divinity accompanies us when we incarnate on earth and guides our experiences through agreements made prior to incarnating. To that end, the personal divinity becomes the prime mover in our lives.

It is called the Ori in Yoruba, Edome in Ewe, Chi in Igbo, Sunsum in Akan, Itongo in Zulu. These are just some of the names that reflect this idea in cross cultural expressions. One way to view it in western terms may be one's conscience. To that end, one's personal divinity is reflected to be multifold residing in parts of the body; the head and the belly being primary places. Iponri is ones inner self in Yoruba and located in the belly as is the Umbellini in South Africa, and Donyeme in Ewe. It is noted in *Possession, Ecstacy, and law in Ewe Voodoo* that it is called one's deep self. This seems to be the African version of the gut instinct or the Asian "hara" where it is one's center.

This idea of the personal divinity is so prevalent that it is the guiding theme behind the divination process itself. It is seen essentially as consulting one's personal divinity to determine alignment with their destiny. In fact, the personal divinity is more important than any Orisha in one's life because it determines your possibilities and limitations this lifetime. Wande Abimbola shares in *Ifa An Exposition of Ifa Literary Corpus* the following verse in Ifa Odu Ogunda Meji:

Iku, arun, ofo egba, ese
Gbogbo won ni nyo Orunmila wo
Won nwi pe ojo kan
Ni awon o pa a
Ni Orunmila ba gbe oke Iporii re kale
Nnkan lo deruba Qrunmila,
Lo ba wale,
O bi oke iporii re leere wo

Death, disease, loss, paralysis and wickedness
were all staring at Orunmila
they said that one day
they would kill him
Orunmila then set down his divination instruments
ready to consult his Ori (soul, Consciousness)
Something frightened Orunmila,
And he came home
And consulted his Ipori (higher self) about it.

Another idea that is prevalent is the idea that since we all can find the divine within, we are all born good and blessed people. It is only our conscious choices that determine whether we experience our highest potential that was in the original plan. We utilize divination to determine the best choices that will align us with our highest destiny.

To that end, a good part of a person's success depends on his or her character, so character development is key for achieving the greatest states of success. Dr. Bonseki Fu Kiah relates in his book *Cosmology of the Bantu Kongo*, that the Kikongo relate the idea of high character and spiritual evolution through the concept of vertical beings vs horizontal beings. Horizontal beings are animals and reflect an animal nature utilizing instinct as its primary tool for addressing the world. Horizontal beings are humans who walk upright and in doing so are intended to use higher mind and reason in how they address the world. One of low character is likened to a horizontal being in that they are not walking upright and are functioning on lower mind or an "animal level." This idea is expressed in the Kemetian tradition as well when studying the divinities with both an animal nature and human one with the prime motive being to cultivate oneself beyond the animal level of existence to that of a divinity or "ascended one."

Mandhlalanga, a Bantu master teacher of the mysteries, recounts the Bantu view point of our existence and the need to develop oneself through interview in a theosophical text entitled *The Wisdom of Africa*, what he calls the " Riddle of Existence". It is expressed through the following:

The Itongo (Universal Spirit) is ALL that ever was, is, or ever shall be, conceivable or inconceivable. The Itongo is ALL things, all things are of IT; but the sum of all things is not the Itongo. The Itongo is ALL the wisdom there is, all wisdom is of IT; but all wisdom conceivable is not the Itongo. ALL substance, ALL power, ALL wisdom is of IT and IT is in them and manifest through them, but IT is also above them and beyond them, eternally unmanifest. Man who is of the Itongo can never know the Itongo while he is Man. All he can know of IT are certain manifestations which come within the range of his perceptions. The pupil is generally taught that the manifestations are three in number. Namely:

1. Universal Mind,
2. Universal Force,
3. Universal Substance or Matter.

But really there are but two manifestations, Mind and Matter. What we call Force is not a separate manifestation. It is simply certain of the lowest, or grosser grades of Mind. Force is simply that portion of Mind which endows Matter with Form. It is that portion of Mind which transmits the idea of Form to the higher grades where Consciousness dwells. Let the Pupil think and he must see that this is so. Colour, size, shape, what are they? Simply light vibrations which when passed on to the Consciousness give the idea of Form. And what is vibration? It is Force. Heat, cold, hardness, softness, varieties of taste and smell are all vibrations, and therefore also Force. If you make Force a separate manifestation, then also must you make those planes of Mind which transfer the ideas of passion or emotion separate manifestations.

In the beginning of a Cosmic Cycle the Itongo first manifested in all the many grades of mind, downward into all the grades of Matter. But at first both Mind and Matter were unindividualised. When, how, or why, only the Itongo can know. Individuality began in the highest planes of Mind -- those planes which touch on pure Spirit. Understanding of what occurred is best gained by the following conception. Think of the Cosmos, just before Individuality began, as a vast, amorphous ocean of Mind and Matter, its surface ripples and upper reaches, those planes of Mind which touch on Spirit; growing denser and denser, downward till Matter, in Etheric form, is reached; downward till Ether becomes Gas, which may be likened to the mineral-charged lower strata of the ocean; downward till gases become liquids (muddy water); finally into solids (thick mud).

The beginning of Individuality in this Cosmic Ocean may be likened to the starting of myriads of tiny "whirlpools" among the ripples of the surface (the Spiritualised Mind). These "whirlpools" under the force of a growing flood-tide, *extended deeper and deeper, till at last all strata were involved in the swirl. Thus we have Individuality set up, extending from Spiritual Mind to the Physical Plane. The "whirlpool" on the surface represents the birth of the Soul. Its extension to the muddy depths represents the Soul's descent into matter. In matter the Soul has reached the aphelion of its cycle, and now it begins its long, slow return journey. By the process of evolution it climbs slowly upward, from mineral to plant, from plant to animal, from animal to man; through all grades and states of human development, shaking off, slowly and painfully as it climbs, the gross accretions gathered during its descent; up through the lower mind to the higher, it climbs, till at last, its cycle complete, it merges with its source, the Itongo, and ceases to be Individual, being one with the ALL.*

This decent from subtle levels to gross existence is also expressed by Dr. Fu Kiau as a V or a descending triangle or pyramid. ▽ Likewise as we have seen in Egypt, Nigeria, Ghana, and even worldwide, the upright pyramid, △ as a highly spiritualized concept representing the concept of initiation to the mysteries as a means of refining one's person for the purpose of transcendence, releasing the gross forms of existence for the more subtle spiritual ones. That is to say becoming a divine being through refinement. When those two polarities are joined, we find a divine symbol found throughout the world. ✡ This symbol represents balance and wholeness as well as the descent and ascent to and from the heavens. It further mirrors the sex act and by extension the relationship of sacred sex to the idea of reaching a heavenly state.

In Ifa, many dieties are individuals who have lived on Earth and through mastery and cultivation became immortal. To that end, each person's ultimate achievement may be to become a venerated ancestor or even a diety themselves. Benard Maupoli reports in *Divination and Deity in African Religions* that Chief Bokono Gedegbe who divined for the King in the Fon Dahomey Kingdom regulated the ethical behavior and teachings of the Bokono throughout the region.

He reports:

Gedegbe knew entire levels of Fa not accessible to anyone else. These higher levels of Fa had nothing at all to say about the demigods or spirits; they were instead about the interaction of the primary cosmic elements themselves, and one was devoted to astrology. Fa, in short, works a depersonalization of the Fon cosmos.

The great fault, in the ethics that is implied in Fa philosophy, is excessive self-will. Fa is not a method of changing one's fate, but of adjusting to it (in the active, not the passive, sense). Knowing his own characteristic engrained failings, the wise man avoids subjecting himself to otherwise inevitable pitfalls. One must learn to accept one's own limits. These "limits," the Fon believe, are chosen by oneself before birth as one's destiny-soul. Maintaining a good relationship with our destiny, knowing its possibilities and inadequacies, enables us to make the very best life possible for ourselves. Ignorance of the powers bearing on us makes us entirely their victim. The fortunate and happy can push their luck too far; the unfortunate can through hopeless passivity make their lot gratuitously agonizing.

This implies the idea of going with the flow of nature as opposed to resisting nature as a means of reducing hardship and achieving one's highest destiny. Therefore, Fa ethics suggests that one's character must be aligned with one's destiny, which is a part of our being. In Ifa, according to Fasina Falade in *Ifa: Keys to its Understanding*, exemplary character is that of a sage and is identified as humility, gentleness, kindness, honesty, patience, level headedness, perseverance, the ability to endure without complaining, being respectful, and hopefulness. Cultivation of these qualities can then provide the foundation for success in life.

We find many of these suggested in the Odu Ose Iwori from the book *Iwe Fun Odu Ifa*.

Baba of Destiny (**Faith**)
Baba of Purity (**hopefulness**)
Baba of Supplication (**prayer**)
Owner of Coolness (**contententment**)
Master of Deliverance (**relief**)

Destiny the praise of name of Ori
cast Ifa divination for Ori
Hopefulness the praise name of Osanla,
cast Ifa Divination for Osanla
Supplication the praise name of Orunmila
cast Ifa divination for Orunmila
Coolness the offspring of Osun cast Ifa divination for Osun
Deliverance the praise name of Osanyin, cast Ifa for Osanyin
When they were seeking after the good place in life called perfect Ire, but while staying in different places not knowing why things had not changed to their liking.
Why is it I have Ire but still feel emptiness inside? They asked Olodumare.
Patience the offspring of Olodumare,
Cast divination for the five of them and told them to combine and always be working together in the same place together and the feeling of fullness and content will be theirs, enough so that it will engulf the world over, (all existence)
They were told to make ebo, large enough that as long as any person who deploys your attributes with earnest in the world will enjoy the fruits of your efforts,
They heard the ebo and performed it fully.
They praised their Awos and their Awos praised Ifa and Ifa justly praised Olodumare
Come meet us in complete satisfaction, it is in complete satisfaction that one is normally found at the feet of the King of Orisa.

Finally, the idea of transcendence and the Perfect State is suggested in the Odu Irosun Iwori when Orunmilla explains how to transcend the trappings of this world and return to your original state. Here it is explained what type of behaviors will move one forward, and which will hold one back. This idea is in direct alignment with the other intercontinental themes of humans transcending this world and returning to an immortal state. This becomes the foundation for character and the foundation for achieving our highest destiny.

Let's do things with joy
Those who wish to go may go
Those who wish to return may return
Definitely, human beings have been chosen to bring good fortune to the world.

Omniscience, the diviner of Orunmila,
divined Ifa for Orunmila,
who was told that human beings would come and ask him a particular question.
He was advised to offer a sacrifice of fishes and two hundred grains of cornmeal (agidi).
Orunmila heeded the advice and performed the sacrifice.

One day, all kinds of people, including robbers and other evildoers, gathered themselves together and went to Orunmila' to complain that they were "tired of going back and forth to earth, Orunmila! Please allow us to take refuge in heaven." Orunmila said they could not avoid going to and coming back from the earth until they had attained the good position that Odudua had ordained for every individual; only then could they reside in heaven. They asked, "What is the good position?"

Orunmila asked them to confess their ignorance. They said, "We are ignorant and would like to be given knowledge by Olodumare (olu wa)."

Orunmila said: The good position is the world. A world in which there will be full knowledge of all things, joy everywhere, life without anxiety or fear of enemies, attack from snakes or other dangerous animals, without fear of death, disease, litigation, losses, danger of accidents from water and fire, without the fear of misery or poverty, because of your inner power, good character, and wisdom. When you refrain from stealing because of the hardship the owner suffers and the disgrace with which this behavior is treated in the presence of Odudua and other good spirits in heaven, who are always friendly and often wish us well. These forces can turn their backs on you and allow you to return to the darkness of the world. Bear in mind that you will not receive any favors, and whatever is stolen will be repaid. All evil acts have their repercussions. Individually, what will be needed to attain the good position is: wisdom that can adequately govern the world as a whole; sacrifice or cultivating the habit of doing good to the poor or those who need your help; desire to increase the world's prosperity rather than destroy it. People will continue to go to heaven and return to earth after death until everyone attains the good position. There are a lot of good things in heaven that are still not available on earth and will be obtained in due course. When all the children of Odudua are gathered together, those selected to transfer the good things to the world are called eniyan, or human beings.

CHAPTER 1   YORUBA THEOLOGY

It is important to have an understanding of Yoruba theology in order to better understand the verses containe in the Ifa literary corpus known as Odu Ifa. This chapter provides a brief explanation of the Yoruba theology. Theology encompasses the theories behind the methods of a particular tradition's religious expression. It has been shown that the African continent has a consistent body of thought. Individual cultures have their particular religious expression. On the continent, these forms of expression rely on theories that are in line with the continent wide thought system. The thought system, then, is like the tree and the individual religious expressions are the branches. Here we are concerned with the theology of the Yoruba. What I am referring to as theology encompasses cosmology, ontology, epistemology, aesthetics and ethics. Theology itself is based on the idea, as expressed by Thomas Aquinas, that there are things in the world and they are in motion. Whatever is in motion must have been put in motion by another thing in motion. Aquinas holds that, "whatever is in motion must be put in motion by another," and that, "this cannot go on to infinity, because then there would be no first mover." Hence St. Thomas argues that in order to eliminate the infinite chain of motions, there must be a first mover and source of all motion, God. For the Yoruba, this "first mover," is called Olorun or Olodumare.

The Yoruba don't see their system of belief as a religion per se. Rather they see their religious system as a practical philosophy (in this book I will refer to the system as religion, understanding its limitations). To them, religious practice is not separate from culture, but is embedded in the culture and daily life. They have no generic concept of religion as a discrete field of human activity. As Frisvold (2006) states:

"Actually, Yoruba religion seems to be "religion" in the same sense as Hinduism is a religion, meaning that religion is not a very good term as it fixes what is naturally volatile in a way that hardly confines to the dynamic mutability of the belief itself. Hinduism is rightly called *santatana dharma* as a reference to the orderly cosmos and the actions man has to do that are in accordance with his or her dharma. It designates a system where man is a part of a bigger order, where the whole cosmos and creation are interrelated. Even having their rites and ways of worship it is not an institution as one find in the case of monotheistic religions. This is evident considering the many cults all of over India based upon a minor deity important for a given village. The Yoruba word for religion is *esin*. This word means, "to serve" and this term is used only when referring to Muslims or Christians. The Yoruba's on the other hand tend to denote and identity ones "religion" by referring to cult belonging. Like by using the term to designate ones religious belongingness *Elèsù*, a devotee of the *Òrìsà Èsù* and accordingly a member of his cult. The Yoruba is not using *esín* to denote their own religion, rather they use *asa ibile* or *oro*, which means "Customs of the country" or simply "Custom"." The *oro* (custom) of the White man was Christianity, but the *oro* of the natives were "*A nse Oro ile tabi baba wa*", meaning "We are performing the Established Customs of our Land and our Ancestors."

Yoruba is one of the three major and second most populous ethnic groups in Nigeria. The people occupy the southwestern part of the country stretching from the upland area to the hinter land of the Lagoon. They speak Yoruba language. The people are traditionally farmers, most of whom are now engaging in some white-collar jobs and trading activities. Like other African societies, the people were predominantly traditional worshippers who worship various gods and deities. They have the world view of a supreme being know as Olorun or Olodumare.

As descendants of a common ancestor (Oduduwa), they share a common worldview. Like many other African societies, the following five categories of religious practices can be observed, as earlier observed by Mbiti (1969):

1. God as the ultimate explanation of the genesis and sustenance of man and all things;
2. Spirits, made up of superhuman beings and spirits of ancestors;
3. Man, including human beings alive and those not yet born;
4. Animals and plants or the remainders of biological life; and
5. Phenomena and objects without biological life.

In addition to these five categories, there is a vital force, a power or energy, permeating the whole universe (ase, ashe, ache, axe). For the Yorubas, every plant, animal, inanimate object and natural phenomenon is a carrier of divine consciousness. God is the source and the ultimate controller of the vital force, but the deities are the intermediaries between man and God. The Yoruba believe all individual manifestations of consciousness can communicate. This extensionist concept, that we are connected to God, eachother, and all conscious beings, is common to many religions, and is the basis for much of the practical aspects of the religion. It is through communication through extensionism, that we pray for the help of the dieties. In addition, we can build up or strengthen our individual level of ase (power to make things happen) through communication. It is believed that this communication benefits both parties.

A few human beings are endowed with the knowledge and ability to tap, manipulate and use the vital forces, such as the medicine men, powerful women (Aje), priests and rain makers. Some use it for the good and others for the ill of their communities and fellow human beings. Those that use their power for ill purposes are considered witches or sorcerers, terms that denote anti-social behavior. In order to attain the help of dieties in the invisible realms, we make offerings (ebo). This is based on the concept of reciprocity. There are numerous rituals such as those for fertility, initiation, rites of passage, marriage and death; for rain making, planting and harvesting.

For the Yorubas, nature is not separate from the invisible realm (orun). The invisible realm is symbolized or manifested by visible and concrete phenomena and objects of nature. According to Mbiti (1969), the invisible dimension presses hard upon the visible, and the Yoruba experience that invisible universe when they look at, hear or feel the visible and tangible world. The physical and spiritual are the two dimensions of one and the same creation. For the Yoruba, it is advantageous to maintain communication with beings in the invisble realm because they can help us and make life easier in the visible realm. The Yoruba believe all that happens in the world (aiye) first is manifested in orun.

Yoruba culture is based on kinship. Yoruba believe in reincarnation (atunwa) and that we reincarnate into our same lineage. This belief along with the centrality of kinship, makes the veneration of ancestors of prime importance. It is believed that we are an ancestor reincarnated. On our path to reunification with the divine source, we pass through many life times. We come with a specific destiny each incarnation, but these specific destinies tie together. Thus it is imperative that we know our destiny. Central to Yoruba religion is the remembering of our chosen destiny which is forgotten through the trauma of rebirth. Ifa divination is about re-learning our destiny.

Yoruba view the cosmos "as a dynamic interplay of such opposites as heaven and earth, day and night, masculine and feminine, physical and metaphysical, body and soul, inner and outer, hot and cold, hard and soft, left and right, life and death, success and failure and so on." (Lawal 1996) However, the Yoruba say that the great mystery of Olorun or God, is unity. It is when Oro (the ase of God) passes into the physical realms and becomes Ela (formless ase ready to manifest) that polarities are created. It is in balancing these forces that harmony at the universal, societal and individual level is achieved. Why is it we have polarities in the universe that make it hard to achieve harmony on earth? The Òdù Òsá Méjì says: "*Ogbon kan nbe ní kùn omo àsá Ìmóràn kan nbe kìkùn omo àwòdì Òkan nínúù re Okan ninúù mi Okòòkàn níkùn ara wa Sefá fún Òrúnmìlà Ifá nlo bá àjé mulèMòrèrè Wón ni nítorìi kìnni Ò ní nìtorì kì nkan òun lègún gègèègè ni* which means: The hawk has one wisdom. The falcon possesses one knowledge. One in my mind. One in your mind. One each in our minds. These were the declarations of Ifá to Òrúnmìlà when going to enter in to a covenant with the witches at Mòrèrè. They asked him why he was doing this. He said that it was for his life to be perfectly organized." (Fáládé 1998). It would seem that the creation of polarities allows the knowledge, wisdom and understanding of Olodumare to be comparted amongst the plethora of individual consciousnesses because for one to have complete wisdom would mean our annihilation. This dividing of knowledge compels us to work together in harmony as expressed by the relationship between Orunmila and the diety Odu.

The Yoruba believe that humans are tripartite beings, made up of spirit, body and soul. Problems may arise from accumulation of negative energy or may have more supernatural origins like witchcraft, ajoogun, etc. Yoruba cosmology dictates that the universe is made up of two realities; The visible material worlds (aiye), and the invisible non-material worlds (orun). All forms of "good" and "evil" are manifestations of invisible realities. This construct infers that the causes of phenomena are supernatural, beyond human power. So there are two ideas here. One is the need to restore balance. Two is the the supernatural origin of things. This is why we appeal to entities in the invisible realm (orun). These divinities can operate in the invisible realm to rectify the problem. However, the Orisa can also afflict us if we are out of alignment with them (as forces of nature).

The Supreme Being, Olorun, is genderless. IT constitutes unity. Olodumare, an aspect of Olorun, is the portal that births the universe. Odu can be interpreted as womb or portal. Olodumare can be interpreted as the rainbow serpent who comes from the darkness of the womb. Our most powerful deity is *Odu*, a feminine diety. The earth diety, *Onile* or *Aye* is feminine too. The power of the babalawo resides in Odu, the feminine diety. As the ashe of God passes to the visible realm through Olodumare, polarities are created. The most significant being the feminine/masculine polarity; electromagnetism and gravity. elctromagnetism, or light energy, is expansive thus masculine and carries the atoms, molecules, particles of creation . It is gravity (contractive thus feminine) that pulls the elements together to create form, like stars, planets, etc. That is why for example EjiOgbe is expansive light energy and Oyeku is contractive dark energy. The balance of the two creates life. This is why we say Eji Ogbe is the father and Oyeku is the mother of all the other odus. One is not more important or better than the other. Another way to see this construct is Obatala as light and Odu as dark. It is the balance between Obatala and Odu that creates life. This construct is put in mythological poetics in the odu Ogbe Yonu:

THE HOLY ODU

...the children of eleiye (Iyami) come to say,
They say, Obatala, they say that it is good.
We are going to ask a riddle.
They say that he has to be able to answer the riddle that they shall ask.
They say that he has to be able to answer the riddle that they shall ask him now.
They say, his house will be safe,
his path will be good,
his children shall not perish,
his wives shall not perish,
nor will he perish himself,
all of the places where he extends his hand will be good.
But if he does not know this riddle,
they will not accept his pleading,
they will be forever angry with him.
But if he is able to give the answer, it is finished.
Obatala says that it is good,
He says for them to ask him this riddle
They say throw (seven times)
Obatala says catch
They ask this answer from Obatala for the seventh time.
They say, Obatala,
they say, when he says catch,
they say, what does she throw him to catch?
Ha! he says, you throw me a chicken's egg.
They say what do you have to catch it with?
Obatala says it's a wad of cotton.
They say for Obatala to throw this chicken's egg into the air.
They say for him to catch it seven times.
Once Obatala has caught it seven times,
they say is it finished now.
They say it is fine now.
They say that they are pardoned.
They say, all of you, the people's children, and you, Obatala,

> they say dance,
> they say sing
> Obatala did it, you saved the people. You saved the people...

I believe this verse, besides describing a ritual that brings peace and harmony to the community through the balancing of opposing energies and mediation, is also at another level describing poetically the larger metaphysical truth of the interplay between the light and dark, represented by Obatala and Iyami.

This metaphysical theory of the Yoruba trickles down to the social level where a balance between men and women is the greatest concern for harmony of the society. This harmony is achieved through cultural institutions that create balance; Ogboni being one of them. The institutions of egbe Ifa and egbe Iyami were also important for maintaining harmony. These two institutions were of equal power and importance politically.

Pierre Verger did research on the question of a "high god" and found that the Yoruba do not worship the "high god." There is no shrine, object, or initiation. A study of the oldest writings on the religion and older Odu verses suggests Olodumare and Olorun are not exactly synonyms. Olorun, Ol Orun. Ol is like owner of. Orun is invisible realm. Very straight forward. Olodumare. Ol odu osumare or Olo dudu osumare. There are a couple other possible elisions, however the general meaning is there - Owner of womb black rainbow serpent. Put the nouns and adjectives in proper order and you have something like owner of the dark womb from which the rainbow serpent came or something to that effect. So there is a hierarchy of beings. Olorun, Olodumare, Osumare, Obatala, orisa, etc.

Olorun as high god or source, Olodumare as the portal created by Olorun to birth the universes, and Osumare as light in the universe or the physical universe itself, Olodumare's "baby."

The cosmology of the Yoruba contains a hierarchy of Gods, with a supreme creator and minor Gods, called irunmole. The irunmole are divided between those who are mostly related to helping humans (benevolent) and that humans are able to control to some degree or at least communicate with. These irunmole include what we call Orisa (Orisha). There are also a group of irunmole that are not benevolent, are seen as volatile and unpredictable and are not communicated with. The following page is a hierarchical structure of the cosmos from Dr. Abimbola:

Yoruba Cosmology

Olodumare
Supreme God/ess [no gender]
"The one who breathed the breath of life into them"
↕
Eṣu
↕ ↕

Ajogun (Malevolent Beings) warlords against humans 200 + 1	Benevolent Beings 400 + 1
most well known are:	Oriṣa (Divinities)
Iku - death	**Ajala** - creates Ori,
Arun - disease	**Eṣu /** gatekeeper.
Ofo - loss	Ifa (Orunmila) – divination
Egba - paralysis	**Obaluaye**
Oran - big trouble	Obatala
Epe - curses	Ogun
Ewon - imprisonment	Oṣun
Eṣe All other afflictions	Ṣango
	Oya
	Obaluaye
	Yemoja
	and so on, 400+1 of them.
	Egungun (Ancestors)
	Ori (Inner Head, personal divinity)
	Eniyan (humans)
	Nature
	Animals, Birds, Trees, Rivers, Hills, Oceans, and so on.

The Yoruba cosmology is divided into a right hand side (benevolent) and a left hand side (malevolent). The High God, Olodumare, is neither good nor evil, male nor female. IT is unity. ITs contact with humans is through the Ori, Eguns and Orişa, especially Eşu and Ifa. The terms 200+1 and 400+1 does not mean 201 and 401, but denotes infinity (there is always one more). Eşu communicates with everyone. He talks with humans, the High God, the Orişa, the Egungun, and the Ajogun. Esu is conflated with evil or satan by Christians and many in the diaspora. However, The Yoruba do not think to assign a separate ultimate cause to evil since they realize that evil is an imperfection, not an entity, the absence of good or being. Evil does not require a cause. Yoruba thought has no room for such an "evil incarnate" or devil who does nothing but evil. There is no structural opposition between good and evil.

The Aje (Eniyan), also called Iyami or Eleye, deal with humans and spirits on both sides of the divide (Abimbola).

To the human, the most important are our Ori (consciousness, soul), our Egun (ancestors) and our "heavenly mates" (Egbe). The Yoruba believe our soul exists here in our bodies but also in orun. All our blessings come from our soul in orun (Iponri). No deity can help us without our Ori's consent. Thus Ori is most important, more so than Orisa. Our ancestors protect us, guide us and nurture us. Nobody cares more about you than your own mother thus ancestors are very important, more so than Orisa. Our Egbe also are very close to us and involved in our lives. Orisha then, are fourth in order of import to our lives.

The ontology (idea of being) of the Yoruba is encapsulated in the concept of Ori, variously associated with the physical head (the cranium), personal Orisa, consciousness, destiny, human soul, and ancestral guardian angel. It can be considered as the Yoruba theory of consciousness, or as the Yoruba theory of destiny, or both. In my conception, our Ori is our soul, which contains consciousness (knowledge, wisdom, thought and emotion) as well as our predetermined destiny and is our connection to source as well as all things containing consciousness. Ori is the most fundamental principle to gain insight into in order to understand Ifá. The word Ori is often translated into the phrase "To receive one self" as the word's composition "O" signifies he or her and "ri" denotes to receive. It can also mean "head" or "summit". Without Ori there is nothing, for ori is individual consciousness. Within the mystery of Ori is another mystery, "Ori Inu," our inner self; the divine spark (soul). A third component of the "Ori complex" is the "Iponri" - our higher self. It is our mirror image that resides in Orun, the Invisible Realm of the Immortals. In order to begin to understand the Ori complex, we must start at the beginning, the Yoruba creation myth.

There are variations to the myth, and in my opinion there really are two separate story lines. One is cosmogenic and the other is political. The two became entwined into the most popular version below.

Yoruba Creation Myth

Orisanla (Obatala) was the arch-divinity who was chosen by Olodumare to create a solid land out of the primordial abyss that constituted the earth and of populating the land with human beings. Olodumare (The Creator) called Obatala (Chief of White Cloth – meaning the fabric of creation) to Ikole Orun (the Realm of the Ancestors) on the day that he wanted to create dry land on the waters of the Ikole Aye (visible realm). Obatala kneeled before Olodumare and said that he did not know the awo (mystery) of creating land on Ikole Aye. Olodumare told Obatala that he would give him the ase (power) to make land on Ikole Aye (Earth). He descended from Orun into Aiye (the visible realm) on a chain, carrying a snail shell full of earth, palm kernels and a five-toed chicken. He was to empty the content of the snail shell on the water after placing some pieces of iron on it, and then to place the chicken on the earth to spread it over the primordial water by doing what chickens do, which is to scratch at the ground. According to this version of the myth, Obatala completed this task to the satisfaction of Olodumare. He was then given the task of making the physical body of human beings after which Olodumare would give them the breath of life (emi). He also completed this task and this is why he has the title of "Obarisa" the king of Orisas.

The other variant of the cosmogenic myth does not credit Obatala with the completion of the task. While it concedes that Obatala was given the task, it avers that Obatala got drunk on palm wine even before he got to the earth and he fell asleep:

Ogun took all the iworo (gold) and forged a long ewon (chain), which he flung towards Ikole Aye (earth). Obatala placed his ase (power) in a pouch and began the descent down the ewon. When he came to the last rung, he could see that he was still some distance from the primal waters.

Obatala removed the igbin (snail) shell from his pouch and sprinkled soil upon the primal waters. Then he removed the five toed etu (guinea hen) and dropped it on the land. As soon as the etu reached the soil, it started scratching the ground, spreading dirt across the surface of the primal waters. Seeing the ground had become firm, Obatala removed an ikin (palm nut) and dropped it on the land. The ikin sprouted and became a palm tree. When the palm tree grew to its full height, it reached the last ring of the iworo 'won(gold chain). Obatala was able to step from the ewon to the palm tree. After climbing down the tree, Obatala started to mold humans from the clay in the earth. As he worked, he became tired and decided that he needed a rest. Taking the fruit from the palm tree, he made palm wine and drank until he was ready to return to work. The humans that he molded while drunk did not look like the others, but Obatala did not notice and he kept drinking until he fell asleep. While Obatala slept, Olodumare gave the task of finishing Creation to Oduduwa (sometimes said to be Obatala's brother). Olodumare waited for Obatala to awaken from his drunken sleep and told him that it was taboo for Obatala to taste palm wine ever again. When Obatala saw what had happened to the humans he had created while he was drunk, he agreed to protect all children for future generations. It is said that Orunmila had warned Obatala not to get his clothes dirty, but they got dirty during his drunkeness. It was Obatala who said that he would never again let his White Cloth become soiled. To this day those that worship Obatala say, "Obatala o su n'na ala, Obatala o ji n'nu ala, Obatala o tinu ala dide, Iba Obatala," which means, "The Chief of White Cloth sleeps in white, the chief of the White Cloth awakens in white, the chief of the White cloth gets up in white, praise to the Chief of the White Cloth."

In the above interpretation, Oduduwa is the founder of the Yoruba people, nothing more, nothing less. However, in the first interpretation there is no Oduduwa. If we look at Odu, we will find mention of a feminine Oduduwa. If we analyze the name Oduduwa it is obvious that we have the word "Odu," which means womb and always is used to express the mystery of the feminine principle. Then we have "dudu" which means black or dark; and "iwa" which means character. So what we get is "character of the mystery of the dark womb." The dark womb being the source of the feminine principle, so something like "manifestation of the dark principle." It seems then, that this female entity at some time was made into the male progenitor of the Yoruba. Could this have happened when the matrilineal system was changed to patrilineal? Whatever the case may be, the making of land is a symbolic reference to the founding of the Yoruba kingdoms, and this is why Oduduwa is credited with that achievement. Oduduwa's progeny were sixteen in number and became Kings. So Oduduwa was the first king of the Yoruba nation and founded Ile Ife, the ancient capital, creating a succession of kings all related to him. Again, this version incorporates history into the creation myth. It establishes the divine nature of the founder Oduduwa. Some say that before the time of Oduduwa, the story did not involve Obatala getting drunk and Oduduwa finishing the job. However, as interesting as this debate may be, it really isn't important to the discussion of Ori.

What is important is the symbolism. The chain is representative of Ogun. How can Obatala get to earth? Ogun opens the way. Ogun pushes the creation to evolve, to move forward. Obatala arrives at Ile Ife and starts cutting his way through the brush, but can't do it with his silver cutlass – the metal is too soft. So Ogun takes over with his iron cutlass. the five toed hen represents Osun. Five is the sacred number of Osun, the Yoruba Goddess of love, fertility and abundance. In the early stages of evolution, diversity is created on the surface of the earth through the interaction, combination and re-creation of the basic elements. This diversity is an expression of the fertility and abundance manifested through the power of Osun. The palm nuts (ikin) represent Orunmila. Obatala can create the land, but needs Osun to "fertilize" it, and Ogun to create civilization. However, Ogun cannot create a polity. For this we need Orunmila, who brings the ethical foundation for society. These Orisa, in combination, represent unity and a balance of forces. Unity and balance (in a cosmos of dualities and diversity) become the central paradigm of Yoruba metaphysical thought. In Awo Fatunmbi's words:

"The world begins with one ... the one that is formed through perfect balance between the powers of expansion and contraction, light and dark, ... the balance between the masculine and feminine powers ... and that one is a microcosm of all that is..."

In addition, the palm nuts grow into the palm tree (the sacred palm of Ifa) that Obatala descends. Within the religion of Ifa, the palm tree is regarded as the sacred tree of life. Most earth-centered religions designate a particular tree to symbolize the transformation of all things as they progress through the cycles of birth, life, death, and rebirth.

Here is an excerpt from Falokun Fatunmbi on Obatala and the metaphysics of the creation myth:

Obatala is the Spirit of the Chief of the White Cloth in the West African religious tradition called "Ifa". The word Obatala is the name given to describe a complex convergence of Spiritual Forces that are key elements in the Ifa concept of consciousness. Those Spiritual Forces that form the foundation of Obatala's role in the Spirit Realm relate to the movement between dynamics and form as it exists throughout the universe. According to Ifa, dynamics and form represent the polarity between the Forces of expansion and contraction. Together, these Forces create light and darkness, which in turn sustains and defines all that is. Ifa teaches that it is the interaction between light and dark that generates the physical universe, and it is Obatala who brings this interaction into Being.

The power of Obatala is described by Ifa as one of the many Spiritual Forces in Nature which are called "Orisha". The word Orisha means "Select Head". In a cultural context, Orisha is a reference to the various Forces in Nature that guide consciousness. According to Ifa, everything in Nature has some form of consciousness called "Ori". The Ori of all animals, plants, and humans is believed to be guided by a specific Force in Nature (Orisha) which defines the quality of a particular form of consciousness. There are a large number of Orisha, and each Orisha has its own awo (mystery).

The unique function of Obatala within the realm of Orisha Awo (Mysteries of Nature) is to provide the spark of light that animates consciousness. To call an Orisha the "Chief of the White Cloth" is to make a symbolic reference to that substance which makes consciousness possible. The reference to White Cloth is not a reference to the material used to make the cloth, it is a reference to the fabric which binds the universe together. The threads of this fabric are the multi-leveled layers of consciousness which Ifa teaches exist in all things on all levels of Being. Ifa teaches that it is the ability of Forces of Nature to communicate with each other, and the ability of humans to communicate with Forces in Nature that gives the world a sense of spiritual unity. It is the understanding of this ability which gives substance to the Ifa concept of good character, and it is Obatala who guides us towards developing this understanding.

Ifa teaches that all Forces in Nature come into Being through the manifestation of energy patterns called Odu. Ifa has identified and labeled different Odu which can be thought of as different expressions of consciousness. But because consciousness itself is generated by Obatala, every Odu contains an element of Obatala's ase (power).

In metaphysical terms, this means that all of Creation is linked to Obatala as the Source of Being. Ifa teaches that all forms of consciousness contain a spark of ase (spiritual power) from Obatala, and it is this spark that links everything that is, to its shared Beginning. Western science teaches that all of Creation evolved from the light produced during the primal explosion at the beginning of time. Ifa teaches that all Creation evolved from the White Cloth of Obatala's robe.

Keep in mind that Orisa and other entities featured in Yoruba myths, itan (stories) and Odu bear deep philosophical connotations that begin at the level of the metaphysical, descending into the aesthetic and then epistemological through to ethical meanings and, eventually, to positive or negative social effects (it is easy to get caught up in the personalities themselves). Individual metaphysical phenomena come together as a unity of substances in a universe of relativistic existence (Okunmakinde). This idea is expressed in the most compelling part of the story; the Snail Shell full of earth-dust.

In the Odu Okanran Ogunda there is another version of the creation myth that is not well known. In this version, it is Orunmila who carries the snail shell full of the substance which creates land upon the primordial waters. The Snail Shell was taken from the seat of Olodumare and given to Orunmila with the authority to create the earth. In the process of creation, Orunmila dipped his hands into the snail shell and took out measures of earth-dust (this dust is called Oro, primordial matter, and the word [sound] of God) with which land was created on the primordial waters.

Odu Osa Ogunda

There-were-no-living-things
Was the priest on earth
That-which-was-suspended
But-did-not-descend
Was the priest in heaven
All-was-just-empty-space
With-no-substance
Was the priest of Mid-Air
It was divined for Aiye and Orun*
When they both exited
With no inhabitants
In the two empty snail shells,
There were neither birds nor spirits
Living in them
Odumare then created himself
Being the Primal cause
Which is the reason we call Odumare
The only wise one in aiye
He is the only cause in creation,
The only wise one in Orun,
Who created humans.
When He had no companion,
He applied wisdom to the situation
To avert any disaster.
You, alone,
The only one in Orun
Is the name of Odumare
The only wise one,
We give you thanks,

The only knowing mind,
You created man.
Listening to one side of an argument,
You judge, and all are pleased.
Ase

In another verse from Osa Ogunda, it says, "Iri tu wili tu wili la fi da ile aye, la bu da ile," which means, "Dews pouring lightly, pouring lightly, was used to create the earth world in order that goodness could come forth into existence at once." The dew drops are particles of Oro – primordial matter - contained in the snail shell (in the creation myth oro is the earth that Obatala was carrying when he descended down the chain). Once empty, the shell remains as the representation of the base of causation from which matter derived. The "goodness" speaks to eniyan – human beings. Eniyan translates as "the chosen ones." This suggests that all humans have been chosen by Olodumare to continue bringing goodness to the earth. The oro then melted and was suspended in mid-air (referred to in the above Odu verse as the "priest of mid-air"). Oro then dropped;

Oro, the cause of great concern for the wise and experienced elders

It sounds, "Ku" (making the heart miss a beat)

"Ke" (as a ponderous object hitting the ground)

"Gi" (making the last sound before silence)

and "La", with a loud cracking sound is transformed into a new state called "Ela."

Orunmila can be considered the anthropomorphic representation of Ela: Olodumare's wisdom (ogbon), knowledge (imo), and understanding (oye); the most powerful particles or elements in the earth-dust or droppings. Orunmila's connection to Ori is fundamental to the Ori complex. He is "Eleri Ipin", the deity of fate. He was present at the moment of creation, and thus knows the destiny of every Ori. He acts as the mediator between a person and their Ori through his ability to speak the words of Ifa as they relate to the individual Ori and its destiny. Ifa is the Oracle. Ela is that invisible energy that moves between the oracle and Orunmila, and between Ori and Olodumare – the umbilical cord. Ela is Oro after it hits the primordial abyss. This means that the substance of creation, when it passes from Orun to the visible realm undergoes a change; it becomes "physical" or "manifested." Oro, as primordial matter, has an innate urge to communicate:

The oro that drops from the elderly is stupendous
It was divined for oro-oro-oro
Who did not have anyone to communicate with and started groaning
HOORO, HOO-RO! (Ogbon, Imo, Oye, descend!)
Olodumare made HOO
(Ogbon, Imo, Oye)
HOO
descended to become Hoo-ro
Ela made Oro digestible and useful to human needs

Ela is the manifestation of the primal urge to communicate. It is the link between human and God; human and human; and human and the universe. This extensionistic conception, prevalent in all religions, is Oro, which manifested is Ela. Its individual manifestation is Ori. The Snail can be viewed as the principle of natural extensionism which forms a basis for that which can be seen and that which cannot; the physical Ori (your skull), and Ori-inu (consciousness, soul). There is a Yoruba phrase, Ori-Ooro, which means, "head at dawn," dawn being the beginning obviously. Thus, Ori is Oro, and Oro is Ori:

THE HOLY ODU

Ori lo nda eni
Esi ondaye Orisa lo npa eni da
O npa Orisa da
Orisa lo pa nida
Bi isu won sun
Aye ma pa temi da
Ki Ori mi ma se Ori
Ki Ori mi ma gba abodi

Ori is the creator of all things
Ori is the one that makes everything happen, before life happens
He is the Orisa that can change humans
No one can change the Orisa
Ori, the Orisa that changes the life of man with baked yam (abundance)
Aye, do not change my fate
Ori do not let people disrespect me
Ori do not let me be disrespected by anyone
My Ori, do not accept evil

This extensionist concept (from God to human), that our Ori is composed of a portion of Oro (each Ori receives a portion with its own special combination of elements contained in the earth-dust – oro - from the snail shell, thus each ori's individuality), is further elucidated in the sayings, "Ori lo da ni, enikan o d'Ori o" (It is the Head that created us; nobody created the Head), and, "Ori eni, l'Eleda eni" (one's Head is one's Creator), and also in the following oriki:

Ori lo da mi
Eniyan ko o
Olorun ni
Ori lo da mi

Ori is my Creator
It is not man

It is Olorun
Ori is my Creator

Olodumare made Hoo, which is comprised of three of the most powerful elements contained in the "earth-dust" sprinkled from the Snail shell – Ogbon (wisdom), Imo (knowledge), and Oye (understanding). "Ro" means descend, as in the chant, "Ela ro, Ela ro, Ela ro." It is said that Olodumare created Ogbon, Imo and Oye as an intermediary force for creating more beings. IT tried to find a place for them to live, but they came back to IT, humming, and Olodumare swallowed them. They hummed inside IT for millennia, so IT had to get rid of them. Olodumare ordered them to "ro" descend, saying, "hoo-ro." Oro, the solid matter, melted and was suspended in mid-air like jelly. Oro then dropped and "la" - cracked into a new state called E-la, or Ela. Ela (the Spirit of Purity) functions in the Ifa divination complex as the embodiment of Ogbon, Imo, and Oye. Ela is the recognized authoritative source of communication and explanation of the nature of Olodumare and all ITs creation (Abiodun).

Who was the first to speak?
Ela was the first to speak.
Who was the first to communicate?
Ela was the first to communicate.
Who is this Ela?
It was the Hoo which descended
That we call Ela.

In Odu Ogunda Ogbe, we find more references to Snail and Oro:
He Made Divination for the Snail in Orun
Aba she kere mu legun, Odifa fun ibikunle to ma nu kan kunle ara le

The-umbrella-tree-is-short-when-young-but-a-little-later-it-will-become-taller-than-the-roof-of-the-house. That was the name of the Awo who made divination for Ibikunle, when she was single-handedly going to populate her house by herself (Ibikunle is a praise name of the Snail and it means the one who produced enough children to fill her house). She was advised to make ebo with hen, rat and fish. She made the ebo and began to produce children to fill her house.

He Later Divined for his Friend Oro

Okon kpoki, Erigidi kpii, adita fun Oro nijo ti Oro wo orun kenge kenge.

One-sharp-sound and one-loud-sound are the names of the Awos who made divination for Oro when he was so ill that he thought he was going to die, (notice the snail is referred to as she and oro as he) when he was looking forlornly at Orun from his spot hanging in the air. He was advised to make ebo with eko, akara, rat, fish and a hen. After preparing the ebo, the Ifa priests told him to carry it on his head (ori) to Esu's shrine. He was further told that on getting to the shrine, he was to back into it and incline his head backwards in such a way that the ebo would drop on the shrine (acknowledging Esu as that liminal space between orun and aiye, dark and light).

As soon as he allowed the sacrifice to drop on the Esu shrine, while still backing up to Esu, a voice instructed him to stretch his hands and feet (hands and feet working in unison; alignment with destiny) forward. First, he stretched out his left limbs and next his right limbs (with Esu's help, he makes the transition from the invisible plane to the visible plane. Left limbs darkness, right limbs light). The moment he did that, the disease (ibi) that had afflicted his body to the point of incapacitation suddenly disappeared. From the shrine, he began to dance and sing towards the house in praise of the Awo. The Awo praised Ifa, and Ifa praised Olodumare. When he began to sing, Esu put a song in his mouth:

Ijo logo ji jo, erigidi kpii, erigidi.

Ijo logo ji jo, erigidi kpi-kpi-kpi, erigidi.

He was singing in praise of Orunmila and his two surrogates for the miraculous healing he had just experienced.

In the ese (verse) above regarding Snail, we see that Snail is also known as Ibikunle, "the one who produced enough children to fill his or her house." This is a praise name. It refers to the the Snail's role in creating everything in the universe, in this case the earth including humans. In the verse following the one about snail, regarding Oro, we find in the names of the Awo, reference to the sounds of Oro dropping and becoming Ela.

Ela speaks through Owe (proverbs, Odu, oriki, chants, ofo ase, etc.), and Aroko (coded symbolic messages- drums, sculpture, dance, song, poetry, etc.). Owe is the horse of Oro; if Oro gets lost, Owe is employed to find it. It is the Spirit of Ela who gives an awo the ase to invoke Odu and all the Spirits who manifest through the oral scripture of Ifa. The historical prophet Orunmila was an incarnation of the Spirit of Ela and the alignment of Ori with Ela is known as "returning to the time when Orunmila walked the earth." This alignment occurs as a result of consistent attention to the Ifa discipline of chanting oriki (Fatunmbi). Oro as the word of God, or in scientific terms, the big bang. Owe is how we as humans imitate that "word."

The Ori Complex

As we continue with the Yoruba creation myth, we now come to the creation of human beings. Obatala, who is equally referred to as Orisa-nla, is said to have been charged with the responsibility of sculpting the human beings - "eniyan" and designing only the body: hence his appellation a-da-ni bo ti ri (he who creates as he chooses). After finishing his work, Olodumare then breaths emi (life force) into the body. The eniyan then proceeds to Ajala-Mopin (Ajala Mopin from the elision aja-ala-mo-opin, meaning, "the dog of light brings me mystic vision"), also known as Irunmole to o nmo ipin (the divinity who moulds ipin). Ipin is that portion of oro, the "God-matter" apportioned to each Ori by Ajala-Mopin. Ipin is destiny. In Ajala's "shop," the eniyan (person) selects for himself his ipin (portion), commonly referred to as Ori-inu (inner head). Presumably, the choice of heads (Ori) is based on what one wants to accomplish in the coming lifetime. This Ori–inu or ipin is the individual's chosen destiny. There is some variance in this part of the myth. Some say you get your Ori from Ajala but then go to Olodumare and tell IT what you want to accomplish in this lifetime, and the deal is sealed. Some say that humans obtain their ipin (portion, destiny) in one of three ways; by kneeling down and choosing it, a-kun-le-yan (that which one kneels to choose), by kneeling to receive, a-kun-le-gba (that which one kneels to receive), or by having his destiny apportioned to him a-yan-mo (that which is apportioned to one). Others, myself included, believe akunleyan, akunlegba and ayanmo are component parts of Ori-Apere. ("one half" of Ori) Regardless, all acknowledge the Yoruba belief in predestination and also establish the belief in Ipin (portion) as a person's destiny which he chooses during his pre-existent state. It is this destiny that is seen as metaphysically constituted in Ori-inu (inner head), and it is this that man comes into the world to fulfill. This belief manifests itself in the maxim, "Akunle-yan ni ad'aye ba" - the destiny chosen is that which is met and pursued (Abimbola).

The Yoruba believe that creation exists on two complementary dimensions: the visible world, called Aiye, the physical universe that we inhabit, and the invisible world, called Orun, inhabited by the supernatural beings and the "doubles" of everything that is manifested in aiye (in Odu there is reference to seven planes in each dimension). These dimensions are not to be confused with heaven and earth. There is not a strict division; they exist in the same space. Aiye is a "projection" of the essential reality that processes itself in orun. Everything that exists, exists in orun also. Actually, orun is the reality and aiye the mirror image. It is necessary to understand that aiye and orun constitute a unity, and as expressions of two levels of existence, are undivided and complementary. There is full identity between them; one is just an inverted image of the other (Teixeira de Oliveira).

The Ori complex is comprised of three parts; the Ori – consciousness and destiny; Ori Inu - the Inner Self; and Iponri - the Higher Self. Much has been written regarding the concept of Ori. I break it down using the theory of extensionalism, which simply states that humans are connected to God in some manner; that there is communication; that we are in fact extensions of God. This idea is common to most metaphysio-religious systems. In Yoruba thought we have the concept of Oro. At the level of the individual, the concept is expressed in the Ori complex (or soul complex) – an extensionist construct that explains the interaction between tangible and intangible existences. As Orun and Aiye exist simultaneously in the same space, so does the human soul in the form of Ori-inu and Iponri. Matter-mass which makes the transition from orun to aiye through the snail shell produces a double existence. The fragments or portion that a person receives (ori-inu) from Ajala-Mopin in his or her Ori is brought with the person to aiye, the visible realm and to Ile (earth). The original stays in orun. This original is called the Iponri or Ipori. It is our Iponri that allows blessings to flow from "above." No Orisa can bless us without permission from our Ori. Why? Because our Iponri is our real self, our beginning and our end. Anything we wish to manifest in life, must be created by our Iponri first in the invisible realm, where all things are created before manifesting in the visible worlds. Thus the popular chant from Odu Ifa:

THE HOLY ODU

Ko soosa
Ti i dani i gbe
Leyin Ori Eni
No divinity
Can help, deliver, or bless one
Without the sanction of one's Ori

Our wishes, wants, fulfillment of needs, prayers, etc., must originate in orun before they can manifest in aiye. Our Ori, the third component of the Ori complex, serves as our individual "Ela," that which connects our dual selves that exist simultaneously in the invisible and visible worlds. Ori is that intangible substance that is the extension, the communication, across the divide. That is why we portray Ori as our personal Orisa, because Ori carries our prayers and communicates our wishes to our Iponri. In this way, our Ori is like an Orisa pot. It is our connection to ase. This is why Ori is the first "Orisa" to be praised; it is the one that guides, accompanies and helps the person since before birth, during all life and after death, assisting in the fulfillment of his or her destiny. Thus the praise name Ori-Apesin - one who is worthy of worship by all. It is said that a person's Ori, besides being the source of ire, is the only Orisa that can and will accompany one to the very end:

Bi mo ba lowo lowo
Ori ni n o ro fun
Orii m, iwo ni
Bi mo ba bimo l'aiye
Ori ni n o ro fun
Orii m, iwo ni
Ire gbogbo ti mo a ni l'aiye
Ori ni n o ro fun
Orii m, iwo ni
Ori pele
Atete niran
Atete gbe'ni k'oosa

Ko soosa ti I da'ni I gbe
Leyin Ori eni
Ase

It is Ori alone
Who can accompany his devotee
to any place without turning back
If I have money, it is my Ori I will praise
It is my Ori to whom I shall give praise
My Ori, it is you
All good things I have on Earth
It is Ori I will praise
My Ori it is you
No Orisa shall offer protection
without sanction from Ori
Ori, I salute you
Whose protection precedes that of other Orisa
Ori that is destined to live
Whosoever's offering Ori chooses to accept
let her/him rejoice profusely
Ori the actor, the stalwart divinity
One who guides one to wealth, guides one to riches
Ori the beloved, governor of all divinities
Ori, who takes one to the good place
Ori, behold the good place and take me there
Feet, behold the good place and accompany me thereto
There is no divinity like Ori
One's Ori is one's providence
My Ori, lead me home
My Ori, lead me home
Ori, the most concerned
My skull, the most concerned in sacrificial rites
Ori, I thank you
Ori, I thank you for my destiny
My skull, I thank you for my destiny

Ori I thank you (mo juba)
Ase, ase, ase o!

As the "personal Orisa" of each human being, our Ori is vital to the fulfillment and happiness of each man and woman; more so than any other Orisa. More than anyone, it knows the needs of each human in his or her journey through life. Ori has the power of Ela, to pass freely from Orun to Aiye and vice versa. It exists on both dimensions:

Ire gbogbo ti ni o nii
N be lodo Ori
A lana-teere kan aiye
A lana-teere kanrun
All the good that I am expecting is from my Ori
He who makes a narrow path to aiye
He who makes a narrow path to orun

What at first glance seems like a very complicated theology, when we gain an understanding of the metaphysics within the mythology, reveals a simple metaphysical principle; the principle of causation. The ability to create in Orun, and have it manifest in Aiye; like Oro becoming Ela. Awo is the development of this ability; either through our Ori, through Orisa, ancestors, etc. Others have expressed the concept of Ori. One explanation worth quoting is by Babasehinde Ademuleya:

"The soul, to the Yoruba, is the "inner person", the real essence of being – the personality. This they call "ori". The word "ori", in contrast to its English meaning as the physical "head", or its biological description as the seat of the major sensory organs, to the Yoruba connotes the total nature of its bearer. A critical study of the term in Yoruba belief reveals the intrinsic meaning and value of the object it is identified with – that is, the physical head – and carries with it the essential nature of the object associated with it – that is the man. To the Yoruba, the physical "ori" is but a symbol – a symbol of the "inner head"

or "the inner person", the "ori-inu" (the inner head). Ori in Yoruba belief occupies the centre of sacredness, and how it is conceived is embedded in the Yoruba myth concerning the creation of man and the role played by his creator, Eledaa (He who created). The Yoruba word for man – eniyan – is derived from the phrase eni-ayan (the chosen one)."

… a wa gegebi eniyan, …
a wa ni Olodumare yan
lati lo tun ile aye se,
Eni -a yan ni wa...

we as human beings,
we are the God's elect,
designated to renew the world,
We are the chosen ones.

Human beings are called eniyan (the chosen ones) because they are the ones ordained "to convey goodness" to the wilderness below Olorun. In other words, divinity abides in humanity, and vice versa (there is another meaning to eniyan, referring to Aje, with the appropriate tonal changes).

Let us now consider the Ori-inu. The African idea of the soul has been conceived and described in different ways. In Yoruba, the idea of the transcendental self, or soul, has been difficult to express in English. Some have called emi soul. Emi is invisible and intangible. This is the life force breathed into each human by Olodumare. Not to be confused with eemi, which is simply breath. Emi is what gives life to the body. When it ceases, life ceases. A Yoruba would say about a corpse, "emi re ti bo" - his emi is gone. Another word sometimes mistaken for soul is okan, which literarily means the heart. For the Yoruba, the heart is more than an organ that pumps blood. It is from where our emotions emanate, and the locus of psychic energy. But it is not soul. For me, the soul is Ori-inu, that portion of the "God-stuff" from the Snail that comprises the "inner person," the real essence of being. If Ori is the mystery of consciousness, then Ori inu is a mystery within a mystery. Ori inu is the elusive inner core of knowing. It is the focus of initiation to get to that "place."

Regarding life-force (emi), that which Olodumare bestows on each individual and an integral component of each Ori-inu, it is known as ase (pronounced awshay). Emi is the life force, but it is made up of ase. Ase is a concept almost as complex as Ori. Ase is a component of the life force breathed into each human being by Olodumare; it is spiritual power; it is the power to create. Pemberton describes it this way:

"Ase is given by Olodumare to everything – Gods, ancestors, spirits, humans, animals, plants, rocks, rivers and voiced words such as songs, prayers, praises, curses, or even everyday conversation. Existence, according to Yoruba thought, is dependent upon it; it is the power to make things happen and change. In addition to its sacred characteristics, ase also has important social ramifications, reflected in its translation as "power, authority, command." A person, who through training, experience, and initiation, learns how to use the essential life force of things is called an alaase. Theoretically, every individual posseses a unique blend of performative power and knowledge – the potential for certain achievements. Yet, because no one can know with certainty the potential of others, eso (caution), ifarabale (composure), owo (respect), and suuru (patience) are highly valued in Yoruba society and shape all social interactions and organization.Ase inhabits the space (shrine) dedicated to Orisa, the air around it, and all the objects and offerings therein. As stated by Pemberton, ase pertains to the identification, activation and use of the distinct energy received by each thing in its original portion. The efficacious use of ase depends on the ase and knowledge, the awo, of the one who attempts to harness it. The power of the word is an important part of harnessing ase."

The day Epe was created
Was the day Ase became law
Likewise, Ohun was born
The day Epe was invoked
Ase is proclaimed
Epe is called
But they both still need Ohun (to communicate)

Without Ohun (voice), neither Epe (curse, the malevolent use of ase), nor Ase can act to fulfill its mission. This is why ase is often likened to "a-je-bi-ina" (potent and effective traditional medicinal preparations which respond like the ignited fire (ina). Je (to answer), da (to create), and pe (to call). Iluti is the power of the Orisa to respond to our call – "Ebora to luti la nbo" – we worship only deities that can respond when consulted (Abiodun). One of the main goals of Ifa/Orisa devotees is to build up their personal ase. The goal of every babalorisa, iyalorisa, santera, santero, iyanifa and babalawo (collectively called Awo), is to not only build up their personal "quantity" of ase, but to develop the ability to tap into the ase of other beings and objects in order to use it. However, it must be understood that, according to Yoruba belief, women are born with the ability to access ase (that doesn't mean they know how to use that ability). This power inherent in women and the secret of the womb, is called "aje." Men, however, must develop this ability through initiation.

In the words of awo Falokun Fatunmbi;

"Awo need to develop the ase necessary to transform ibi (misfortune) into ire (good fortune). They must possess the ability to effect change in the visible world by manipulating forces in the invisible world. "The word "Ela" literally means "I am light" from the elision e ala. The ability to become one with the Spirit of Ela is the ability to use Ori as a portal between the visible world and the invisible world. When an Awo is in an altered state of consciousness the thing that passes between dimensions is pure unformed ase symbolically referred to as ala or white light. As this ase comes from Ile Orun to Ile Aiye through the Ori of the diviner, it takes shape and is formed by the ofo ase [oro, power of the word] inherent in the oriki spoken by the diviner while in an altered state of consciousness."

The innate urge to communicate contained in Oro and manifested as Ela is observable in ritual. The importance of Esu cannot be overstressed, as it is Esu who determines the efficacy of any ritual, from iwure (prayer), to chanting Odu verses (oriki ire), to ebo and to initiation ceremonies. Esu is in a powerful position as one's good fortune or bad depends on what he "reports" to Olodumare. A hierarchical structure emerges in divine communication. Even if Esu carries the message of an Orisa to Olodumare, Olodumare will check with one's Iponri (higher self, twin soul in Orun) to see if it has the desired ire (good fortune) asked for by the person. If the person's Iponri says yes, then Esu delivers the message to the original Orisa who made the request on behalf of the person. Esu facilitates the movement from orun to aiye as he is the line in between them. Esu and Ela are inseparable.

Another aspect to divine communication is the use of color. The use of color against color creates a mathematical equation. This graphic design uses symmetry, rhythm, emotion, and balance. The Yoruba word for this is "iwontunwonsi" (moderation). An example would be the white and red of Sango. The red signifies raw power, and heat. The white coolness and wisdom. Sango is balanced, moderated – iwontunwonsi – through color. This concept is expressed In the following Yoruba saying derived from Odu: "Efun ewa osun l'aburo" Beautiful lime chalk (white) is camwood's (red) senior (Mason). The Yoruba metaphysics of extensionism, is a somewhat complicated structure of divine communication, but a close relationship between all involved (Ori, Esu, ancestors, Orisa, etc) insures its efficacious nature.

In addition to controlling the release of ire (good fortune), our Iponri determines the Odu under which we are born, which in turn determines which Orisa energy a person will live under in the particular life in question (Orisa are born in Odu). When we tell Olodumare what kind of experiences we want to have in a lifetime, we are choosing experiences that will help us hone our souls; we want to work on our weaknesses, so as to do our part in the elevation of our collective ancestors (egun). Thus Olodumare will place us under the influence of the particular Odu/Orisa that will best provide us with those experiences in a way that ensures lesson learned.

The concept of personal taboos (ewo) in Ifa/Orisa is related to our dual existence (ori-inu as double of iponri) A person should not ingest or have anything to do with the particular elements (including colors) that make up his or her ipin, ori-inu (Opefeyitimi). These ewo are contained in the Odu of our birth. It is through divination that we learn what we need to know about our Ori, our destiny, taboos, potential pitfalls, dangers, etc.

For further explanation of Ori-inu, ase, and Iponri we return to Baba Falokun Fatunmbi:

In Yoruba psychology, consciousness originated from lae-lae (i.e. eternity)—the mystical source of creation. This idea is part of a body of thought on the structure of being and of the universe, and these thoughts are referred to as Awo (i.e. mysteries). These ideas were formulated at the dawn of Yoruba civilization, and were contained in 256 verses each known as an Odu. Knowledge of these ideas was kept away from the public domain and guarded jealously by the priests of Ifa (the Yoruba religion). They were only passed on via oral tradition from one priest to a descendant priest. It is only recently that some of these ideas have started to be written down by Yoruba scholars.

According to Awo, a part of which is paraphrased above, everything in the universe was created from the ontological tension between the opposing forces of expansion and contraction, light and darkness. The contracting forces are centripetal in nature, and therefore absorb light, and the expanding forces are centrifugal and so generate light.

To the Yoruba, light comes from darkness and darkness from light. Both are seen as an expression of ase, a spiritual potency sustaining all of creation. In human beings, the seat of ase is located within ori-inu (i.e. inner head), which is the spiritual consciousness of self and the home of the unconscious mind. The balance of opposing energies in ase generates a spherical pattern in consciousness. This is symbolized by the circular format of opon-ifa, a divination board used by priests to restore alignment between ori (i.e. the physical head, also the seat of the conscious mind) and iponri (i.e. the super-soul, imbued with eternal life, which resides in orun). This board is essentially a map of the polarities of forces in consciousness.

Referring to the opon-ifa model of the structure of consciousness, ori is to the south, opposite iponri in the north. To the east is ara (i.e. the body) and to the west is emi (i.e. breath of life). In the centre of these forces is the inner head (ori-inu). It is the home of the unconscious mind and the seat of destiny.

It is believed that, just before birth, every ori negotiates an agreement with Olorun (i.e. God—literal translation is owner of the sky), outlining their goals for that lifetime. At birth the details of this agreement are removed from the realm of conscious thought and hidden in the unconscious domain, within the inner head (ori-inu) and iponri in heaven. One's destiny, therefore, is to remember the original agreement and work towards achieving those goals. Any deviation from these goals creates a misalignment between iponri and ori and results in disease. Healing is sought through divination, a process of remembering and of realignment with destiny.

This is a very lucid explanation and worthy of including in its entirety. What we want to accomplish through divination and in our daily lives, is the balance of the four quadrants which intersect at Ori–inu, the center spot on the opon Ifa. It is worthy to note at this time that the Ori-inu is also the interstice of all Orisa. Obatala (the arch-divinity) came down the chain with the Snail Shell. Ogun not only took over where Obatala left off, but also works alongside Ajala-Mopin. Ogun, carves the faces of the Ori's after Ajala moulds them, including the eyes, which are then "activated" by Esu, who also activates the facial muscles, in effect giving us the emotions. Remember also, that Esu is the "membrane" between darkness and light. Ogun's relationship to Ori is found in still another Odu verse from Osa Meji:

Ori buruku ki i wu tuulu
A ki i da ese asiweree mo loju-ona
A ki i m' ORI
oloye lawujo
A da fun Mobowu
Ti i se obinrin Ogun
Ori ti o joba lola
Enikan o mo
Ki toko-taya o mo pe'raa won ni were mo
Ori ti o joba lola
Enikan o mo
A person with a bad head (Ori) isn't born with a head different from the others
No one can distinguish the footsteps of the madman on the road
No one can recognize the head destined to wear a crown in an assembly
Ifa was cast for Mobowu,
Who was the wife of Ogun
A husband and a wife should not treat each other badly
Not physically, nor spiritually
The head that will reign tomorrow,
Nobody knows

The participation of Obatala and Ogun in creation is attested to by the fact that most of the ese Odu about creation are found in Odu's containing either Ogbe or Ogunda or a combination of both

(Ogbe is the Odu that incarnates Obatala, and Ogunda incarnates Ogun).

Oshun is the "owner of the beaded hair comb," and the Orisa of hair stylists. Besides adding to the power and beauty of the human face and head which is the focus of much aesthetic interest in Yoruba culture and art, hair-plaiting carries an important religious significance in Yoruba tradition. The hair-plaiter (hairdresser) is seen as one who honors and beautifies Ori, the "pot" for Ori-inu. One's head is taken to be the visible representation of one's destiny and the essence of one's personality. It is believed that taking good care of one's hair is an indirect way of currying favor with one's Ori Inu. Thus, the Yoruba have created a wide range of hairstyles that not only reflect the primacy of the head but also communicate taste, status, occupation, and power, both temporal and spiritual.

The Ori inu is comprised of three parts which are accessed through our Ori. The first spot is our forehead which is what many refer to as the third eye. The second is at the top of the head which is connects us to our iponri and Ela (khundalini), and the third is at the base of the skull which connects head and heart, a condition necessary for attaining elevated levels of consciousness. It is through the base of the skull that one connects with Orisa (goes into possession).

Yoruba religion focuses on the worship of the Orisa because of the belief that they act on behalf of Olodumare, who is too exalted to be approached directly. Yet Olodumare is indirectly involved in the day-to-day life of an individual through his/her Ori Inu. This is why it is of central importance to maintain balance and harmony between the three components (ori, ori-inu, iponri) of the Ori complex. This preoccupation over rides any worship of any Orisa, and even of one's ancestors. In the past, every adult Yoruba had an Ori pot or an ibori, which is kept inside an Ile Ori (house of the head). It is encased in leather and adorned with thousands of cowrie shells.

Many people consider the Yoruba concept of Ori as fatalistic. If one's Ori contains one's destiny, which is pre-determined in Ajala-Mopin's workshop, then how can it not be fatalistic? If every activity we engage in on earth has been pre-ordained at the point when we chose our ipin-ori (portion or lot) with Ajala-Mopin before coming into the world and cannot be altered, then how is it not a fatalistic theology?

The first thing to consider is that Ori is divided into two parts; Apari-inu (represents character) and Ori-apere (represents destiny). So far we have only considered Ori-apere. This division into two parts is why, at the beginning of this paper, I said, "It can be considered as the Yoruba theory of consciousness, or as the Yoruba theory of destiny, or both," and is the source of much confusion regarding the Ori complex. As stated previously, Ori-apere, the half that consists of destiny, consists of three elements: a-kun-le-yan (choice), a-kun-le-gba (freewill) and a-yan-mo-ipin (destiny)

Akunleyan were choices you made at the feet of Olodumare regarding what experiences you wanted on earth. For example, how long you wanted to live, what kinds of successes and failures you wanted, the kinds of relatives, etc. Why not choose to be the only child of wealthy parents? Because life is not measured on how comfortable it was, but on the degree of honing of the self that was accomplished; The continuing quest for perfection; the elevation of soul. Akunlegba (notice legba in the phrase) is the element of free will. The freedom to make choices while on earth. Watch out, Esu/Legba is watching! Akunlegba also relates to those things given to us to help us fulfill the choices made in Akunleyan. Ayanmo is that part of our destiny that cannot be changed. For example, day of death, our sex, the family in which we are born, etc. But even here, in Ajala-Mopin's domain, we make a choice as to which of the Ori's we want. It is when coming into the world, when we pass through omi-igbagbe – the water of forgetfulness; the boundary between orun and aiye (Esu), that we forget our chosen destiny.

These concepts show that although there is some determinism involved, there is plenty of room for one to influence one's fate. There is another element called ese. Ese literally means "leg," but in this context means "strife," "hardwork," or "struggle." Ese introduces the principle of human agency:

Opebe the Ifa priest of ese (legs)
Divined for ese on the day he was coming from Orun to Ile (earth)
All the Ori's called themselves together
But they did not invite ese
We will see how you will bring your request to fruition
Their meeting ended in quarrel
They then sent for ese
It was then that their meeting became successful
That was exactly as Ifa had predicted
No one deliberates
Without reckoning with ese
Opebe, the Ifa priest of ese
Cast Ifa for ese
On the day he was coming from Orun to Ile
Opebe has surely come
Ifa priest of ese
ase

This principle is further elucidated in a verse of EjiOgbe:
"Do your work"
"I am not working"
This was the Ifa cast for the lazy person
He who sleeps until the sun is overhead
He who relies on that which is possessed through inheritance

exposes himself to suffering
If we do not toil and sweat profusely today
We cannot become wealthy tomorrow
"March through the mud"
"I cannot march through the mud"
"If we do not march through the mud
Our mouths cannot eat good food"
These were the declarations of Ifa to the lazy person
He who possesses strong limbs but refuses to work
He who chooses to be idle in the morning
He is only resting for suffering in the evening
Only toiling can support one
Idleness cannot bring dividend
Whoever refuses to work
Such a person does not deserve to eat
If a lazy person is hungry, please let him die
Dead or alive, a lazy person is a useless person

Human agency is a central part of Yoruba theology. Besides not working hard, another path to failure is that in which a person, not knowing their destiny, will work against it, thus experiencing futility even if working hard. This is why we turn to Ifa through Orunmila – Eleri-ipin, for guidance as to whether or not one is on the right path. However, one is free to make use of ese (hardwork) and ebo (sacrifice, offerings) – which requires freewill – to change their fortunes. Since Ori is limited to one's material success – nowhere in Odu does it say that Ori pre-determines moral character or personal ethics - it does not affect all our actions. Although we come into the earth with either a good Ori – olori-rere (owner of a good Ori) – or a bad one – olori buruku (owner of a bad Ori) – an individual's destiny can be changed through the help of spiritual forces such as Orisa, Egun, etc. Ebo is a form of communication between the natural and supernatural realms, and involves the establishment of a reciprocal relationship with those forces. One's destiny may also be affected by the Ajoogun - malevolent forces. In addition, there is a concept called "afowofa", were one is the cause of one's own problem. Such actions are empirically observable. So a person is held responsible for those actions for which he is the cause, but attributes to his Ori those which transcend him (Balogun).

Orunmila lo dohun a-dun-hun-un
Emi naa lo dohun a-dun-hun-un
Orunmila ni begbe eni ba n lowo
Ba a ba a ti i ni in
Ifa ni ka ma dun huun-huun-huun
Ori elomii mo
Ori eni ni ka maa dun huun
Orunmila ni begbe eni ba n n'ire gbogbo
Ba a ba a ti I ni in
Ori eni ni ka maa dun hun-un
Orii mi gbami
Mo dun huun aje mo o
Orii mi gbami
Mo du huun ire gbogbo mo o
Ori apere
a-sakara-moleke
eni Ori ba gbebo re
ko yo sese
ase

Orunmila said complaint, complaint, complaint…
I said it is all complaint
Orunmila said if ones colleagues are rich
If we are not yet rich
Ifa said we should not complain
To another person's Ori
We should complain to our own Ori
Orunmila said if one's colleagues are getting
all the good things of life

If we have not got...
We should complain only to our Ori
My Ori, deliver me
I complain of money to you
My Ori deliver me
I complain of all the good things of life to you
Ori nicknamed Apere. Nicknamed A-sakara-moleke
Whoever's offering is accepted by their Ori
Should really rejoice.
Ase

Orunmila's involvement in the Ori complex cannot be overstressed. One of his praise names is "A tori Eni ti ko sunwon se" - One who reforms bad heads. In Odu Ogbe Ogunda, Ifa says there were seven duties one had to perform before he left orun for aiye or ile:

1. Divination
2. Performing of Ebo
3. Job distribution and giving of Ewo (taboos)
4. Digging the pit of loss
5. Removing the rag of poverty
6. Wishes
7. Choice of Ori

According to the Ifa verse, these duties takes place at four different locations. Perhaps relating to the four parts of the opon Ifa. These duties together comprise our destiny. However, we forget our destiny on the way out of the birth canal. This makes it extremely difficult to complete it. However, Orunmila, as Eleri-ipin (witness to destiny) through Ifa, can help us make the necessary corrections in our lives to get back on path. Other difficulties are that, as we are making our way from Orun to Ile, the Ajoogun (malevolent forces) try to take things from within our Ori, laziness and other character flaws, and failure to make ebo.

THE HOLY ODU

In Ogbe Ogunda, Ifa says:

A grinder makes three works
It grinds yam
It grinds indigo plant
It is used as a lock behind the door
cast Ifa for Oriseku, Ori-Elemere and Afuwape
When they were about to choose their fates in the domain of Ajala-Mopin
They were told to make ebo
Only Afuwape made the ebo requested
He, consequently, had ire gbogbo (all good fortune)
The others lamented, they said that if they had known where
Afuwape had gone to choose his Ori
they would have gone there to choose theirs
Afuwape answered that, even if they had chosen their Ori's
in the same place, their fates would still have differed

Only Afuwape had shown good character. By respecting his elders and doing his ebo, he brought the potential blessings within his destiny to fruition. His friends Oriseku and Ori-Elemere had failed in showing good character in refusing to make ebo and, because of that, their destinies were altered. The most important influence on one's destiny is one's character and personal ethics – iwa. Iwa pele, or iwa rere, good or gentle character. That's why the Yoruba say, "the strongest medicine against curses and spells is iwa pele." It is through adhering to the ethical standards of Orunmila that we can achieve spiritual growth. These ethics are embodied in two concepts, Iwa–pele (good or gentle character) and Ori-tutu (coolheadedness or wisdom). It is through the development of these two attributes, improvement at the personal, social level that we can improve at the spiritual level, which, according to the Yoruba, will elevate our collective ancestors, our entire lineage (Egun).

Here we come to the end of the philosophical movement from the metaphysical meaning descending into the aesthetic and then epistemological through to ethical meanings and, eventually, to positive or negative social effects, which effect the metaphysical in a unifying cycle. The ethics of iwa pele. If your life is a mess, before blaming witchcraft, family, or co-workers, examine your nature, your character. If you are selfish; if you are arrogant, if you are disrespectful, no amount of ebo will fix your problems. If you give happiness and share your possessions, if you are humble and thoughtful, you shall receive. Eniyan, the chosen ones, to bring good into the world. This is the social effect, which brings us full circle back to the metaphysics of Oro.

Ayanmo ni iwa pele; iwa pele ni Ayanmo

Destiny is character; character is destiny

At this stage it should be evident that the Yoruba concept of creation, cosmos, divinity and self are sophisticated and elaborate and not lacking in any level, especially not the metaphysical. These complex sources contain a vivid belief in "otherworldly beings" as well as theories, speculations and philosophies of a purely metaphysical nature, dispelling notions that African religious systems are devoid of a theology, or that African societies are not particularly interested in anything else than the terrestrial plane and the practical conditions concerning healthy and happy life.

In the creation myth, creation was ascribed to a class of spirits called *Irúnmòle* or *Ìmólè*, which is a reference to the forces of nature in their primordial manifestation. The word it self means "House of Light". These terms are used both as a designation for a given class of spiritual beings in reference to the ray given off from stars, like *ímólè ìràwò*, meaning "light of star", *ímólè òòrùn* meaning "light of sun" and *ímólè osupa* meaning "light of moon". Actually, the stellar lore or the teachings of the *Ìràwò* is also found within *Ifá* divinatory systems and teachings and constitute a complex lore known as *Gẹ́dídí*, similar in its principles to classical astrology (Fatunmbi). Aiye and orun is more a concept of a metaphysical nature. The Earth-Heaven distinction in a more materialistic form is usually named *ilẹ̀* (earth) and *sánmọ̀*(sky/heaven).

The concept of two realms, *àiyé* and *òrun* is an interactive one in which both the visible and visible occupy the same space and can affect eachother. This interaction and natural state of being joined together is disclosed in the mystery of *Odù*, also known as *Igbádù* or *Igbaíwà*, meaning "The Calabash of Existence" as its most common translation. But the word *Odù* also refers to darkness (*O dù*) or the Womb (*odù*) as well and are sometimes translated to "The Womb of Creation" (Fatumbi 1993). Both translations are meaningful and also demonstrate the level of flexibility in the Yoruba language. The image of the calabash divided in half horizontally is a powerful and central image of the cosmology, separating the sky from the earth or orun from aiye. Ori can also be represented by the same calabash, which suggests our ori is a microcosm of creation itself.

This same complexity is found everywhere in the wisdom of *Ifá*, denoting an understanding of creation, life and death as being part of a greater order than the socially ordered structure of human created society. If the calabash of existence or the calabash of consciousness is broken Orunmila and Esu can solve the situation. As one *ese Ifá* says: "Ifá was going to mend the life of the king of Ifẹ̀. As one mends a broken calabash"(Abimbola 1997). Important concepts of our tradition are change, adaptability and improvisation, understanding and prevailing through suffering, and through wise counsel and understanding to be able to achieve good fortune in the end.

Another important concept is coolness. The primary metaphorical extension of this term is self-control, having the value of composure in the individual context, and social stability in the context of the group. These concepts are often linked to the sacred usage of water and efun (and other substances drenched with associations of coolness and cleanliness) as powers which purify men and women by return to freshness and clear thinking. It denotes a purification, balance, an ability to remain aloof in crisis or triumph (Thompson).

In the words of Thompson; "Manifest within this philosophy of the cool is the belief that the purer, the cooler a person becomes, the more ancestral he becomes. In other words, mastery of self enables a person to transcend time and elude preoccupation. He can concentrate or she can concentrate upon truly important matters of social balance and aesthetic substance, creative matters, full of motion and brilliance. Quite logically, such gifted men and women are, in some West and Central African cultures, compared in their coolness to the strong, moving, pure waters of the river."

A very important ritual is a bath made up of herbs and other elements that restore coolness. Order is of central importance and is brought about by restoring balance. It is through divination that we determine how to restore order and balance individually. It is Orunmila, Esu and Iyami that we appeal to for this restoration. No condition is seen as permanent or fixed; all things are in a state of change – as dictated by a natural order mirrored in the changes present in the yearly cycle of seasonal changes. *Ifá* is based in geocentric holism that includes the empirical realm as well as the unseen.

Reflexivity and improvisation are another important tenet that we need to understand in order to better understand the religious system and the odu corpus. "As media of change and transformation, rituals are conceived as "journeys", …the journey…highlights the subjective experience of participants, their capacity for reflexive self-monitoring, and their transformation of consciousness through play and improvisation" (Drewal 1992). This is highly crucial for understanding Yoruba ritual, the role of the individual, and this also explains the many differences and variations to be found from community to community. Diversity is celebrated by the Yoruba. Change is not resisted but accommodated thus dogma is seen as dangerous to survival as adapting to change is seen as integral to it. Òrúnmìlà is the sage who knows how to speak with the totality of creation and aided by Èsù is able to heal and restore the individual as well as the community either by inducing understanding or providing solutions to problems,

This aspect of the religion, improvisation and diversity, is not understood in the diaspora as a normalization of ritual and compliance are valued due to insecurity brought about by the loss of knowledge of ritual, etc. However, what the individual brings into the movement of the world in a drama of interchange between individuals, between individual and the community, between the community and the otherworldly often requires an openness of the participants to allow spirit to express itself how it sees fit.

According to Drewal and Drewal (1983) regarding the fluidity of the Yoruba religious system, it can be seen as a melting together of descent and divination which will naturally give rise to a vast number of possibilities, according to personal, communitarian and regional needs and beliefs as well as to what other forces and cults the particular region has incorporated or what has been considered as most helpful. This great diversity was also expounded upon in William Bascom's seminal research on *Ifá* (1969).

Incantation is an important aspect of ritual and are infused in odu verses as well as incantations such as ofo awure (incantations for ire). To understand odu verses, one must understand the function of incantation and its placement in the verses of odu. Yoruba theology contains the concept of interactionism, which states that, "The Yoruba world is permeated by numerous vibrations. The African views the world as a continuous cycle of life and death. For the Yoruba, the universe is a fusion of the material and the spiritual in a rhythmic cycle. Consequently, science and religion are intertwined. Incantation can, therefore, be defined as systematic utterances meant to manipulate physical and non-physical forces to actualize a desire for self or others" (Odusola 2000). Mastering the use of incantation is a big part of the apprenticeship of the awo.

To o n'to 'luwo
To fe n'to jugbona
Ase ale
Ase owuro
A dia fun Arugbo
Abi ewu ori ke ke ke
Ko ta ko ra
O gbe iwo ase re dani
Won ni o lo so
O lohun o lo so
Won ni o l'aje e
O lohun a l'aje e
Won ni lee ti ri t'ohun fi nsoro
Ti nfi nse
O ni e o mo pe ohun awo loso
Ohun awo loro, ohun awo lase
ase
To speak and what is spoken becomes a reality belongs to the Ori of the Ifa priest
To implement what is spoken belongs to the secretary (jugbona)
Order of the night
Order of the morning
Performed Ifa divination for the old man
With gray hair all over his head
Ifa did not buy nor sell

He holds his horn of ase
He was accused of wizardry
He said he wasn't a wizard
He was accused of witchcraft
He said he was not a witch
They asked why does he predict
And his predictions come to pass?
And he answered that the voice of the diviner is wizardry
The voice of the diviner is a divine seal of potency.

"Incantation is designed to concentrate and vitalize thought and will power through sound with a view to translating intention or desire into material reality" (Jegede 2010). The universe was created from Oro, the sound of "God." Thus, sound is at the center of creation and creating.

There are different kinds of incantations, the basic divide being positive and negative. For example, when making a bath mixture we are using positive incantations (Ela rowa) which are based in adoration (iba) and elements that enhance the potency of the ewe (plants) and activate their ase. It is another principle in Yoruba theology that states the use of primordial words (ofo ase) gives one the power to manipulate. All things have primordial names. The object can be controlled if one uses the primordial names. This Onomastic principle is why we do our chants in Yoruba and not in English (Olatunji 1984).

This dual quality of incantation and medicines and charms made using incantation is alsomentioned by Awolalu who says: "the mysterious power in a medicine may be used for good or evil end" (Awolalu1996). With herbs one can cure illness or provoke illness, bring good fortune or cause bad fortune. *Ifá* calls for a lifestyle of moderation and this is also a view held by the majority of the *Onisegun* (medicine men) (Buckley 1997). Illness is understood on premises of the threefold color scale, "blackish", "reddish" and "whitish" as encountered in the discussion about witches, so it is in medicine and thus ties in with Yoruba metaphysics as related to the geocentric and holistic understanding of the world. This is related to phenomena of the earth and the body simultaneously where blackish refers to matters hidden, reddish to matters dangerous and white to matters fertile. This is seen both in the black fertile earth of ilé and the reddish earth covering it in seasons where rain is absent – the rain seen as the white that fertilizes or mingles with the red. Thus the symbolism of color is also important to the interpretation of odu verses. The cosmos with earth as its center is not much different than the fertilizing of an egg in the mothers womb, where the whitish of the father (sperm) and reddish of the mother (menstruation) are met and develop in the blackness of the womb, hidden from sight (Buckley).

Another metaphysical principle central to the structure of odu verses is the principle of transference, or irrevocability. This principle states that historical events and natural laws are transferable through utterances (Jegede 2010). Many incantations are based in this principle. We find this especially in Odu verses, where the "oriki ire," the incantation for the manifestation of the good fortune in the verse, is a historical account of the problem/solution polarity. If a particular action or actions was used at some time in the past for a certain outcome, then it can be used again, provided we can harness it by the use of incantation. Yoruba ritual is based upon the repetition of a given theme. "one of the purposes of repetition is to establish extraterrestrial connections and a framework for order and predictability" (Lawal). However, all change is constant, so a repetition must also include dynamism.

The dynamic change present in ritual performance are a natural consequence of the Yoruba world view, which can be partly explained linguistically by reminding that a word can both signify the action and the one executing the action as well as a condition – as in the example of *awó* which means secret, but are used both as a term for the diviner as well as the secret he is holding. Drewal comments in this regard: "(they are) turning the static equation between two related "things" into a double-voiced process. "To signify" is to revise that which is received, altering the way the past is read, thereby redefining one's relation to it" (Drewal 1992). In other words, the Yoruba ritualist is not concerned about an exact replica of events in the past; it seems more that the past is brought in so it can both guide the community as well as open up for communication and advice for those who are living. "Yoruba ritual is not a rigid structure that participants adhere to mindlessly out of some deep-seated desire for collective repetition in support of a dominant social order." The point is that the ritual creates a fertile ground for a discourse between the community and the otherworldly, after all *aiyé* is not a remote heaven, but the sphere of movement and spirit, in proximity to *ilè*. Ritual is used to reinstall social order or maintain harmony. It serves as a reminder to the community of their origin and it contains lessons and blessings from *aiyé* (Jegede 2010).

The principle of cause and effect is also part of Yoruba theology. According to Odusolu (2000):

"An incantation arranges facts and clues into an electromagnetic circuit of cause and effect such that it brings about material and spiritual fulfillment when the rhythm circuit is completed by the accent of utterance"

Ancestors (*Egúngún*) and how we interact with them is another area of complexity whose understanding will assist in our understanding of the odu corpus as the relation death has with wisdom, power and healing are an integral component of the Ifa. *Egúngún* is regarded as the collective spirits of the ancestors who occupy a space in orun, hence they are called *Ará Òrun* (Dwellers of heaven). Almost all divination sessions will include an offering to the ancestors regardless of what Ifa says we must do.

The hierarchy of beings are segmented into four categories. These are; *Ará Aiyé*, meaning the living, *Oku-òrun*, the ordinary dead ones that have not been elevated to an aware state in the afterlife, *Egún* referring to a venerable spirit that is aware in the afterlife and Egúngún, which is the male ancestral spirit. The priests of the cult are called *Oloje* or *Ojé* and the priestesses *Iya-Agan*, which are usually priestesses of *Oyá*, who has a special relationship with Egúngún being the mother of this spirit. This is also evident in the initiations to *Oyá*, where the first part of the ritual is done by the *Egúngún* denoting the deep connection between *Oyá* and this cult. The dead are considered to be our most important source of advice in life. Developing and maintaining a strong relationship with the ancestors is the cornerstone of Yoruba belief.
Many people ask how it is that we venerate our ancestors not knowing if they have been reborn back into our lineage.

"When a man dies his heart (òkon) goes to heaven and it is this that men worship. It is the man's head (orí) that is reborn as a little child. When this child grows old and dies, his own heart goes to heaven. There are always only a certain number of people in the world. When the head (orí) of a man is reborn it becomes the heart of the child, and it is the heart of the dead man that is now worshipped, because it is in heaven and can go to God (Olódùmarè) and beg for us. Sometimes the head is born into the heart of a small child before the person who is still alive wants to return to heaven and he will soon die" (Buckley. 1997).

Ikú is death in the sense of loss of *emí* or life sustaining breath, the end of terrestrial life, but is not *Egúngún*, The great difference between these beings are also understandable through the *Òdù Ifá*, where *Ikú* is said be manifest in the family of *Òdú* related to Oyeku while *Egúngún* is said to be manifested in the *Òdù Oturupon Méji* (Santos 1975). The *Òdùs* that speak about *Egúngún*, beside *Òtúrúpòn Méji* are *Ìwòrì Òyèkú, Ìwòrìdí, Ìwòrìkó Rekú (Ìwòrìsá), Òbàrà Òsá, Òwònrín Aséyìn (Òwònrínsá), Ogbérikúsá (Ogbésá), Òkànràn eléégun (ÒkànrànÒgúndá)*.

Some verses will mention many characters who affect us such as the *ajogun*, forces of destruction, such as loss, misery, death, illness, tragedy and violence. However, there is no such thing as "evil" in a western sense amongst the Yoruba; you have wrong actions and foolish actions, nothing is premeditated evil as such. Further it is said that the calabash of *ajogun* is held in the hands of *Ìyámí* and only *Èsù* knows the secret of how to unlock this calabash of malevolent forces. Man releases these forces by simply making the wrong choices. The wrong choices need to be pointed out and here the malevolent forces enter the arena. However, the verses relating to ajoogun will provide the actions necessary to repel them. In other words, the wisdom of the right action and behavior. In this way, Ifá is the great healer of all people, the one who heals with understanding and insight bringing less strife and more happiness to our lives.

Another category of entities that are found in odu verses are the *Òrìsá* (Orisha, Orixa). The word *Òrìsá* seems to be compounded of *Orí* meaning head (consciousness) and *Sà*, meaning to select or choose (Mason 1992). There is also the theory that it is derived from *rì*, which means to see and *Sà* and then means "One who sees the cult." In addition, there is reference in odu to the beings known as *Òrìsà* are referred to as, *"Awon to o ri sa"* which means, "Beings who were
successful in their collection". The collection referred to is from an itan regarding the collection of ase that Olodumare dispersed and the Orisa went in search for.

According to Salami (2008):

"Yoruba deities can be categorized as Orisa and Ebora. Orisa are those that came down from heaven. They were created by Olodumare and no one can lay claim to have had any of them as a child. However, Ebora are those that were either born in heaven or on earth and became deified as a result of their exploits on earth. The two categories of deities is what is termed "Irunmole." Ifa distinguishes major orisa as those that invented the usage of "efun" (chalk), and "osun" (camwood), or a combination of the two as part of their dressing. Some of those major Orisa are Obatala, Oranife, Osun and Orunmila. Orisas may be termed to be the senior, powerful compared to Ebora, but events much after the establishment of these important dieties has shown that Eboras also may be very powerful. Among the major Ebora, Osoosi, Ogun, Olokun, Egungun, Oro, and Erinle are well known even today"

Òrìsà Ìmólè, Ebora - Divine beings

Àwon irínwó irùnmalè ojù kòtún
Atí àwon ibgà male ojù kòsì
The four hundred *Irúnmòle* from the right side
The two hundred *Irúnmòle* from the left side
(Santos 1975)

Irùnmalè and/or *Ìmólè* can be understood as the primordial beings released from the womb of creation, each one with their designated powers. "The right side, otun, represents the physical strength of the male, and the left, osi, the concealed spiritual power of the female" (Joseph 2003: 20), According to Santos (which differs from Salami's explanation), the four hundred *Irúnmòle* from the right side are the *Òrìsà* and the two hundred *Irúnmòle* from the left side is the *Ebora*. The left side, the concealed powers are also related to the phenomena of Eniyán or Eleye, referring to the powers of witchcraft and "capable of assuming the form of birds whenever they want to work against Man's interest." (Abimbola 1997: 152) The left side is also reputed to be associated with *ajogun*, which are forces considered disruptive to man's happiness. *Ajogun* are influences like: "*Ikú* (death), *Àrùn* (disease), *Ègbà* (infirmity) and *Òfò* (loss)." The only being excepted from this distinction is *Èsù* who came from both sides. Santos makes a further distinction in separating the beings that came from the right side to be under the dominion of *Obátálà* and being the progenitor of a class of spirits referred to as *funfun* or white, meaning that these spirits are calm, humid, observant, orderly and thrives upon silence (Santos 1975).

The various Òrìsà can be seen as matriarchal or patriarchal founders of cities, lineages or craft guilds, such as Oshun is the patron of hairdressers and Ògún is the patron of blacksmiths and artists. Which orisa are "better" than others depends on the geographical region and lineage one belongs to. "If one asks the worshippers of each of the other Yoruba major deities, one finds that each group claims that its own god is the most important one" (Abimbola 1976).

According to Beir (1980):

The Yoruba people see the multiplicity of gods merely as aspects or facets of *the same* divine force. The *orisha* are not the messengers of God, or his subordinate beings (as missionaries have sometimes assumed) they are part manifestations of the divine spirit, the *orisha* being variously accessible to different people. They are different routes leading to the same goal Myths about Yoruba *orisha* can serve different functions and can therefore be divided into the following four categories :

(1) Myths of a basically religious nature, from which we actually learn much about the Yoruba world view.
(2) Folk-tales in which the protagonists happen to bear the names of the gods.

(3) Myths about the orisha that have an historical, rather than a religious function.

(4) Finally there are the numerous inventions of the Ifa oracle, whose major function is to provide a precedent, with the help of which the priest can advise his client on the right course of action to take. Sometimes existing religious myths can serve this purpose, but on many occasions the stories of the Ifa oracle are tales with divine protagonists, specially created for the purpose of assisting the process of divination.

Obviously the categories will overlap. All have in common considerable merit as literature. The religious myths are often told in sparse language and no attempt has been made to decorate them here. It is often the stark simplicity of the telling that gives them their sense of archaic authority. The less serious myths, the more folkloristic themes, are often more playful and elaborate in their language (Beir 1980).

The Yoruba believe that health problems and other problems usually arise out of imbalance. Ifa uses plants, incantations and rituals to bring us back into balance. Odu verses incorporate the ase of regaining balance. Usually, the imbalance is a breach of equilibrium between us and the spirit world which leads to misfortune. However, the Yoruba system of healing is not simply magical. The knowledge of the properties of plants, animals and other objects is scientific as well as magical.

The Yorùbá people attach much importance to their animals and that animals occupy an important place and space in human existence and life on the globe. Babalola (1973) and Ojo (1973) have compiled some Yorùbá folktales. Their folktales reveal that there is a close and deep relationship and interaction between the animals and the Yorùbá. In all their folktales there are no limits to the interaction of man and animals. They do speak, eat and relate freely with each other without any barrier. This illustrates the Yorùbá worldview in relation to their animals. To gain a solid understanding of odu verses, the symbology of animals has to be considered, as when mentioned in odu verses, usually are important to understanding the message of the verse, or relate important information regarding medicines and charms that are important to the client in divination.

"*Bí a ò rígún* If we don't see the vulture
A ò gbọdò ṣ ebo We must not offer sacrifice
Bí a ò rákàlà If we don't see ground hornbill
A ò gbọdò ṣ orò We must not perform rituals.

In essence, the Yorùbá rely extensively on animals for their own well-being. Next to using the animals in various rituals and sacrifices, they also play a central role in Yorùbá traditional medicine. Medicines are made of a whole animal or part of it. For example, the feathers of akuko and agbe are used for charms and medicines for good fortune. There is a particular
rat, called *edá*, which is used by folk healers to cure infertility because of its nature to reproduce within a very short time. Even being as small as it is, it brings much offspring. A part of the incantation goes *Àbímọlémọ ni teku edá* 'Edá rats procreate frequently'. This quality makes the rat an essential medicinal ingredient for infertile women to make them fertile. The issue of childbearing among the Yorùbá is a serious one and they do everything to make sure that a married woman bears children. They hold the belief that anyone without a child lives a meaningless life"
-Ajibade George Olusola.

In addition, animals many times are metaphors for certain Orisha. Recognizing when an animal is a metaphor for an Orisa adds to one's ability to interpret the verses of the Odu corpus. With the knowledge imparted in these first chapters, the foundation is established. All it takes now is time and dedication.

CHAPTER 2   INTERPRETING THE VERSES OF IFA

Odu Ifa are complex and exist at different levels of existence which makes it difficult to provide a succinct explanation of what is odu. One way to conceptualize odu is to consider them as deities themselves, as they arise from the matrix of the source of creation Bascom 1969). This interpretation suggests that odu are not only geometric energy patterns, but are manifestations of divine consciousness with whom we can communicate. Another conception is that the 256 odu at the level of universal energy are portals between the invisible realm and the physical realm. We saw that in the creation myth, Oro descends from invisible realm and becomes Ela. This occurs through Olodumare, the womb of creation or the portal through which God creates the physical universe(s). I envision this grand portal like a honeycomb, with 256 cells. Each cell of the "honeycomb" is a portal for a specific form of Oro or energy. Thus at the metaphysical level, each odu is a portal which transfers a qualitative energy. As human consciousness, we come through one of these portals, which endow us with certain properties (also determines our "guardian" orisha). When we receive our odu through Ifa initiation, it is this odu that is revealed. Regarding divination, in a general sense, the odu from divination is the energy that is affecting us at the time of divination. This provides the foundation to any specific questions the client might have. Oro we recall, is "the sound and light," or "the word of God." As it passes into the physical realm thru Olodumare, it becomes Ela. Orunmila is a physical manifestation of Ela. Ela is the ase of God in an unformed state. In this way, the odu verses provide the opportunity to take a specific energy or energy pattern and form it into something physical. That is the "magic" of the awo based in the theological foundations of our faith.

There is a wide range of possible interpretations of the verses of odu Ifa. The verses of Ifa provide historical information, medicinal information, ecological, poetic as well as divine instruction to solving problems (divination). Here we are interested in Odu Ifa as divination oracle. The oracle itself is viewed by some as the word of "God." To me this is a result of Christian and Islamic influence. I see the oracle as divinely inspired, but not as the "word of God." More like the wisdom of the ancestors. However one chooses to conceptualize the oracle's source, there is a method to its interpretation. Here I am not going to go into what the diviner's method is as far as passing the message of the oracle to the client, but how the layperson can begin to understand the verses of Ifa.

Ifa divination is not like other forms of future seeing or fortune telling. Although divination can and will speak of the future (as well as past and present), it is understood that the future can change and probably will due to the countless decisions we make everyday that affect the future. Ifa divination is always done in the context of one's destiny. Again, Orunmila is the witness to destiny and any question we ask the oracle is always in the context of the person's destiny. This means that we don't ask Ifa for example, to help me land the job I am pursueing, but first we ask Ifa if the job is in alignment with my destiny and if it is, the odu will provide the information on what we can do to improve our chances of getting it (even if we don't ask in this fashion the odu revealed will answer in context of destiny whether we realize it or not). The verses provide information on how to receive assistance from the invisible realm, where all things manifest before they do in the physical realm. Usually, that assistance from dieties in invisible realm requires an offering, based on the theory of reciprocity and communication.

However, along with information regarding which dieties will help with our problem and what offerings are to be given, every verse will also have information regarding what the person must do in the visible realm to solve the problem. Usually it refers to a change in some detrimental form of behavior as well as possibly a personal or general taboo the person is violating.

The verses of odu Ifa have a particular poetic structure. Most verses of Ifá begin with the name(s) of priest of Ifá that historically solved the person's problem. These are usually praise names and are very important as praise names contain ofo ase. This is the first part of the overall structure. Without these names, the verse is ineffective as far as from the viewpoint of divination. The names of the diviners usually provide clues on how to solve the issue. This is the most problematic thing for us in the diaspora who don't speak the language. Understanding the meaning of the names of the diviners is important to understanding the metaphysics of the odu as well as the client's problem and solution.

The next part of the structure is the name(s) of the client. They usually provide clues as to what the problem is (or actually was). The third part relates what the person(s) problem was, which provides us with the problem the client might be having. It is this part that the client usually responds to. The fourth part relates what the diviners had told the person to do to bring the ire; to fix the problem. In this part we find the ebo prescription, taboos, etc. the next part of the structure relates whether or not the person followed the advice given her/him.

After this, comes an account of the results, positive or negative. For example, if the person did everything asked what was the result, or if they didn't what was the result. This part is key. If the verse says the person didn't do the things he/she was told to do, usually this means the diviner doing the divination in the present needs to double her/his efforts to ensure the client understands what is being asked of them and why. The next part provides the clients and priests' reactions to what transpired. This is the part that usually says the client praised the babalawo, and the babalawo praised Ifa, etc. The last of the eight parts is the conclusion which restates the main themes of problem, solution, and result, focusing on the manifestation of the result. Within the verse is a part that is the "oriki ire" or incantation, the part that invokes the good fortune in the Odu verse. Usually it is the conclusion. Not all verses contain the eight parts; sometimes they are reduced to four. Verses are usually sung or at least the oriki ire part should be sung.

Some verses relate the creation myth, or stories regarding Orisa, stories with moral or ethical teachings, or historical information. However, most verses are an account of a problem some person or entity had in the past, and how the problem was solved. The use of a solution that worked in the past to solve the same problem today is based on the Yoruba concept of transference, as discussed in the last chapter. Let's look at a couple of verses to see the structure.

Iwori Ose:
Iwori, please look at money
Iwori please look at okun beads
Iwori, look at beads before looking at brass ornaments
These were the declarations of Ifa
To the person whose efforts were being thwarted in his home
But who felt the enemy was outside
He declared he harbored no ill intentions towards the youth
Nor towards the elders
He said that with carefulness
He would expose those working against him

With extreme caution

The first part of the verse gives the names of the awos which provides clues to solution of the problem. It would seem the client is looking the wrong direction, the solution of course being look in the right direction. Also there is symbolic message in beads and brass ornaments. The second part provides the name of the client which many times speaks to the problem. In this verse, there is no guess work as the name of the client is skipped and we go straight to the problem. The next part is the incantation as well as the advice given. The longer version would provide what happened – the results, but we can assume from what we have, that the person followed Ifa's advice and solved the problem. The advice in this case is to pray for forgiveness or ask for forgiveness from those you falsely accused or thought were working against you, and to proceed with caution and smarts to expose the real enemy. The inference here is that perhaps the person was too quick to blame someone because of panic or lack of patience, etc., the person needs to calm down and outwit the enemy. This verse doesn't even mention the ebo. Usually verses come with an ebo to gain the help of dieties in the invisible realm and the behavioral modification or work we need to do on earth. This verse suggests the solution is pretty straight forward. However, I would ask Ifa if indeed there is ebo that might provide additional help, starting with Esu to not confuse me and illuminate the enemy.

Owonrin Ogbe:
Hukuhuku is the sound of the Oro cult
Geregemo is the sound of the masquerade
Nobody knows the secret of rainfall
More than Sango
Pankere is the awo of Olubesan
Olubesan is the awo of Erigi-masa
A child was advised to take care of his pronouncements
He didn't

The child instead focused on his business concerns
the work a child does at night
And that done during the day
It only takes Esu Odara one afternoon to reverse it
May Esu Odara not overturn our ire

Again the first stanza speaks of the awos who divine on the problem and provides clues to the solution. the first wo lines suggest the person might be confused as to the source of things. The line regarding Sango suggests the person is not listening to advice do to arrogance. The next part, that of the client, again goes right to the problem. The client disregarded the advice and felt he knew better. He focused on making money, on his business. This is not a bad thing, but he was advised to also take care of his pronouncements. The next part gives the results of the client's action. The person is working hard but won't succeed. Usually this is because the person is working against his/her destiny but in this case it is Esu blocking their success because they did not follow Ifa's advice. The last line suggests ebo to Esu and a change in behavior to fix the problem.

The most difficult part, which takes time, dedication and study to accomplish, is the symbolism in the verses. The Yoruba use animals, plants, inanimate objects, geographical locations, etc. as symbols. For example, yams are a symbol of abundance. They are the top economic item in the village and truly the wealth of the village largely is determined by the yam harvest. They are also sweet. So in a verse, if yams are mentioned, we should recognize it as a symbol. Many bird feathers represent good fortune; in fact they are very powerful in this regard. Birds themselves usually represent Iyami. Hunter represents Ogun, etc. This is what separates the average reader of odu from the advanced. Of course, the other thing that separates the average reader from the advanced is the knowledge of the theology/cosmology; that is not too difficult, but learning all the symbols will take time and effort.

THE HOLY ODU

Let's consider a verse and see how we interpret symbols.

Obara Meji:
Òbàrà, what did you sell that made you so rich?
I sold pumpkins
The-vulture-was-bald-not-for-fear-of-razor
Python, the diviner of Àgbaalè,
The-blacksmith-does-not-want-war-removed-from-the-face-of-earth.
It was those who cast Ifá for Èjì Òbàrà.
The child between all of them
On the day in which they were going
To cast Ifá (dafa) at the home of Olofin,
These four were always casting Ifá
For Òlofin every nine days
Whenever they were coming,
Olófin would give them food and drink
But, one day,
Olofin picked four pumkins,
And he opened them.
He put money inside one of them.
He placed ókùn and iyùn inside another one.
He put láàràngúnkàn, the clothes of king inside the third one.
He put other valuable things of the city of Ifè inside the fourth one
after he finished with this
Èsù rubbed his hands on the marks
Created by the knife in the surface of the pumpkins,
and the marks disappeared.
When Òbàrà and his friends arrived,
Olofin did not give them food and drink like was his custom.
After they have been resting for a good time
Olofin gave them a pumpkin for each one of them.
Three were curious on what they should do with
the pumpkins.

They said, "Òbàrà why don't you take them?"
And so it was like they all
pushed their pumpkins on Òbàrà.
When he arrived at home,
He gave the pumpkins to his wife,
And he asked her to cook them.
But his wife said,
"What can I possibly to do with all these pumpkins?"
She also refused them and left them for Obàrà.
When hunger did not allow Òbàrà to rest,
He went to the kitchen,
And he put a cauldron on the fire.
When he cut one of the pumpkins,
The money came out in great quantity.
When he cut the other three,
He found all the valuable things that Olófin had put
inside them.
It was how Òbàrà became a rich man.
When another period of nine days ended,
When they had gone together again to the house of Olófin,
He had begun building a house,
And he got married with a new wife.
He bought a black horse,
And he also bought a red horse.
Òbàrà became a famous man in whole world.
He began to dance,
He began to rejoice,
Bells were rung in Ìpóró,
The Àràn drums were played in Ìkijà,
The drum-sticks were applied incessantly to different
types of drums, in the city of Ìserimogbe.
Òbàrà began to praise Awo,
And the Awo praised Ifá
And Ifá praised Olodumare
He opened a little his mouth,

And Esu put a song in it.
He said that it was just like the Awo predicted
They employed their good voices praising Ifá:
"Òbàrà, what did you sell that made you so rich?
I sold pumpkins
The-vulture-was-bald-not-for-fear-of-razor
Python, the diviner of Àgbaalè,
The-blacksmith-does-not-want-war-removed-from-the-face-of-earth.
It was those who cast Ifá for Èjì Òbàrà,
The child of all
On the day in which they were going
To cast Ifá in the palace of Olófin.
They no longer put Òbàrà last.
He is the first of all.
Èjì Òbàrà, catch a black horse,
Èjì Òbàrà, catch a red horse.
Pumpkins
Èjì Òbàrà, what did you sell
That made you so rich?
Pumpkins "
ase

The names of the awos are vulture, python and blacksmith. The vulture represents the Mothers, the blacksmith obviously Ogun. The python represents a little known but very powerful Orisa (Osumare). The Mothers, in the form of Oshun, the embodiment of the feminine principle; Ogun as the embodiment of the masculine principle, and unity symbolized by the python (ere). The python is the symbol for Osumare, who appears as the rainbow. Frequently represented as a pair of serpents or a single serpent with two heads, Osumare is associated with wealth and prosperity. Curiously, the word "mare" ('the immense, infinite, or eternal') appears in both Osu-mare and Olodu-mare. It is said in ancient myth that the rainbow is a message from Olodumare to his mother - the python - in the underworld. Here we find the ancient idea that Olodumare, the light, came out of the dark - his mother in the underworld.

The clues as to the solution then, are to regain balance whithin the client's Ori. This is symbolized as the center of the divining board (opon). The balance of forces inside the individual, the alignment of Ori-inu (inner self) with Ori (destiny) and Iponri (higher self) leads to spiritual and material wealth and prosperity - abundance - (ire gbogbo). Central to the tenets of Ifa is the necessity for practitioners to establish a good relationship with the world that we inhabit. Ifa practitioners have faith in a form of reincarnation where the individual repeatedly returns, after death, to greet the earth, while part of that individual's essence always resides in heaven as a spiritual double.

The Ifa concept of fair exchange means also that by greeting the earth with good character, ("Iwa pele" which means good or gentle character, is formed from the elision Iwa Ope Ile - I come to greet the earth) the natural world will welcome us and support us. We will live in harmony with the seasons, environment, and the other inhabitants of the earth. Clearly understood also, is that if we disrespect our environment, abuse and squander the gifts and blessings that we enjoy while on earth, suffering will be the outcome. Living in an honorable path requires that the practitioner develop specific attributes of good character and moral behavior. This entails personal responsibility, a gentle nature, and a humble disposition. But besides that, one must balance the inner forces. The purpose of Ifa is to balance all the elements of consciousness. We have that here in vulture, blacksmith and python.

The things put in the pumpkins have their esoteric meanings as well. Pumkins (another symbol of abundance) are one of Oshun's elements and the objects put in the pumkins are symbols of fertility, wealth, health and peace. Let's just say that Obara's Ori (consciousness) is being elevated big time. Obara was humble in that he was always made to cast Ifa for Olofin last. He didn't say anything, just kept his cool. Pumpkins also have their esoteric meaning, and the fact that the other awo and his wife didn't want them denotes a certain lack of character on their part. The red and black horses - Esu's colors are red and black. Horses represent a high title, like Olofin or Oba. Esu takes care of those who do proper ebo. Obara did not argue with the others about them sticking him with their pumpkins, and Esu rewarded him. He didn't fall for the trickster. As we can see, there is much symbolism which needs to be recognized in order to completely understand the message. Let's look at another verse for its symbolic references. This verse is in the structure of ofo ase or ofo awure - powerful incantations used to make preparations that bring good fortune.

Iwori Meji:
It is the Agbe bird that carries blessing to Olokun;
it is the Aluko bird that carries blessings to Olosa
It is the Odidere bird of Moba river, the-offspring of the one carrying calabash of trade who carries good fortune to the king of Iwo;
Ela Iwori, carry good fortune to me on my way
The owner of Esinminrin river full to the brim;
Let wealth come to my residence now!
Wherever the Oka snake hides, it meets two
hundred prey there to feed on
The manner of crawling of the python does not
make it go hungry;
It is where Esu stays permanently that his own blessings are brought to him
It is the house that the weaver stays at while
the Okerekere moves to him
It is at the house that the seat awaits the
sitting-buttock;
The dump-pit is a perpetual beneficiary

There is no day the dump-pit does not receive
its own gift
Mighty Creator please gives me my own blessing/gift
All Waters pay homage to Olokun
All swampy lands pay homage to the river deity
All the labour that erosion ends up doing
It is the river deity that is the beneficiary
It is Osin (dove) that commands them to serve me;
It is anybody's clothes that a chamelion wears;
Both the forest and the jungle team up to spin the Eegun cotton wool;
Both the young and old in the town, come and serve me with all blessings;
For the erosion serves the river deity with all blessings,
All blessings

The three most powerful birds used in Yoruba magical incantations are the agbe (the blue turaco), the aluko (the purple/indigo woodcock) , and the odidere (african grey parrot). When these birds are in a verse, it is a powerful symbol of good fortune (ire). Other birds, as mentioned, usually represent the Iyami (especially vultures, finches, woodpeckers, crows). In addition, there is a third group of birds that represent Orunmila or masculine energy; asa (eagle) and awodi (hawk). These are birds that fly very high, are aggressive predators and never become victims of hunters (due to their high flying and quickness). The verse or ofo awure above has a particular structure in which natural facts are used to invoke the ire. This is an example of the principal of transference in Ifa. It is common in the incantation part of verses. This structure also relies on the onomastic principle in context of Yoruba theology.

Another area where symbolism is prevalent is regarding the ebo. For the purposes of this book, ebo interpretation is not important, as it is not needed to understand verses. Ebo interpretation is part of the training of the diviner. However, some information on ebo symbolism is provided here as it is helpful in understanding what diety a verse might be saying will help fix the problem.

In addition to general offerings for different forms of good fortune or bad, dieties, such as Orisa, also have general offerings. Sometimes verses include the offering but don't specify who is to get the offering. The offering itself can give us clues as to what entity can help us with our problem. Clues can be in the name of the client or the diviner in the verse, or sometimes the ebo is given. For example, if the ebo given is dog, the ebo is most likely for Ogun. Here are some general outlines of offerings for different entities. If these elements are in a verse, it might be a clue as to the diety that can help with the problem.

Ori:
Pigeon
Kolanuts with four valves
Bitterkola
Water
Coconut
Shea butter
Efun
All edible foods

Orunmila
Hen
Female goat
Rat
Fish
Pigeon
Eko (corn pap)

Sango
Bitterkola

Cock
Ram
Gbigiri (bean soup)
Roasted beans

Ogun
Palm wine
Dog
Pounded yam
Roasted yam
Bean cakes
Cock

Obatala (Orisanla)
Snails
Efun
White beads
Lead
Shea butter
Vegetable prepared with shea butter
Goat (white)
Hen (white)
White kolanut
Pounded yam

Oshun
Hen, with tied legs
Female goat
Eko (corn pap)
Yanrin vegetable
Corn wine

Esu (esu eats everything so more difficult, but some of his symbolic things are listed here)
Club or baton

THE HOLY ODU

Stone known as Yangi
Red and black things
Knives, blades, etc.
Palm oil
Cock
He-goat
Beans
Amala (yam flour meal)
Pounded yam

Osanyin
Alligator pepper
Ewe
Goat
Ground and cooked white beans
Sanponna (Obaluaye)
Iron club
clothes soaked in camwood
Palm wine
Camwood
Corn pudding (Egbo)
Ekuru

Orisa oko
Cowry shells
Sword
Cam wood
Efun
Bees
Palm fronds
staff made of silver or decorated with white beads '''
He-goat
Melon soup

Osoosi

Hunting bow
Bamboo leaves
Kolanuts with three valves
Cock
Boiled beans

Yemoja
Palm nut shells
Corn pudding (Egbo)
Sugar cane
Melon seed and garden egg soup (osinsin)
Ekuru

Oya
Buffalo or buffalo horns
Axe
horsetail switch
Goat
Hen
Mashed yam with palm oil
Corn pudding
Honey comb
Cotton wool
Okro leaves

Egungun
Cloth
Switches and whips

Egbe
Sugar cane
Pounded and cooked beans
Honey
Foods kids like
Iyami

THE HOLY ODU

Vulture and other birds
Chicken eggs
Entrails and organs of animals
uncooked animals

An understanding of the theology, the structure of verses and the symbolism is what leads to a deep understanding of the verses of Odu. The following chapters provide verses as well as general themes and messages of the particular odu.

CHAPTER 3 SIXTEEN MEJI ODU

ÈJI OGBÈ

Èji Ogbè is the first odu and represents alignment with destiny. This person is doing the right thing at the right time with the right people. *Èji Ogbè* is considered the most important of the *Òdùs* being associated with light and plenty – and is intimately linked with destiny. Potentially this sign speaks about man and his connection with destiny. It is a *Òdù* sacred to *Obàtálá* and represents the principle of expansion, pure light and enlightenment. *Èji Ogbè* speaks of the positive and negative forces that permeate the earth. This odu explains that both good and bad aspects of life are interconnected in fulfilling our destiny. One translation of *Èji Ogbè* is "eji n mo gbe n go gbe enikan" (I support the positive and negative dimensions of every issue in life). The main ire of this odu is success and honor. This odu demands MODERATION IN ALL THINGS. Every positive thing must be counterbalanced by an equal negative. This is why although we all aspire to be within the energy of *Èji Ogbè*, we must do ebo to protect us from the negative. One of the main ideas of this odu is that all things are possible. Hope, faith, gratitude, discipline and work will bring success. Another major message is if planning any kind of change, like moving, changing jobs, etc. don't do it. It will lead to bad result.

It represents high ethical standards which will be rewarded with enlightenment and abundance. Time heals the pain of any matter. We have cut off our own head to make us grow, like the banana tree (rebirth of consciousness). In this odu is born Orisa-nla a.k.a. Obatala. Ifa says an offering of a large catfish to one's Ori and feeding Esu will lock in the ire in Ejiogbe. This person must stay close to and listen to Ifa, observe ose Ifa and offer kola nuts to ikin on his day. It is Ifa that brings the ire, not one's own will in this case. The down side of this odu at the individual level, is the propensity for those under this sign to grow in arrogance, as they start to think they are the source of the ire and stop listening to spirit. This odu warns us to stay humble. Should receive Egbe and feed it regularly. Children of *Èji Ogbè* crave attention and many times that attention brings jealousy. They must resist that need for attention. Again, humility will turn the bad luck into good. If suffering poverty or failure, usually it is a result of self deceit. In ibi, this person might have a problem with ajogun. The person might have a defeatist attitude to their problems. A change of attitude is needed and ebo to Ifa and Esu to appease the ajogun and for ire to manifest.

Gbogbo ola omi ti nbe laye
Kole to ti Olokun
Gbogbo iyi odo kole to ti osa
Lodifa fun Obatala oseere igbo
Lojo ti yio je alabaalase
Ti gbogbo Irunmole nleri pe
Awon yoo gba okan ninu oriki re
Orunmila Agboniregun yehun
Esu lalu elegbara ogo yera
kosi ifa ti ni yi koja EjiOgbe

alase ni a fia ase fun
gbogbo odo keekee kee ti oba so pe
ti o okun ko si laye
gbogbo won nii gbe lau-lau
bi papa bajo, eruku asoloju won
motoro ola lowo Olosa ibikeji odo
mo rije bee ni no yo rara
tani ko mope ola Olorun nikan
loto ni ije dojo iku eni
ase

All the honor of the earthly water
None can match the honor of Olokun (the Goddess of the Ocean)
All the glory of the river, none can match the glory of Oosa
(Goddess of the Lagoon)
This was divined for Obatala Oseere-magbo
The day he was crowned the head of all Irunmole (divinities)
All the divinities were jealous and promised
That they will take one of his numerous honors and glory
Orunmila Agbonniregun did not alter any word
Esu lalu elegbara stayed away
None of the odus have honor comparable to EjiOgbe
Honor is given to whom it's due
Ejiogbe, you are the greatest of them all
If the little river wants to claim superiority over the ocean
It will dry to its source
If the bush is burning, those who need to go into hiding must do that
I ask for prosperity from Oloosa, the second in command to Olokun
I am filled with blessings
Everybody knows that the blessing of Olorun is sufficient for us
ase

Eji Ogbe alerts us to the importance of medicines (akose) and incantations (ofo). There are positive ofo - ofo rere or ogede, and negative – asaan. Herbal concoctions that may also include other elements - animal or mineral, etc., are used in conjunction with the power of the word, ofo ase, to cure illnesses, control natural phenomena, etc. Incantations are powerful and the awo must protect her/himself. After chanting the Awo should lick some palm oil to "cool" the tongue. There are several classes of ofo for protection. The following is an incantation for protection from negative kickback.:

Ofu la a pasan
Arabamu la ape ogede
A dia fun Orunmila
Nijo t'iku ohun arun nkan 'le baba ni lilo
Orunmila ni bo ba se pe bi ise ti omo tohun ba ni
Odundun ni ki ibi o ma lee dun nile e mi
Ko ma lee dun lara a mi
Tete lo ni ki ibi o ma lee te ile e mi
Ko ma lee te ona mi
Ibi tutu la a ba rinrin
Ero pese ni tigbin
Igbin o nile olojo o wo
EjiOgbe, gbe ibi kuro lori i mi!
Gbede ni ide igba olorii!
Ase

Ofu is the name of asaan (negative incantation)
arabamu is the name we call ogede (positive incantation)
They were the ones who performed Ifa divination for Orunmila
When death and disease besieged his house
All evil forces lurked around his house
Orunmila said if it was for him and his children
Odundun says the evil should not be in my house
And should not come near my body
Tete has said that no evil should befall my house

And that no evil should befall my body
Rinrin is seen only in a cool place
Snail is always cool
Snail has no house where evil forces can enter
Eji Ogbe remove evil from me!
Shea butter container is always at ease
Ase

NOTES:

ÒYÈKÚ MÉJI –

Òyèkú Méji is the Òdù that brought darkness and night into creation. Death came to earth in this sign, as did all things concealed and hidden. It is the principle of contraction. The main ire of this odu is wealth and family. In Ire (positive manifestation), Òyèkú Méji brings a blessing of Alaafia (peace), and strong protection from enemies. In ibi (negative manifestation) it would mean a premature ending of a cycle or premature death. Death itself is not to be feared, but welcomed. The Yoruba say, "Earth is the marketplace; Orun is home." What we don't want is to die before the time we set when negotiating our destiny. Sometimes, although rare, Òyèkú Méji warns us we are in danger of this malfortune, but also provides the solution (unless it is our predetermined time of death).

One translation of Òyèkú Méji from the elision "o yeye iku" means spirit of the mother of death. It is a reference to the idea that nothing in the Universe is created or destroyed, but simply transformed. Death represents any end of cycle for example the end of poverty, the end of ill health, the end of confusion, and the end of loneliness. In this context, death is a positive and also represents the end of cycles for example, the end of infancy, the end of childhood, the end of adulthood, and ultimately the end of this life as a stepping stone for the next life. Another translation is "Oye Iku" – wisdom of death. This odu teaches us the meaning of death. Ebo to Obatala, Esu and Ifa (gong) to defeat all enemies. For those born of this odu, success is guaranteed so long as the person remains humble. Humility is the key to success. Must do early morning prayers for it to manifest. This person is driven by ambition, but must be careful to not go overboard. Long life and Orunmila's protection are the main ire's of this odu. Warns of the need to respect elders. Warns of character defects. Must give Ori palm oil, never water.

Òtóótó
Òróoró
À diá fùn Èjì Óyè
Èyí tó mòo rí Èji Ogbé Ègbón è lójú fín
Ebó n wón ní ó se
Òyékún gbébó `nbé
Béè nì ò rúbó
Èsú àìsébó
Ègbà àìtùèèrù
Èyìn ò rí bòyèkú se dojú dé?
Ase

Òtóótó
Òróoró
Cast divination for Èjí Òyè
The one that was that always arrogant to Eji Ogbè his brother
He was warned to offer sacrifice
Oyeku heard about the sacrifice
Yet he did not offer it
The Evil of not offering the sacrifice
The ill not giving the prescribed booties
Come and see how Oyeku mèji eyes become closed
Ase

Verse 2
Ifa fore,
wọn ni keleyi rubọ nbẹ.
Ifa ni yio gbagbe gbogbo ohun toju ẹ ri,
yio di gbagbe patapata.
Bẹẹ ni, o ni:
Ọgan lo da inu orọmi sinu.
Ọlọrọ nirọmi ọran sikun a dia fun Alapa n yawe,
ọmọ amu eegun eja rubọ nitori ọmọ,

maja maja la kalapa.
Alapa o ku ewu, ọmọ ku ewu,
Alapa o ku ewu ọmọ ẹja, ero Ipo, ero Ọffa,
ẹ wa ba ni ni jẹbutu ọmọ, jẹbutu ọmọ,
nla n ba ire lẹsẹ ọbariṣa.
Ifa ni ọmọ sun bọrọ,
ti gbogbo ọrọ rẹ yio si di gbagbe.
ase

The termite mound keeps its contents inside (Only you know your own situation)
delapidated wall, child of he who used fish bones for ebo
in order to have children
divined for Alapa
She was told to do ebo
She complied
maja maja is how we sing the praises of Alapa
Alapa, greetings for just having a child
greetings for just having a child
People of Ọffa, people of Ipo
come meet me surrounded by children
Surrounded by children
this is what we receive at the feet of the King of the Orisa
ase

NOTES:

ÌWÒRÌ MÉJI –

Ogbe, birth. Oyeku, death. Iwori, transformation. Spiritual transformation. Fire. Passion. Conflict. From the elision Iwa-Ori. The character of consciousness, suggesting that the innate character of consciousness is to continually transform. *Ìwòrì Méji* is a sign that speaks about difficulties, especially related to enemies and envy and is accordingly a sign that speaks about personal transformation and the challenges of spiritual growth.

The conflict usually manifests as slander. This person should be cool headed and do ebo to Esu against slander. The main ire of this odu is career success and achievement. The dieties that make this possible are Ori, Ifa and Ile Aiye. This person either needs to be initiated into Ifa (Tefa) or must receive Ifa and propitiate him often for career success. This Odu, as can be seen by its name, centers around consciousness. Iwori is a fire sign and one of Sango's odus. Continuous transformation is difficult and requires the humility to reject our own dogma. Those born under this Odu see things clearly. They dream a lot, and have talent for being diviners or spiritualists. They are successful in a way that surprises people, even themselves. However, there is a tendency for their successes to be short lived. They should be tight lipped, and not jump to conclusions which is a fault of this person. Victory is at hand for this person, she/he just needs to be dedicated, honest, humble and hopefull. Ebo to Obatala for long life.

Iwori teju mo ohun ti nse ni
Bi o ba te Ita tan
Ki o tun iye e re te
Iwori teju mo ohun ti nse ni
Awo, ma fi eja igba gun ope
Iwori teju mo ohun ti nse ni
Awo, ma fi aimowe wo odo

Iwori teju mo ohun ti nse ni
Awo, ma fi ibinu yo obe
Iwori teju mo ohun ti nse ni
Awo, ma ji kanjukanju jaye
Iwori teju mo ohun ti nse ni
Awo, ma fi warawara mkun ola
Iwori teju mo ohun ti nse ni
Awo, maseke, sodale
Iwori teju mo ohun ti nse ni
Awo, ma puro jaye
Iwori teju mo ohun ti nse ni
Awo, ma se igberaga si agba
Iwori teju mo ohun ti nse ni
Awo, ma so ireti nu
Iwori teju mo ohun ti nse ni
Awo, ma san bante Awo
Iwori teju mo ohun ti nse ni
Awo, bi o ba tefa tan
Ki o tun iye e re te o
Iwori teju mo ohun ti nse ni
ase

Iwori take a critical look at what affects you
If you undergo Ifa initiation (Itelodu)
Endeavor to use your wisdom and intelligence
Iwori take a critical look at what affects you
Awo, do not use a broken rope to climb a palm-tree
Iwori take a critical look at what affects you
Awo, do no enter into the river without knowing how to swim
Iwori take a critical look at what affects you
Awo, do not draw a knife in anger
Iwori take a critical look at what affects you
Awo, do not be in haste to enjoy your life
Iwori take a critical look at what affects you

Awo, do not be in a hurry to acquire wealth
Iwori take a critical look at what affects you
Awo, do not lie, do not be treacherous
Iwori take a critical look at what affects you
Awo, do not deceive in order to enjoy your life
Iwori take a critical look at what affects you
Awo, do not be arrogant to elders
Iwori take a critical look at what affects you
Awo, do not lose hope
Iwori take a critical look at what affects you
Awo, do not make love to your colleague's spouse
Iwori take a critical look at what affects you
Awo, when you have been given Ifa initiation
Initiate yourself again by using your wisdom and intelligence
Iwori take a critical look at what affects you
Ase

Verse 2
Ogodo Owu lo gboke Odo
Lo payin kekeke si Oloko
Adifa fuu Alantakun
Eyiti yio mo se ohun gbogbo bidan bidan
Bidan ni mose ti mofi
nlaje awo rere logodo owu
To gboke odo to payin kekeke
Si oloko, bidan bidanni mose
Ti mofi nlaya ti mofi nbimo
Awo rere logodo owu to gboke odo to
Payin kekeke si oloko
Ase

The bright cotton wool
At the bank of the river
Beams its sparkling whitish smile at a farmer

Divined for Alantakun (Spider)
When he was going to perform things like magic, like magic
It was like magic, I have my wife
It was like magic, I have my children
My Ifa priest is a good priest,
The one whose nickname is "The bright cotton wool"
At the bank of the river
Beams its sparkling whitish smile at a farmer
It is like magic I will aquire all the good things of life
Ase

NOTES:

ÒDÍ MÉJI –

Òdí Méji is the fourth Odu, and completes the four cardinal points of the universe. All birth is re-birth in a theology containing the idea of reincarnation (atunwa). *Òdí Méji* is a sign related to fertility and rebirth represented by the vagina. It also speaks about difficulties, especially in terms of unsolved issues in the past. Odi is symbolic of motherhood and childbirth. It comes with the blessing of a baby, probably female. It is Yemoja's Odu. People born of this Odu need to always remember to keep their feet firmly planted in practicality. Where Iwori focused on our inner consciousness, Odi is more focused on our outside environment. As the womb is a space with very obvious boundaries, this odu also provides messages regarding restrictions, limits, etc. The major blessings of this odu are long life – ogbo ato - and Ifa's protection. Within *Òdí Méji* we find the saying, "a single link never breaks." Sometimes you will see ileke Ogun (Ogun's beads) with an iron link, symbolizing this idea of spiritual strength. It is said Yemoja is the "mother" of Ogun, a reference to the source of Ogun's strength. Ogun protects the person for whom this odu is revealed. Should receive Ogun for protection. Use your ability to speak well to defend yourself. Develop your assertiveness through voice – ofo ase. Truthfulness and sincerity is the key to long life for this person. There is always the threat of illness. Ebo to Esu for protection from illness (for the whole family). Speaks of success in court cases, because this person is a really good talker. This person can be restless. Must learn patience. Also don't let others use you or push you around in any way. This person might have lost their independence. Ebo will get it back. This odu brings babies into the world. Ebo for a stable relationship.

Ifa ni ka fi otun we Osi
Ka fi osi we Otun
Baa ba fi Otun we Osi

Ka fi Osi we Otun
Owo eni kii mo kedere
A difa fun Awemo
Nijo ti n lo ree weri ola lodo
Awa weri Ola a raje
A weri Ola a raya
A weri ola a bimo
Awa weri ola saiku
A weri Ola a nire gbogbo
 Ase

Ifa says we should use the right hand to wash the left hand
And use the left hand to wash the right hand
If we refuse to use the right to wash the left
And use the left to wash the right
One's hands will not be fresh and clean
Cast Ifa for Awemo
On the day he was going to wash his Ori to make wealth in the river
We have washed our Ori and got wealth
We washed our Ori and got wives
We washed our Ori and have children
All of us have washed our Ori for longevity
We washed our Ori and got all good fortunes
 Ase

Verse 2
Oodu ni koyi gbirigbiri jana
Adifa fun won ni Idi kunrin
Abu fun won ni idi birin
Ebo omo ni won nse
Igbati idi di meji ni ire omo de
Igba idi di meji lawa nbimo
Ase
Ojo nla ta di sasa

A difa fun won ni di okunrin
A bu fun won ni di obirin
Nijo ti won nmekun oju se rahun omo laye
Idi ni a apa asa
Igba ti idi ba di meji
Ngba ye la dolomo
Obatala , oseremagbo
Majeki gbogbo olusin re yagan
Ase

Success depends on perseverance;
See how rain drops in time wear out granite?
Thus declared the oracle of Ifa to the husband
The same was declared for the wife when they felt sorrow daily
For lack of children
Commence your effort
From bottom upwards
For when two ends meet
A child is born
Obatala Oseere Magbo
Never allow all your devotees to witness barrenness in the world and the world to come
Ase

NOTES:

NOTES:

ÌROSÙN MÉJI –

Ìrosùn Méji is a sign that speaks about traps and a need to listen to advice. It warns against arrogance and provides direction on how to complete one's destined goals. The main ire of this odu are success, long life and happiness. Irosun Meji is fifth in the order of Odu. The cycle begins anew. Birth, death, transformation, rebirth. Irosun is birth at a different level of consciousness, we could say. One translation of the word Irosun is menstrual blood. Menstrual blood is one of the most powerful ritual elements that exist, so that tells you something about this Odu. Irosun is a reference to ancestral lineage. Irosun leads to fulfillment of potential through ancestral support. Its negative manifestation is resistance to ancestral support, or resistance to developing potential (self-denigration). *Ìrosùn Méji* is one of Sango's odu. It is here he learns the lesson of humility. The humility to understand we are not always right and to consider other people's opinions. Sometimes it is saying there is a family problem that needs to be fixed. Ifa says at this time heed advice. Be careful with any actions at this time and don't do anyone any favors. Be careful with who you choose to sleep with. If afflicted with confusion, it is the person's Ori that needs to be propitiated.

Another translation of Irosun is "ire osun." Osun relates to consciousness, to Ori. It denotes the protection of Ori. Thus, Ori and its protection is a very important concept in this odu. This person should receive Ile Ori. This person must look to Ori to end confusion or hard times. People born under this Odu are usually very popular. They are subjected to emotional and financial difficulties throughout life. They might suffer depression or lose interest in their activities. They should consult Ifa for guidance. They must never give their Ifa blood ebo. Palm oil and kola to keep ajogun away. This person should move slowly, learn patience and always remember that nothing is permanent. They will overcome all difficulties by the right ebo, and keeping their minds clear of evil thoughts or ideas. They have to learn to show appreciation. They are persistent and that persistence is the source of their ire. They need to propitiate their Ori regularly. Don't forget the ancestors! A yearly family ritual to the ancestors is a must. There is a plant, called ewuro, that is used to make a very popular stew in Yorubaland. The thing about ewuro is that it is extremely bitter. It is used for stomach problems as well as weening children off breast milk. However, when ewuro is crushed, and crushed, and crushed, in water, it becomes sweet! It then becomes the main ingredient of one of the most cherished meals in Yorubaland and beyond. So, of course, there is a chant in coordination with the plant, that is something any child of Irosun should know. Basically it is the light at the end of the tunnel. It takes a lot of work to turn ewuro sweet, but it always ends sweet. Just like the problems we might encounter in life will always end sweetly if we work hard and do the right thing. This person has a problem showing appreciation and complaining even when things are going well. This person requires an attitude adjustment so the ire can flow. In *Ìrosùn Méjì*, Ifa says that this person is not having economic success. The person's business is not moving forward; Work is not going well; Everything is falling apart for him/her. Ifa says this person is not living up to expectations. Things are difficult, the person can't pay his or her debts or even make enough money to break even. But Ifa says if this person offers ebo, the fight with poverty will be overcome, (s)he will begin to make progress, make money, and become surprisingly rich. It will happen suddenly, and the person will forget his or her problems and rejoice. Ebo to Ori and Ifa to open the way for the ire to flow.

Ada nko a da roko
a da nko a da rodo
ada wa mo foro
a dia fun Ẹlẹkọ Idanre
eyi ti o lọrọ kọjọ ale o to lẹ
Ifa ma mọ jẹ kọrọ ale temi o lẹ mi

Ifa ma je koro ale temi Ifarinwale Ogundiran
ma je ki o le nti o lowo lowo.
ase

Where is cutlass?
It has gone to the farm
Where is cutlass?
It has gone to the river
Ada wa mo foro
help us to understand the case of the Ẹkọ (corn pap) seller of Idanre
who was destined to have success in the latter part of her life
Ifa don't allow the latter part of my life to be hard
Ifa don't allow me _(name)_ to be poor in the twilight of my life
Ase

It is said that this ẹlẹkọ Idanre, she used to package and sell ẹkọ [corn pap]. Idanre is a town in Nigeria. So this woman when she bought corn on credit to make ẹkọ, she would tell the owner of the corn, "When I'm done preparing the ẹkọ and I have finished selling it, I will pay you back." When she had finished selling ẹkọ, she hadn't made enough money to repay the owner of the corn. Can a person who can't pay her debt to her creditors find money to buy food? Can she live up to her potential? Ah! She was building up debt everywhere. This is how she would do it, she would borrow corn on credit from this person. Then she would be too ashamed to come back to him/her and would run off to borrow from someone else. She wondered, "how did my problem become this serious?" She put two and two together and went to consult a babalawo. The babalawos cat Ifa for her, the babalawos said she should offer a sacrifice. They said everything that she is experiencing, she will overcome and become a very rich person indeed. She will become rich in a very curious way, and her money will last her a lifetime. Ah! Everything that Ifa prescribed for the sacrifice, 4 pigeons, a large he-goat, and a she-goat, she offered them as a sacrifice. When they [the babalawos] had finished their work, they said, "Where is our money? Please you must pay a fee for out services." They didn't demand a price, but they said she should offer them something. She said, "Ah! I don't have any money." The babalawos continued to ask for payment. She hadn't made any profit from the ẹkọ that she had been selling. They said, "Ok. We are going off to do the work of Ifa. Before we come back, have our money ready!" She said she didn't have the money ready. They said, "Ah! See this woman, you say you don't have money. Wasn't your ebo offered, and wasn't it accepted?" She said, "I haven't made any money, but I will have your money ready by the time you return." Then the babalawos left, and when they came back after 3 months, Ẹlẹkọ Idanre had become rich! She had the most expensive clothes made out of very rich material. Ah! They said, these are the clothes of a rich person. Rich people are the ones who wear them. She used the fabric to make costly clothing. She posed elegantly on a stool next to the wall like this. Someone who struggled to sell one basket of ẹkọ before, she is selling ten baskets now. Even with ten baskets, she would run out of ẹkọ to sell. Ah! This is how she came into the money she used to pay them. The babalawos said, it is as the babalawos said, it is as the babalawos predicted:

They sang, "Ẹlẹkọ Idanre how did you make all of this money? Ẹlẹkọ Idanre how did you make all of this money? She offered a sacrifice, it was accepted, she used expensive cloth to make fancy clothing, she posed elegantly on a stool next to the wall. Ẹlẹkọ Idanre how did you make all of this money? Ẹlẹkọ Idanre how did you make all of this money?
Ah! She said, when she made this money, she repaid her debt.
Ase

Verse 2
toro ewon Oduduwa
Eni ara ro ni i raro mo
Babalawo Rere li d'Ifa fun Ori

Ori nti orun bo w'aye
Won ni ki Ori ru'bo
Ori ru'bo
Ori t'o'w' aye t'o' l'oun o ni l' owo
Osun, mo f'Ori mi sun o, Ifa je ki nl'owo l'ode aye
Ori t'o'w' aye t'o' l'oun o ni l'aya tabi l'oko
Osun, mo f'Ori mi sun o, Ifa je ki nl'aya tabi l'oko l'ode aye
Alata, mo f'Ori mi sun o, Ifa je ki n'ire gbogbo l'ode aye
ase

T'oro ewon Oduduwa
Whoever feels comfortable behaves so
Rere's priest divined for Ori
Ori was coming from "heaven" to earth
Ori was advised to make ebo
Ori made ebo
Ori that comes to earth and says he would not be rich
Osun (he who listens and blesses), I tell you my desires
Ifa make me rich in life
Ori that says she or he would not have a husband or a wife
Osun, I tell you my needs, Ifa let me have a good wife or
a good husband in life
Ori that comes to earth and says he/she would not have Ire
Alata I tell you my needs, Ifa let me have all Ire in my life
ase, ase, ase o!

NOTES:

OWONRIN MEJI –

Death as in Oyeku, but at another stage of evolution. Esu and Sango are prominent in this Odu. It represents unexpected change, chance and free will. It speaks of sudden change that can be chaotic. *Òwònrin Méji* from the elision "owo n rin." suggests something that is brought to or received by the hand, meaning this person will make something out of nothing. They are a hard workers and their hard work will pay off. *Òwònrin Méji* is a sign related to the mystery between *aiyé* and *òrun*, it is related to the mystery of Òsó and speaks about victory over adversity. The main ire of this odu are achievement and honor. Ebo to Iyami for protection of what he/she has built from being destroyed. This odu brings the message that what we want isn't always what we need. Insisting on what we want against Spirit giving us what we need is inviting Esu as the Trickster to teach you a lesson. This person needs to make a change in their behavior. They are too arrogant and disrespectful. Esu will also bless us in Owonrin Meji with great wealth if we bravely follow his advice. This person should receive Esu Odara and propitiate him constantly for success and protection from ajogun. This person's success is dependent on developing relationships with people.

Iba to yeye
Iba Ojugbona
Iba Akoda
Iba Aseda
Iba pa-npa-sigidi-adaso-mamero
Afeyi ti mo ba da se
K'oro ma saigba
Ase

The unsmoothness of the road breaks the snake's back
Divined for horse
Divined same for ram

When they were on Ifa mission to the palace of Ooni
Inclusive of the horse and the ram
Awo in the palace of Ooni (Ife king)
Divined for Ooni
When he lacked the iba (ase) from his father (eguns)
Iba to baba guidance.

Owonrin is the encounter with Esu that pushes us to re-examine our core beliefs. This encounter is disruptive, confusing, uncomfortable, challenging, resistant, puzzling, perplexing, unwelcome, and difficult, but it is what keeps us from becoming stagnant. This person, if in business, will have great success and should charge a high price for what they are selling. This person needs to develop a good social network for success and care for their reputation. Ebo against slanderers. Possible ebo and omiero to drive away ajoogun. If this person is planning to marry, it is a good choice of spouse; they will be happy. Warns of problem with one's property. Ifa says this person must be respectfull of their elders and their eguns.

Idasiki ona nii rejo leyin
Adifa fun Esin
A bu f'agbo
Nijo ti won nsawo rele ooni
Atesi, atagbo
Awo ile Oooni Alanakan-esusu
A difa fun Ooni
Nijo ti o r'iba ile baba re mo
Iba baba
Iba yeye
Iba Oluwo

Iba to yeye
Iba to yeye

Iba to Ojugbona
Iba to Akoda
Iba to Aseda
Iba to the big savior (to Ikin Ifa tree)
Unless I do not give appropriate iba
Will my doings not be sanctioned
Ase

Owonrin Meji speaks of giving reverence to one's ancestors as a way to become stronger spiritually. Owonrin Meji is an "unstable" Odu. Stability is found in the foundation which is your ancestral heritage, your lineage. To go through life without a connection to your ancestors is to have an unstable foundation.

Osa pe ire aje
Irunmole pe ire omo
Orisa pe ire aiku
Orisa pe ki a ru ebo
Nibi a gbe ri agbalagba mokanla l'ori ate
O ri ona ti orisa gba ti fi je be?
A ji n'igboro, a rin n'igboro
O burin bu omi'gboro we
Be ni nbu omo igboro bo'ju
Da fun owonwon omo a se'gi l'owo
A ji n'igboro, a rin n'igboro
O burin burin bu omi'gboro we
Bi nti nbu omi'gboro we
Be ni nbu omi'gboro bo'ju
Da fun owonwon omo a se'gi l'owo
Da fun ejo omo a p'ate s'oro
Owonwon jo o l'owo, ejo jo o l'oro
Eyin o mo pe ile wa l'a l'oro?
Orisa pe ire aje ire omo ni on yio bun'ni se o
Nibi a gbe ri agbagba mokanla

Osa su ni be
Osa says so
Irunmole fi le le
ase

Osa bring me money
Immortals bring me children
Orisa bring me long life
Orisa accept my offerings
Where we see eleven elders on the tray
Do you see the way that orisa says that this is so?
One who wakes in the city, one who walks in the city
One who walks and walks and uses city water to bathe
So he is using water to wash his face
One who walks in the city, one who walks in the city
One who walks and walks and uses city water to bathe
As he is using city water to bathe
So he is using city water to wash his face
Cast for owonwon, child of one who cuts wood to have money
And cast for snake, child of one who hunts birds to have riches
Owonwon danced, he had money; snake danced, she had riches
Don't you know that in our house we will have riches?
Orisa says a blessing of money and a blessing of children is what he will give us
Where we see seven elders
The Immortals condone it
ase

Ifa says ibori (head cleaning) is needed. Ifa says this person needs to appeal to Iyami (the Mothers) for ire. Esu is creating confusion in this person to force them to look at themselves, the way they see the world, and let go of their assumptions in order to expand their consciousness. This confusion is a result of the conflict between "urban and rural life" (peacefulness and daily stress). Ifa says this person needs to make ebo to Iyami and Ogun, creating unity as symbolized by the snake. The reference to bees is to honey as part of the ebo, which refers to Osun as head of the Iyami. The ebo brings a blessing from the mothers and the mushrooms signify the Egun (ancestors), so a blessing from the ancestors.

ÒBÀRÀ MÉJI

Obara means strength, or "Spirit of Strength." The unexpected change encountered in Owonrin that led to an expansion of consciousness (Esu), leads to inner transformation in Obara (Sango). That is, the successful management of the change brought by Esu, the opening of the door and our walking through it with courage and guided by spirit, leads to the next odu in line, Obara, which is the transformation of the person's consciousness by the fire of Sango. This odu brings the blessing of prosperity. *Òbàrà Méji* speaks about poverty and difficulties, but also the end of these things by learning empathy and avoiding exerting one's will on others. *Òbàrà Méji* in its negative manifestation (ibi), is when we try to dominate others. Egotism is an inflated sense of self; the opposite of humility. The positive energy of this odu is the transformation that leads to putting our ego in check. This Odu reminds us that human will cannot become stronger than that which created human consciousness. This principle is the foundation of iwa pele (good or gentle character). This Odu contains the story of Sango's transformation into Orisa. It was accomplished by his ownership of his faults, and his sincere and successful effort to gain humility. This person must avoid acting with vanity, boastfulness and stubbornness. These will bring misfortune. Ebo to Esu against unforeseen events ruining one's plans.

For the client, Odu *Òbàrà Méji* denotes being in a state of uncertainty, unable to make decisions. For a client in business, Ifa says that to have a house full of customers and friends, she or he will have to do ebo and follow Orunmila. The client for who this Odu comes up in ire, should move on any project they have planned. If he or she is going to travel, they will be succesful. He or she must have patience with business partners, or clients. He or she will be rewarded. This person might be having financial difficulties and surrounded by enemies who plot his or her destruction. With ebo, financial difficulties can subside, and enemies defeated. The client will find out who his enemies are and what created his problems. Must not be dishonest, self centered or greedy. A change in behavior and ebo to Esu, Ori and Ogun to clear away confusion, put an end to strife and open the way for ire. Warns of someone coming into the life of this person bringing trouble. This person might have been abandoned, but ebo will bring the person(s) back. This person needs to focus on themselves and less on the group. If married, cooperation will lead to success. If not married, it is in this person's best interests to get married and settle down. This odu speaks of prosperity. The riches will come from Oshun. The client might need to do ebo to Oshun. A river wash along with the offering to Oshun is recommended. However, Ifa warns this person against focusing solely on wealth; that this person likes to show off, and this vanity will bring trouble. This person should focus on building a home and starting a family.

Òsòló awo Awòn
Ló díá fún Awón
Níjó ti n lo rèé werí Olà lodo
Ará ro Òun báyìí?
Wón lára ó rò ó
Wón ní sùgbón kó rúbo fún Òsún
Ó bá rúbo
Ará bá dè é
Ní bá n bímo
Ló bá kó omo è lo fún Òsún
Wón níkú ò gbodò pa omo Awòn
Ayé ye é
Oshun n tójú è
Ní n gè é
N ní wá n jó n ní n yò
Ní n yin àwon Babaláwo
Àwon Babaláwo n yin Ifá
Ó ní béè làwon Babaláwo tòún wí
Òsòló Awo Awòn

Ló díá fún Awón
Níjó ti n lo rèé werí Olà lodo
Òsòló mòmò dé ò
Awo Awòn
E ò mò Órí rere Àwòn n wè?
 Ase

Osolo, babalawo of Awon
Did divination for Awon
On the day he was going to wash his Ori in the river for wealth
"Will life would be easier for me?" he asked
They said it would be easy for him
But advised him to do ebo to Osun
He made the offering
Life then pleased him
He began having children
He took all his children to Osun
"Death is not to kill the children of Awon," they instructed
Life was pleasant
Osun took good care of him and his children
And caressed all
He was dancing and rejoicing
He was praising his Babalawo
His Babalawo was praising Ifa
He said it was as his Babalawo said
Osolo, babalawo of Awon
Divined for Awon
On the day he was going to wash his Ori in the river for wealth
Osolo is really here
He is the priest of Awon
Do you not know that everything you have is because Awon washed your Orí in the river?
ase

Verse 2
Gunnugun o tori abe rari
Ere awo Agbaale
Alagbede o fogun o tan laye
A dia fun Eji Obara
Tii somo ikeyiin won lenje lenje
Nijo ti won nlo
Lee sebo suru suru nile Olofin
Awon mereerin yii nii maaaa sawo
Fun Olofin ni Isiisan
Bi won ba wa
Olofin a fun won ni ije ati imu
Nigba ti o di ojo kan
Ni Olorun ba mu elegede meta
O la won O ro kikida owo sinu okan
O ro ileke okun ati iyun sinu okan
O ro laarangunkan aso oba sinu eketa
O ro akonkotan ohun oro nife sinu ekerin
Igba ti o se bee tan
Ni Esu ba fowo nu oju
Ibi ti won ti pa awon elegede wonyi loju
Ni oju obe ba pare laraa won
Igba ti Obara ati awon oree re
Olofin o fun won lonje bii ti se ri
Leyin ti won ti jokoo fun igba pipe
Ni Olofin too fun enikookan won ni elegede kookan
Awon meta iyokuu ni kin ni awon o wa
Fi elegede se o
Won ni Obara oo lo ko onle
Bayii ni gbogbo elegede naa si Obara
Igba ti Obara dele
O ko awon elegede wonyi fun iyawo re
Pe ki o lo se won
Sugbon obinrin re naa ni

Kin ni awon o fi elegede se
Oun naa ko awon elegede naa si Obara lorun
Igba ti ebi o je ki Obara o gbadun
Lo ba bo si idi aaro
O gbe ikoko ,ori ina
Igba ti yoo dobe de okan ninu awon elegede naa
Ogede owo lo da sile yin
Igba ti o ge meta yoku
O ba gbogbo dukia ti Olofin ro sinu won
Bayii ni Obara se ti o fi di olowo
Nigba ti ojo keesan
Ti won o tuun loole Olofin o fi pe
O ti bere si kole
O fe obinrin kan si i
O ra esin dudu kan si
O si ra pupa kan pelu
Okiki Obara waa kan ka gbogbo aye
Ijo ni njo
Ayo ni nyo
Agogo n Ipooro
Aran nikija
Opa kugukugu lojude Iserimogbe
Obara waa nyin awon awoo re
Awon awoo re nyin fa
O yanu koto
Orin awo lo bo sii l' enu
O ni bee gege ni awon awo oun
Nsenu reree pefa
Gunnugun o tori
o tan laye
A difa Eji Obara
Eyi tii se omo ikeyiin won lenje lenje
Nijo ti won nlo abe rari
Ere awo Agbaale

THE HOLY ODU

Alagbede o fogun
Lee sebo surusuru nile Olofin
Won o le f'Eji Obara seyin mo o
Iwaju lo gbe
Eji Obara, gbesin dudu
Eji Obara, gbesin pupa
Elegede mere,
Eji Obara ki lo ta
To o fi dolowo
Elegede mere.
Ase

Òbàrà, what did you sell that made you so rich?
I sold pumpkins
The-vulture-was-bald-not-for-fear-of-razor
Python, the diviner of Àgbaalè,
The-blacksmith-does-not-want-war-removed-from-the-face-of-earth.
It was those who cast Ifá for Èjì Òbàrà.
The child between all of them
On the day in which they were going
To cast Ifá at the home of Olofin,
These four were always casting Ifá
For Òlofin every nine days
Whenever they were coming,
Olófin would give them food and drink
But, one day,
Olofin picked four pumkins,
And he opened them.
He put money inside one of them.
He placed ókùn and iyùn inside another one.
He put láàràngúnkàn, the clothes of king inside the third one.
He put other valuable things of the city of Ifè inside the fourth one
after he finished with this
Èsù rubbed his hands on the marks

Created by the knife in the surface of the pumpkins,
and the marks disappeared.
When Òbàrà and his friends arrived,
Olofin did not give them food and drink like was his custom.
After they have been resting for a good time
Olofin gave them a pumpkin for each one of them.
Three were curious on what they should do with
the pumpkins.
They said, "Òbàrà why don't you take them?"
And so it was like they all
pushed their pumpkins on Òbàrà.
When he arrived at home,
He gave the pumpkins to his wife,
And he asked her to cook them.
But his wife said,
"What can I possibly to do with all these pumpkins?"
She also refused them and left them for Òbàrà.
When hunger did not allow Òbàrà to rest,
He went to the kitchen,
And he put a cauldron on the fire.
When he cut one of the pumpkins,
The money came out in great quantity.
When he cut the other three,
He found all the valuable things that Olófin had put
inside them.
It was how Òbàrà became a rich man.
When another period of nine days ended,
When they had gone together again to the house of Olófin,
He had begun building a house,
And he got married with a new wife.
He bought a black horse,
And he also bought a red horse.
Òbàrà became a famous man in whole world.
He began to dance,

He began to rejoice,
Bells were rung in Ìpóró,
The Àràn drums were played in Ìkijà,
The drum-sticks were applied incessantly to different
types of drums, in the city of Ìserimogbe.
Òbàrà began to praise Awo,
And the Awo praised Ifá
And Ifá praised Olodumare
He opened a little his mouth,
And Esu put a song in it.
He said that it was just like the Awo predicted
They employed their good voices praising Ifá:
Eji Obara, gbesin dudu
Eji Obara, gbesin pupa
Elegede mere,
Eji Obara ki lo ta
To o fi dolowo
Elegede mere
Ase

NOTES:

ÒKÀNRÀN MÉJI

Okanran from the elision "okan ran." Okan – heart; meaning from the heart. With tonal change and proper context, it also means "mind." The Yoruba consider the heart and mind a duality that must be balanced like all other things. For the Yoruba, the heart is more than an organ that pumps blood. It is from where our emotions emanate, and the locus of psychic energy. Sango speaks a lot in this odu and so this person has leadership qualities, but must deliberate thoroughly before acting. *Òkànràn Méji* brings lots of ire but also enemies. This person can be hot headed and emotionally unstable. The mind is part of the Ori complex. Both the heart and mind have their own peculiar consciousness and if not in alignment and in balance in the individual, will cause problems. Okanran represents the rebirth that occurs when we place our head and heart in alignment. Emotions have a function. The function of emotions is to tell us when we are either in alignment our out of alignment with our higher self. However, we are not our emotions. So feeling anger, confusion, depression, disappointment, etc., - all the negative emotions - are simply a message from Esu saying, *"change your behavior!"* but changing behavior is very different from acting out. When someone makes you mad, you can hit them to make them stop or you can consider why they are making you mad. Anger is always the result of seeing someone behave in a way that you do and don't want to admit, or a way that you want to and are mad because they are getting away with it. For example, when we see injustice, we are sad and take action to fix the problem, but when we see someone being arrogant we get angry because we know that we are capable of being arrogant and have not risen above the problem. That is a hard truth to embrace, and it is the lesson of Okanran. As stated in Odu, It's a lot easier to change one's destiny than one's behavior. People with this odu have to avoid being stubborn and unreasonable.

Okanran also speaks of new directions; thinking outside the box. Osoosi speaks and shows and helps us come up with new ideas. There is the need to be realistic and not be swept up in pie in the sky promises. This Odu most certainly calls for head cleaning. This odu brings above all else the ire of comfort and stability. This person is destined for success and must stay close to Sango. Should be initiated to Sango, for it is Sango who will bless this person with success and progress. Must not be arrogant or disagreeable especially with superiors at work. The person must not eat sheep or ram. It is the perfect time to start a business or related venture. Travel or moving to another place is good for this person. Ibeji is prominent in this odu. Possibility of giving birth to twins. Ebo to Esu for victory over adversaries, and Sango to uncover who the enemy is. This person needs to be more humble around their superiors to be successful at work. If going through hard times, possible ebo to Iyami, Ifa and Esu.

Okinrin kara nini ku eni
Da f'oba'le'fon
Omo a j'ate ki'je
Omo'le'fon ni
On ti se t'on le'i bi omo
Ti omo on fi po, ti o fi si ni iru?
Nwon ni k'o rubo
Kil'on a ru?
Nwon ni o ru igbin mokanla
Nwon ni k'o ru egba mokanla
Nwon ni o ru agbedo adie
Nwon ni o ru eiyele
Nwon ni k'o mu obi mokanla
Nwon ni k'o ma e bo oke ipori e
Oba'le'fon, o k'ebo, o rubo
O k'eru, o tu
K'o se be tan

O bere si omo bi
Nwon ni obe ate ni k'o ma se
Fun oke'pori e
K'o se be tan nu
Omo na o l'enu ma
Omo o l'enu ma
Obe ate t'on je t'on'i bi'mo yi
Nna l'on o ma je lo titi
Nibi ti oba'le'fon gbe nje ate nu
Oba'le'fon wa nyo ni njo
"Oba'le'fon was rejoicing, he was dancing"
Ni nyin awon awo
Awon awo nyin'sa
Pe be ni awon awo t'awon s'enu re wi
Okinrin kara nini ku eni
Da f'oba'le'fon
Omo a j'ate ki'ije
O l'a gbo ru ebo
Atukan eru
Ko I pe, ko I jinna
O ri mi n'jebutu omo
Bi osa ti wi nu
Nigbati a ri agba kan soso
Osa su ni be
Irunmole fi le le
Ase

Child of one who ate unseasoned stew for seven days
There was the child of the house of ifon
What should he do so that he could have children
That his children would be many and that he would have a line of descendants?
They said he should make an offering
What should he offer?

They said he should offer eleven snails
They said he should offer 22,000 cowries
They said he should offer a hen
They said he should offer a pigeon
They said he should take eleven kola nuts
They said he should make an offering to his divination set
Oba'le'fon collected the offering, he made the offering
He appeased the Gods
When he had finished doing so
He began to beget children
They said he should cook unseasoned stew
For his divination set
When he had finished doing so
His children were uncountable
The children were uncountable
The unseasoned stew that he ate in order to have these children
Is what he still eats today
This is how oba'le'fon began to eat unseasoned stew
He was praising the diviners
Their diviners had spoken the truth
Child of the one who ate unseasoned stew for seven days
He said, we heard and made the offering
We appeased the Orisa
You will see me in an abundance of children
As Osa has spoken
When we see only one elder
Osa says so
ase

The "unseasoned stew" is a reference to poverty. This person is suffering from poverty or infertility. Ebo to Ori to end poverty. The number 11 (eleven snails, kola nuts) is Osoosi's number, so ebo also to Osoosi to illuminate new directions, possibilities out of our predicament. The "divination set" is reference to Ifa. The B'ori ritual must include Orunmila. This person needs to align their head (Ori) with their heart (Okan), and their Ori with their Iponri (higher self). This is accomplished by successful B'ori, alignment with destiny and good character. Osoosi shows us the straightest path to alignment with destiny. This ese Odu, is a great chant for abundance and fertility. Alignment with destiny will bring this person abundance and/or fertility.

Ifa ko o je ebo
naa o fin ko je ebo o da
ko je ebo naa orede orun bure bure
Sokoto mo jalawa
Adi ifa fun aluko ogogoro
Nijo ti n lo re saroji fun n ife oodaye
Ojo p aluko
Are idi e d odi
O d asure
Jeki asibi dasure fun mi ati gbogbo ololufe gbogbo Ifa
Ifa ko o jebo naa fin ko je ebo o da ,koje ebo naa orede orun burebure
Okanran kan nihin
Okanran kan lohun
Okanran mejeji pakun kale oju won kpon
Kanrin kanrin di fa fun Laalu
Tii somo kunrin ode
Oruko ti a i pe Esu
Ase!

Make my sacrifice auspicious
Let the ritual be accepted
And let my undertaking go up to the place of divine realm
My mission will succeed
Thus declared Ifá oracle

THE HOLY ODU

When the tall cock, the diviner
Came to Ifá for advice
As he set out for ancient Ife
To make rain for the drought struck city
When tall cock succeeded
It rained and rained
Till he was soaked
Wings and tail
Soaked and confused
Wishing to bless
Instead he cursed
May evil intents turn to good deeds for me and my well wishers.
Make our sacrifice auspicious, Ifá
Let the ritual be accepted
And let my undertaking go up to the place of divine realm
If Okanran is cast on the right
And Okanran is cast on the left,
The configuration result in
Okanran meji
Is it fraught with grave consequences?
Thus declare Ifa oracle to Laalu mighty lord of the cross roads
Whom we call Esu
May all my well-wishers, my family members, friends and relatives live long Ifá
May we live to a ripe and old age.
ASE.

NOTES:

NOTES:

ÒGÚNDÁ MÉJI

Ògúndá Méji is a sign sacred to *Ògún* and provides wisdom regarding masculine energy and its function, as well as war and victory and the idea of clearing a path, be it to spiritual growth or to a more mundane effort. *Ògúndá Méji* clears obstacles. It represents progress towards fulfillment of destiny. It is the primal impetus for evolution at all scales, levels and dimensions. In *Ògúndá Méji* we have the blessing of accomplishment above all else, but also progress, growth, success and family. We also have a warning of disputes, hostility, violence, and deceitful friends. This person must be honest and straightforward in his/her relationships. Ifa and Obatala are also very strong in this odu and it is through them that the ire comes to this person, always at the right time. Children of *Ògúndá Méji* are very creative and usually own businesses that create jobs for others. They are powerful and courageous, tireless and optimistic. They have many children. In *Ògúndá Méji*, there are many references to Ori. *Ògúndá Méji* from the elision "ogun da" meaning the Ogun divides. To divide something is to create something new. For example, when someone builds a road through the forest they are dividing the forest in an effort to create civilization. Ogunda is the impulse to build, create and protect those things that shift human consciousness as we evolve from stone age to bronze age to computer age, etc. Ifa says if planning to hire someone or invest in your business, this is very good time. It is a great time to start a new venture with a partner but must work in cooperation. Ebo to Ori, Ifa, and Ogun for success and prosperity. This odu speaks of an obstacle blocking this person's ire. Ebo to Ogun and Esu to remove the obstacle. The financial problems will give way. Must be open to other's opinions; stubbornness will bring trouble. Ogunda calls for honesty, courage and honor; it is the call of the warrior, the vow of the hunter.

Kanranjangbon awo inu igbo
Ijokun woroworo awo odan
Maawo maawo awo ojola
A dia fun egiri alo
Ti yio jagbo obi
Ki egiri alo
O too jagbo obi tan
Ifa nire gbogbo
A maa wole to ni
Kanranjangbo awo inu igbo
Ijokun woro woro awo odan
Maawo maawo awo ojola
A dia fun egiri alo
Ti yoo jagbo orogbo, atare, aluko, agbe, odidere, akamalagbo lekeleke, okin alade
Ki erigi alo
O too jagbon gbogbo nkan wonyi
Ifa ni ire gbogbo
A maa wole to ni.
Ire gbogbo ko ma wole tomi loni, losun yi, lodun yi
Ki ogun ma o maa dowo fun gbogbo wa
Ase

Kanranjangbon (what is focused and wise) is the wisdom of the forest
Ijokun woro woro (what is calm and brave) is the wisdom of the deep forest
To be crawling is the secret intelligence of the python
These were the ones who divined Ifa oracle for the most powerful divinity (erigi alo)
Who discovered the secret of the obi (the kolanuts)
When the most powerful divinity discovered the secret of obi
Then Ifa said;

Let all blessing, prosperity, good health, long life, strength, harmony
Intelligence and peace be my lot and the fortune of my household
Kanranjangbo (what is focused and wise) is the wisdom of the forest
Ijokun woro woro (what is calm and brave) is the wisdom of the deep forest
To be crawling is the secret wisdom of the python
Cast Ifa oracle for the most powerful master (erigi alo)
Who discovered the secret of orogbo, ataare, iyereosun, opon ifa, ikodide, aluko, agbe, lekeleke, okin alade and akalamagbo
After the most powerful master learned the secrets of orogbo, ataare, iyereosun, opon ifa, ikodide, aluko, agbe, lekeleke, okin olade and akalamagbo
Let me live long, expand my territory,
let my life be radiant,
give me a place of rest and peace,
attract to me the blessing of nature
Ase

Verse 2
Otere, ile ayo
Otere, ile ayo
Eyi o y'ara'waju
Ero ehin fi'ye si'le
Da fun yemoja atalamagba, moas'ogbogbogb'ayo
Yemoja, o ti se ti aiye le'i ye'un?
A ka'wo eri, o te e mo'le
Nwon ni o ru egba metala
Nwon ni o ru akuko adie
Nwon ni o ru eiyele
Nwon ni k'o ni egbo
Nwon ni o ni ewa
K'o ma'i bo oke'pori'e
Yemoja k'ebo, o ru'bo
O k'eru, o tu

Yemoja ba bere si omo bi
O sa bere s'omo bi
O la, o lu
Ni nba njo, ni nyo
Ni nyin awon awo
L'awon awo nyin'sa
O ni be ni awon awo t'on s'enu re wi
Otere, ile ayo
Otere, ile ayo
Eyi o y'ara'waju
Ero ehin fi'ye si'le
Da fun yemoja atalamagba, moas'ogbogbo'ayo
On ni, b'o ri'yan, a jo,
Yemoja
B'o r'agbo, a yo
Osa su ni be
Irunmole I le le
Nibi ti a gbe ri ogunda
Ase

That which made for the success of those who went before
Must be noted by those who come afterward
Mother of the children of fish, what should she do to be able to have a pleasant life?
She put her hands on her head, she went to the diviners
They said she should offer 26,000 cowries
They said she should offer a cock
Offer a pigeon
They said she should take mashed corn
They said she should take boiled corn
And she should offer them to her divination set
The mother of the children of fish collected the offering, she made the offering
The mother of the children of fish began to bear children

She began to bear children
She became wealthy, she became rich
She was dancing, she was rejoicing
She was praising the diviners
She said her diviners had spoken the truth
That which made for the success of those who went before
Must be noted by those who come afterward
She sang, "if she sees yam loaf, she will dance
If she sees a ram, she will rejoice"
Yemoja
Osa says so
Where we see Ogunda
Ase

NOTES:

ÒSÁ MÉJI

Òsá Méji is a sign sacred to the *Iyami* and the female powers (Aje). It also speaks of many riches, fertility, as well as the descent of the spiritual beings to *aiyé*. It is a sign speaking about chaotic forces external to self, rather than from within as in the case of *Òwònrin Méji*. The principle ire of this odu is financial success and abundance in general. Oya is born in *Òsá Méji*. So then this Odu speaks of ancestors, and the awesome power of the Mothers. The power of women in *Òsá Méji* is the gateway to the land of the ancestors. Oya is the Orisha of withcraft, she is a shapeshifter, the Buffalo woman who can be the hunted or the hunter. This Odu is heavy with witchcraft and must be handled with caution. This Odu speaks to rapid change.

Osa creates radical change in one's circumstances. The Feminine principle in Ifa is the awesome power to create and destroy. In order to create the new you, we gotta destroy the old you. *Òsá Méji*, being the manifestation of sudden radical change, must be respected. Whereas Owonrin is the chaos within, Osa relates to chaos brought from outside infuences - Oya as the tornado, the hurricane; the winds of change that destroy a particular form so that a new one can be created. She cleanses and transforms. *Òsá* from the elision "o oosa," means spirit of the Lagoon. It is a place of tranquility and stillness, like the center of the hurricane. It suggests the need to find that calm center in the chaos. In traditional Ifa, the lagoon is one place used for spiritual baths. It is used to wash away the past negativity. In this case the bath is needed because they are running away from problems without dealing with them directly. *Òsá Méji* also has the meaning, "run away." The translation here of run-away is reference to the need to stop avoiding a problem. In ire, Osa brings changes that lead to abundance. In ibi, the client is running from responsibility, or resistant to change, a lack of courage and steadfastness, leading to illness. Many times, the client needs spiritual help against bad dreams, ajoogun, "witches" or dark deceased interfering with the client's sleep. Ebo to the Iyami who are always close to this person, as well as Egun might be needed. Ifa might be talking about enemies. In this case ebo to Sango for strength. This odu portends much ire. This person will not want for money. Ebo to Oya at the river, including river bath and ebo to Ori for the ire to manifest. Those incarnated under this Odu tend to be hard to control and act sometimes without restraint. They have difficulty applying themselves fully to any task or job; ebo to Esu at regular intervals to fight this tendency. They tend to not eat well, skipping meals, etc. They tend to travel alot. They are good managers because they don't take risks. This odu portends relationship problems. This person will receive all ire by sticking close to Ifa and following his advice. People will emulate this person. This person is good at conflict resolution and PR work. Ifa predicts success, but the client must change conceited, arrogant attitude and learn humility. If experiencing hard times, ebo to Ifa of plenty of bananas. This odu implores us to treat women with respect.

...It was then that Olorun gave women the power and authority so that anything men wished to do, they could not dare to do it successfully without women.

Odu said that everything that people would want to do,
If they do not include women,
It will not be possible.
Obarisa said that people should always respect women greatly.
For if they always respect women greatly, the world will be in right order.
Pay homage; give respect to women.
Indeed, it is woman who brought us into being
Before we became recognized as human beings.
The wisdom of the world belongs to women.
Give respect to them then.
Indeed, it was a woman who brought us into being.
Before we became recognized as human beings.

ase

Kereje Owinrin
Owinrin kereje
A difa fun ope yekete
Ti nwon sawo rode iwere
Won ni ebo ni ki o se
Ki o le baa laaje laje
Bi ara ode owere
Kereje Owinrin
Owinrin naa kereje
A o loomo lomo
Bi ara ode iwere
Kereje Owinrin
Owinrin naat kereje
A o lohun gbogbo
Bi ara ode iwere
Kereje Owinrin
Owinrin naa kereji
Ase

Kereje Owinrin
Owinrin Kereje
This was divined for the short palm tree
When he was seeking wisdom and knowledge in the city of Iwere
He was instructed to do sacrifice
So that he could be attracted to prosperity, blessings and wealth, in greater measure than his contemporaries
He would be blessed, more blessed and most blessed
Like the people of the city of Iwere
Kereje Owinrin
Owinrin Kereje
We shall be have a good wife, a better husband; a most cherished partner

Like the people in the city of Iwere
Kereje Owinrin
Owinrin Kereje
We shall be blessed with children
Like the people of the city of Iwere
Kereje Owinrin
Owinrin Kereje
We will be blessed with all good things
Like the people who dwell in the city of Iwere
Kereje Owinrin
Owinrin Kereje
Ase

Isa n salubo perepewu
A difa fun agbe eyi ti o ti le sa roko
Eyi toko sa rele
Ebo ni won ni [k]o se
O si gbebo nbe, o rubo
Niru ebo ni fi ti n gbe ni
Aitete ru teṣu a da ladanu
Ko pe
Ko jinna
Ifa wa ba ni laarin isegun
Aarin isegun
La ba ni lese obarisa
Ta ba waiye
Nṣe laa ni gba
Ifa je [ki] n nigba rere
Eleda mi ko gbe mi o
Ki n nisimi.
Ba ba waiye ṣe la nisimi.
Ase

Isa n salubọ
Cast Ifa for the farmer
who ran to the farm,
and then ran back home.
He offered the sacrifice that was prescribed for him.
He did everything asked of him.
Failure to sacrifice to Eṣu on time renders the effort a waste.
Not long after that,
Ifa met me in the midst of victory.
We find victory at the feet of Olodumare
When it comes to life,
we are supposed to enjoy a good lifetime.
Ifa let me have a good life.
Ori favor me, that I may have rest.
When we come to life, we should have rest
ase

NOTES:

ÌKÁ MÉJI –

Ìká Méji is a reference to the idea of drawing in power in anticipation of making effective prayer and effective invocation. "Ka" means the drawing in, or pulling together. It is the principle of contraction, the feminine principle. It refers to the gathering of personal power, ase (ashe, ache, axe). It is the deep breath we take just before chanting oriki. It is accessing internal ase and it is the foundation of the power of the word. Remember, "Owe (ofo ase, oriki, Odu, proverbs, etc.) is the horse of Oro (unmanifested ase)." *Ìká Méji* speaks about ones latent or achieved personal powers that can be used for ones growth or destruction. It also speaks about sickness and hidden enemies. This person should receive Ifa and give offerings to Ifa regularly for the blessing of ase. The main ire of this odu is long life. Ika in ire can be the source of power in healing, protection, transformation, and the creation of abundance. In its negative manifestation (ibi), it is the source of self-hate, gossip, cursing, etc. Ika informed by negative thoughts creates a negative world; Ika informed by positive thoughts creates a positive world. Ika is the first step in forming consensus reality. It is the foundation of the collective power of Egbe. It is also associated with Iyaami because power over the world is the birthright of the Mothers. Olodumare gave this power to Odu who in turn gave it to the Iyaami. Ika usually portends to difficulties in general. Ebo to Ogun, Orunmila and/or Ori is usually divined to alleviate the difficulties. Sometimes this odu portends death. Ebo to Ifa, Esu and Sanponna to rectify. This odu comes with the knowledge to save the person from death, illness and loss, as well as all Ajogun. This person must avoid negativity in thought, actions and words. This person might be having problems holding on to their accomplishments. Portends twins for this person. Ifa says this person is surrounded by haters; needs ebo for protection from this negativity and also must not do negative things to others. This person has a secret and needs to do ebo so it doesn't get revealed. Possibly suffers from mental illness due to multiple Oris.

Káwó fún mi
Kí n kásè fún o
A díá fún Oníkàámògún
Omo Aláaka káwó ikú
Wón ní ó sá káálè ebo ní ó se
Wón ní ó fi aaka kún ebo è rú
Kò kú
Kò rùn
Kà saì kábi kúò
Akika
Akika kà saì kábi kúò
Akika
ase

Káwó fún mi
Kí n kásè fún o
Cast Ifa for Onikaamogun
The child of Alaaka kawo iku
He was asked to take care of the ground and offer ebo
He was told to add Aaka to his ebo
He did not die again
Neither did he fall sick
What would roll away all bad fortune?
Akika
Akika would roll away all bad fortune
Akika
Ase

Verse 2
Ifa je bo na o je
Ela je bo naa o rode orun gbure

Iba rere awo ina
Lodifa fun ina
Won ni ko rubo ko baa lee lase
Maje ki nku , erigi alo
Jenkelewi
Difa fun ojigolo
Ti nlo o dena daje
Aje ki I pa omo ese je
Ifa golo nmo se yun
Ifa golo nmo se bo
Fife ire ni I foju jo ina
Difa fun olokun eseri
Inaki sekun dale
Ifa giyan ni mo se yun
Ifa giyan ni mo se bo
Ki ajinde ara ma je fun gbogbo wa bayi ifa
Ase

Ifa, let my ritual go to the heaven
Ela, let all my supplication be at the presence of Olorun
Men will pay obeisance to you
Even from afar
Thus declared the ifa oracle to Fire
But you must offer sacrifice, added the oracle
So your sovereignty can be everlasting
Let not the members of my house hold and me die before our time, the great master
Do this gently
So declared ifa oracle to the stealthy one, which is another name for the divine cat
On setting forth to ambush witches
Witches do not devour cats
For it is like to like (birds of a feather fly together)
Such as this witches are towards cat

Gently I went
Safely I returned
Just as you foretold, Ifa
Some flowers flourish and bloom
Like wondrous flames of fire
And so will you
Thus declared ifa oracle to Olokun
Worshipped in the city of Esiri
As our lady of oceans
Monkey too is far more clever
Than leopards and tiger added the oracle
Softly to go
Safely to return
Grant my loved ones and my household good health, wealth, success, safety, protection, progress, long life and happiness
Ase!

NOTES:

ÒTÚRÚPÒN MÉJI –

This odu brings much ire. This odu is close to Oshun, and this person should be too. *Òtúrúpòn* creates the maintenance of health. The Odu clearly invokes infectious disease as part of the cycle of degeneration and rebirth, but disease carries with it the potential for immunity from future contact with contagions. The immune system uses disease as a cleansing process. *Òtúrúpòn Méji* is a sign speaking of the birth of the cult of *Egúngún*, about witchcraft and the occult. It is also a sign speaking about the reasons for weak health and diseases. A weak immune system can lead to serious illness and death. Disease can mean an unhealthy relationship with nature. In *Òtúrúpòn Méji* lies the answer as to the source of disease, and the info needed to maintain a strong immune system. Usually when we heal from an illness, we come out stronger as our body now has the antibodies needed to fight off the disease. In ibi, Oturupon leads to the spread of disease past its function as a cleansing and strengthening process. Those born under this Odu are rugged and tough with surprising endurance. They are bold, determined people who plow forward like a Mexican boxer. They can be stubborn to a fault. Must avoid thinking they are smarter than everyone else. A change of attitude is needed; ebo to Esu for help in this area, but the biggest ebo in *Òtúrúpòn Méji* is the sacrificing of our arrogance and the adoption of humility. This person has the full protection of Orunmila from her/his many enemies, but must act with respect and humility. Ebo to Ori and Ifa for prosperity. *Òtúrúpòn Méji* speaks to childbearing. To have healthy and well behaved children, offerings to Egungun (ancestors) and Orisanla (Obatala) should be done. We usually use an alias (Ologbon) for this sign when on the mat so as not to invoke disease. This person must avoid visiting any sick person at this time. Ase

Pepe, awo ile;

Otita awo ode;
Alapaandede lo kole tan,
Lo kojuu re sodoodo,
Ko kanmi, ko kanke.
O waa kojuu re sodoodo;
A dia fun Oyeepolu,
Omo isoro nife,
Eyi ti iyaa re o fi sile
Ni oun nikan sos lenje lenje.
Igba ti Oyeepolu dagba tan,
Ko mo ohun oro ilee babaa re mo.
Gbogbo nnkan re waa daru.
O wa obinrin ko ri;
Bee ni ko ri ile gbe.
Lo ba meeji keeta,
O looko alawo.
Won ni gbogbo nnkan oro ilee babaa re
To nda a laamu.
Won ni ki o lo
Si oju oori awon babaa re
Ki o maa loo juba.
igba ti o se bee tan,
Lo waa bere sii gbadun araa re
O nlaje,
O lobinrin,
O si bimo pelu.
O ni bee gege ni awon awo oun wi.
Pepe, awo ile;
Otita, awo ode;
Alapaandede lo kole tan,
Lo kojuu re sodoodo;
Ko kanmi, ko kande,
O waa kojuu re sodoodo.
A dia fOyeepolu,

Omo isoro nife,
Oyeepolu o mokan.
Bepo le e koo taale ni,
Emi o mo.Bobi le e koo fii lele ni,
Emi o mo.Boti le e koo taa le ni,
Emi o mo.
Oyeepolu o mokan.
Gbogbo isoro orun,
E sure wa,
E waa gboro yi se.
Ase

Pepe, Ifa priest of the inside of the house;
Otita, Ifa priest of outside;
It is the sparrow which builds it's own nest
And puts its entrance face-down in a curve;
The nest neither touches water nor rest on dry land;
But it's entrance points down in a curve
Ifa divination was performed for Oyeepolu,
Offspring of those who perform the ancient rites of Ife;
Whose mother left all alone
When he was very young.
When Oyeepolu grew up,
He did not know all the rites of his family.
His life became unsettled.
He sought a wife to marry but found none.
And he did not have peace in his own home.
He therefore added two cowries to three
And went to an Ifa priest to perform divination.
He was told it was because of the ancient rites of his family
Which he had forgotten
That he was in such confusion.
He was told to go
To the graves of his fathers,

And ask his ancestors for power and authority,
After he had done so,
He started to enjoy his own life.
He had money,
He married a wife,
And he produced children as well.
He said that is exactly what his Ifa priest predicted.
Pepe, Ifa priest ot the inside of the house;
Otita, Ifa priest of the outside.
It is the sparrow which builds it's own nest
and puts it's entrance face-down in a curve.
The nest neither touches water nor rest on dry land;
But it's entrance points down in a curve.
Ifa divination was performed for Oyeepolu,
Offspring of those who perform the ancient rites of Ife
Oyeepolu did not know anything.
If oil is the first thing to be poured on the ground,
I do not know.
If kolanut is the first thing to be put on the ground,
I do not know.
If wine is the first thing to be poured on the ground,
I do not know.
Oyeepolu did not know anything.
All the divinities and ancestors of heaven,
hasten here,
And help us perform this ritual.
Ase

Verse 2
Alabahun Ogangan re ati Ikoko ore ni won
Baba Alabahun o si ni Oosa kan tin maa bo ninu oko re
ko to ku, igi Apa ni
Ibe naa loosa naa wa
Nigba baba Alabahun wa ku

Alabahun wa ri ohun ti n fi bo lodun yii
Lo wa lo ba ore re
O ni, "Iwo ore mi," o ni, "iwo nu o
Oun mo pe o feran eran jije
Gbogbo ebi ti n pa o yii,
to ba ti de nu oko baba oun nisiyin o reran je daadaa"
Ikoko lo yaa, nigba ti ebi si n pa a,
nan ba lo,
igba ti won dohun
Ikoko ni "ore mi eran oun da?"
O ni, "ah, o lo gun igi yii lo ni,
to ba ti gun igi yii,
o lo ri won bi won se po lo lookan
Alabahun si ti dogbon ke okun sile
To ti pokun so
Lo ti pokun si pe ko le so
Lo ni, "Iwo ore ko gun igi, lo ri ki… ko gun igi lo
Kokorun bo bi okun un"
O ni o ri beran se po to
Bore re si gungi,
lo ba korun bo ibi okun un,
bo se yegi fun nu un
Bokun ṣe fun Ikoko lọrun nu un
Nigba [ti] o ku bi emi kan si lorun
lo ba ge okun yen, 'gban' lore jan mole,
lo ba du u, lo fobe du si lorun
Sigi pe…
"Iwo igi yi o, oun bo o, Baba oun o"
La sa setutu,
o sa bo bi won se maa n bo o
Lo ba tan ore re pa
Ifa ni keleyii o sora fun ore,
kan ma ba tan pa a
Loju Ologbon Meji

B'Ifa na se so nu un o
Ase

One only knows wisdom, one does not know tricks,
one who knows tricks does not know deceit
cast Ifa for Alabahun Ogangan (Turtle)
the one who used guile to offer Hyena as a sacrifice to the Apa tree
on his father's farm
Alabahun Ogangan (Turtle) and Hyena were friends. Turtle's father had an Orisa that he worshipped in his farm. It was an Apa tree. That is were the Orisa was. When Turtle's father died, Turtle began looking for what he could use to worship the Apa tree that year. He went to meet his friend Hyena. He said, "Hey my friend! I know how much you like to eat meat. I'm sure you're hungry now, but if you come with me to my father's farm, you will see so many animals to eat." Hyena gladly accepted the offer, and since he was hungry, they left. When they got there, Hyena said, "My friend, where are all these animals?" Turtle said, "Ah, go climb that tree. When you reach the top, you will see just how many animals there are." Turtle had already made a kind of noose and tied it to the tree so he could hang Hyena with it. He said, "My friend, climb up the tree. Get up there nad put your head through that loop and you will see so many animals to eat." So his friend climbed the tree, he put his head through the noose, and Turtle pulled on the rope. That is how Turtle used the rope to strangle Hyena. When Hyena had almost drawn his last breath, Turtle cut the rope. GBAN!, his friend fell to the ground. Then Turtle used a knife to cut Hyena's throat and slaughter him. Then he said to the tree, "O tree! I am worshipping you! Father, I am honoring you!" and did everything required of him for the ritual. He tricked and killed his friend.

NOTES:

ÒTÙRÁ MEJI –

Òtùrá Meji is the source of mystic vision. Mystic vision puts one's Ori in alignment with source (Olodumare). *Òtùrá Meji* is the foundation of an individual's sense of destiny and purpose in the world. The main ire of this odu is success, but this odu brings an abundance of ire. Odu *Òtùrá Meji* brings peace of mind and freedom from anxiety. Orunmila and Esu are prominent in this odu as well as Osanyin and Iyami since this odu is related to the use of the tongue (the vehicle of ofo ase) and where incantations are born. *Òtùrá Meji* is a part of the last cycle of birth, death, transformation and rebirth. Otura is birth. Odu are sequential, like chapters in a story. In Otura we manifest mystic vision. We have gained the ability to tell the difference when it is ego, mind or Ori talking in our heads. From here we can then follow Ori, spirit. When we are following spirit, we are sure that what we are doing is the correct thing. There is no fear or doubt. This state leads to the next odu Irete. The metaphysical principle in Irete is determination. So as the story unfolds anew in each cycle of four, the mystic vision gives us the confidence that we are doing the right thing, so we gain renewed determination to do it. That determination leads to the next odu Ose, which is abundance, prayers delivered; which leads to the last odu Ofun, prayers answered. In its negative manifestation, this odu speaks about deserters and lies. "*Èsù* is the father of the lie and *Òtúrá* is its mother." It can be the source of an inflated sense of self importance, or identifying with something other than source, such as greed, nationalism, racism or moral superiority. Obatala is strong in this odu. This person must apply wisdom and patience at all times. Taboos must be adhered to. This person is very blessed, but ethical behavior is a must for the ire to manifest. Must not hurt other people's feelings with careless comments. Must have a forgive and forget attitude. This person must know when to rest, for he/she can easily suffer physical or nervous collapse due to overexertion. This person should make offerings to Esu frequently for protection. This person is or will be blessed with a very good spouse. Possibly has relatives working against him/her. Watch who you help out; they will pay back with evil.

Igbonwo mejeeji ni o see gbagbon s`aja
Dia fun Alukandi
Tii s`eru Olodumare Agotun
Oba ateni ola legelege f`ori s`apeji omi
Igba ti o ntorun bo wale aye
Ebo ni won ni ko waa se

The two elbows cannot be used to place
A basket onto the ceiling
This was Ifa`s message for Alukandi
The messenger of Olodumare
When coming from Orun (heaven) to Aye (earth)
He was advised to offer ebo

Alukandi was one of the very many messengers of Olodumare. He was usually sent by Him to deliver special messages to the human race at regular intervals. All these messages he had delivered without any fault and also without questioning the rationale behind them. The attitude of Alukandi had endeared him to many Irunmole in Heaven. Whenever there was any message to be delivered, the Irunmole would quickly suggest the name of Alukandi to Olodumare. He would then be sent, and the message would be delivered as quickly as possible.

During the course of delivering Divine messages to human beings, Alukandi came to realize that there was great love and affection for human beings who live on earth by both Olodumare and the Irunmole. Alukandi could not understand why this should be so; was it not the same human beings who kill, maim, hurt and destroy each other at the slightest opportunity? Why should

Olodumare be in love with those who destroy the environment; polute the air and water; kill insects, rats, fish, birds and beasts at will?; wage war on each other for no other justifiable reason than to show supremacy over one another? Why should Olodumare be in love with those who were not in love with Him; who disrespect Him and His Irunmole; and who had not shown any remorse?

Initially, all these baffled Alukandi. They later turned to confusion for him. In his confused state of mind, he was determined to punish them for all what he perceived to be misbehaviour of the human race.

When the time came for Alukandi to come down to earth to deliver Olodumare's message, he saw this as the opportunity he needed to take advantage of to deal a deadly blow on all the ungrateful human beings. When he was coming on his assignment, he asked for special powers and his request was granted.

On his way, he decided that he would show no mercy to anyone; why should he show compassion to those who destroy Mother Nature at will? He concluded within himself that they did not deserve his pity.

The day he arrived on earth was a market day. As soon as he set his feet on earth, he declared:

Igbonwo mejeeji ni o see gb`agbon s`aja
Dia fun emi Alukandi
Tii s`eru Olodumare Agotun
Oba ateni ola legelege f`ori s`apeji omi
Igbati ohun ntorun bo wale Aye
Emi Alukandi, Alukandi
Eyi to ba wu mi ni n o pa
Alukandi!

The two elbows cannot be used to place a
Basket onto the ceiling
This was Ifa's message for me Alukandi

The messenger of Olodumare Agotun
When coming from Orun to Aye
Behold, here comes Alukandi, Alukandi
Whoever I like will I kill
Alukandi!

    Before anyone could realized what was happening, Alukandi released the special power given to him in heaven and began to kill anybody and everybody in the market. Pandemonium everywhere! Everyone ran for dear life! Nobody could really explain what went wrong. The next day, people came to pick the corpses of their loved ones for burial. Uncertainty enveloped the world. They all gathered in small groups to make meaning of what had just taken place. They could not. At last, they approached the Oba who in turn fixed a general meeting to take place in the market on the next market day.

  On the appointed day, the whole market place was filled to the brim. Those who lost their loved ones were first given the opportunity to speak. While they were expressing their ordeal and agony, Alukandi arrived and declared:

Emi Alukandi, Alukandi
Eyi to ba wumi ni n o pa
Alukandi!

Behold, here I come Alukandi
Whoever I like will I kill
Alukandi!

    The whole market scattered instantly. Everybody ran helter-skelter. Many were killed by Alukandi himself, many more were trampled to death. In all, more than a quarter of the population died.

  From that time, it became a regular occurrence every market day. Nobody dared to go to the market anymore. Chaos and anarchy took over completely. Nobody wished to go out in the day time, talk less of night time. Anyone who wished to live long needed to fear Alukandi.

One day, some elders gathered themselves together and went for Ifa consultation in order to determine exactly what was going on and at the same time, find a permanent solution to it.

The Awo told the elders that what was going on was misuse of power and opportunity. They were told that Alukandi thought that he could fight for Olodumare and the Irunmole. The Awo assured the elders that nobody could fight for them but rather, Olodumare and Irunmole do their fightings when the time was right and appropriate. He assured them further that Alukandi would surely fail because he was not sent on the assignment he was carrying out. He advised the elders to offer ebo with one matured he-goat and money. After this, he told them to feed Esu Odara with one big roaster. The elders complied immediately.

As soon as the ebo was offered, Esu Odara petitioned heaven and complained that Alukandi had been misusing the special powers given unto him. He said that he had wrecked untold havoc on earth. He insisted that only the withdrawal of that power would do. Olodumare sent other Irunmole to go and investigate what Esu Odara had said. They confirmed all his reports and the special powers given to Alukandi were withdrawn.

Unknown to Alukandi that he has lost his special powers, he was busy planning his adventure on the next market day. Esu Odara was equally busy gathering people together to confront Alukandi on the next market day. Esu odara assured the people that their arch enemy had no more power to wreck any havoc on them. He told them to stand firm.

On the market day, Alukandi came as expected. As soon as he came he declared:

Emi Alukandi, Alukandi
Eyi to ba wu mi ni n o pa
Alukandi!

Here I come Alukandi
Whoever I like I will kill
Alukandi!

Instead of panic, Alukandi met resolute determination. Instead of fear, he met courage. They all responded in unison, saying:

Iwo Alukandi, Alukandi
Iwo kii beeru Olorun
Alukandi!

Translation:

Behold, you Alukandi
You have no fear of God at heart
Alukandi!

Alukandi was shocked and surprised. He made to rush them but instead, he realized that he had no power to do anything. The next thing he saw was the people tying his hands and legs together. He was unceremoniously sent back to where he came from – heaven. When he arrived, he was not allowed to return to earth again, ever.

Igbonwo mejeeji ni o see gb`agbon s`aja
Dia fun Alukandi
Tii seru Olodumare Agotun
Oba ateni ola legelege, f`ori s`apeji omi
Igba ti o ntorun bo wale aye
Ebo ni won ni ko waa se
O koti ogbonhin s`ebo
Emi Alukandi, Alukandi
Eyi to ba wu mi ni n o pa
Alukandi!
Iwo Alukandi, Alukandi
Iwo kii beeru Olorun
Alukandi!

The elbows cannot be used to place a basket onto the ceiling
This was Ifa's message for Alukandi
The messenger of Olodumare

When coming from heaven to earth
He was advised to offer ebo
He refused to comply
Here comes Alukandi, Alukandi
Whoever I like, will I kill
Alukandi!
Behold, you Alukandi
You have no fear of God at heart
Alukandi!
 Ase
Eye n sunkun Eji
Awo Eselu-Mogbe
Difa fun won ni Eselu-Mogbe
Opo gbe ibule derin-mi awo Ijado
Difa fun Oba Ijado
Okan soso omokun
O bo sini omokun
O mo roro
Difa fun Oba Eselu-Mogbe
Eyi ti eewo yoo ma aba niwa je
Ase

The bird is crying for rainfall
The Awo of Eselu-Mogbe
He was the diviner who cast Ifa for the people of Eselu-Mogbe
The pillar fell and became a hippopotamus
the babalawo of Ijado city
Cast Ifa for the king of Ijado
Child of "Only the Okun bead"
And "It showed its redness"
He also cast Ifa for the king of Eselu-Mogbe
The one whose taboo had been ruining his character
Ase

NOTES:

ÌRETÈ MEJI –

Irete from "ire te" meaning "to press" good fortune; or "ire ate" good fortune is on the mat. *Ìretè* is the stubborn determination to create ire, to move towards self-transformation. *Ìretè Meji* is a sign sacred to *Obalúwayé*, the god of disease. In its negative manifestation (ibi) it would be stubborness regarding needed change, or inappropriate goals. In *Ìretè Meji* we find the idea that it pays to stoop to conquer - humility leads to success. The main ire of this odu is financial success. This person is good at turning a profit. This Odu denotes dedication to Orunmila, and this person needs to wear ide Ifa. Children of *Ìretè Meji* must be devotees of Orunmila. This will lead to good fortune (Ire). Head cleaning (bori) will be needed from time to time to help with stress as well as humiliation from evil forces. Children of this Odu must learn how to relax; they become bored, impatient and are easily fatigued when under pressure. If this Odu comes up and the client or a family member is sick, the solution is at hand - ebo to Sanponna and Iyami. Iyami are prominent in this odu, and if this person is going through difficulties, the source might be Iyami, but ebo will fix it. This odu is also close to the mother earth diety, Onile or Aiye, and this person has the support of the earth diety. Ebo to Orunmila and Sango for long life. This odu warns against pursueing wealth at the expense of spiritual growth. This person must treat their spouse well. This person needs to consider who she/he has around them. This Odu speaks of enemies. This odu denotes obstacles that must be overcome with wisdom and understanding. The person is working against there Ori; that is, against their destiny. This odu denotes determination, which is a good quality, but if taken too far becomes stubbornness. In order for our Ori to fulfill its destiny and rise above any pitfalls that may occur by chance or design (through our choice of destiny), it is important to consult Ifa, adhere to Ifa's advice and, when appropriate, offer the sacrifice (ebo). In other words, we cannot simply walk through life and let things happen; we have to take an active role. We must act in order to advance ourselves and our Ori. Without action, Ori is stagnant. Action can take many forms, literal and symbolic, from observing ewoo (taboo), to performing certain acts, changing our behavior, and leaving a food offering. Whatever the action, it is a source of energy for us and our Ori.

Okan awo Oluigbo li difa f'Orunmila
nigbi Orunmila mi lo si Ife
Won ni iye eniti Orunmila ba te ko ni Iku
Ewe tete, eyele meji ati beebee ni ebo
O gbo o ru
Won gbo ewe tete sinu omi kio fi fo Ori
Ase

Okan awo Oluigbo cast Ifa for Orunmila
when he was going to Ife
He was told that anyone he initiated would not die young
Tete leaves and two pigeons as ebo
He listened and performed the prescribed ebo
The tete was crushed in water for washing his Ori
Ase

Iwo ate
Emi ate
D'ifa fun baba a lese ire
Ma a l'ori ire
Won ni ko ru'bo si ilaiku ara re
O ru'bo
Ko i pe
Koi jina
E wa ba wa laiku kangere
Ase

You are a presser (an initiate)
I am a presser
Divined for the Baba with good feet
but not with a good Ori (destiny)
he was advised to make ebo for good fortune
He made the ebo
Not too long
Soon after
Join us in everlasting lives
ase

    Ifa let's us know that with a good foundation (feet) even if our Ori is not good we can make ebo in order to lead a fruitful and fulfilling life. It's important to understand that ebo is sacrifice, and that sacrifice is performed not only by "giving" something tangible, but sacrifice can also be an action.
Ase

NOTES:

ÒSÉ MÉJI –

Òsé Méji creates abundance through prayer. It is a sign that speaks about good fortune, victory, abundance, fertility and the erotic. It is symbolically associated with fresh water. Ifa says that abundance and fertility are a result of the proper use of ofo ase (power of the word) in prayer (aladura). *Òsé Méji* speaks about all kinds of fragility in the world. It is a time of changing conditions in business and relationships. It's a good time for making money and finding love. In its negative manifestation (ibi), Ose would be the drive to material wealth at the expense of spiritual growth. In Yorubaland, children are the number one form of abundance. In *Òsé Méji* we find the allure of the erotic as an expression of the desire to procreate. The word *Òsé* from the elision "o ase" means spirit of the power. In the odu *Òsé Méji* the power spoken of is the spiritual power that manifests as Ofo ase or the ability to have our prayers heard by the Immortals in Orun. This Odu denotes plenty of children, victory over enemies, and plenty of good fortune. Those born under this Odu are destined to be initiated, probably as Oshun priestess or priest. The person is destined to take a position of honor and responsibility within their chosen profession. Here, Orunmila learned about the mysteries of abundance. Oshun is considered keeper of the mysteries of abundance. Oshun enticed Obatala for this secret and gave it to her worshipers. Desiring spiritual growth will lead to abundance. If the right ebo are made, children of *Òsé Méji* will live to a ripe old age, provided they take care of their health. It also calls for strengthening spiritually, getting closer to Orunmila and Obatala, and strengthening one's professional capabilities in order to prosper in life. Must avoid high handedness so as not to lose position. This person will be blessed with a great spouse. The client may have a problem with enemies, and needs to make ebo to Sango and Orunmila in order to triumph.

Inu u won ni o daaIwa a won ni o sunwon
IFA a won ni o sunwon
Ni o je ki won o pe won lo ile ree jeru wa
Dia fun Yerepe
Tii somo Onikaa merindinlogun
Yerepe o o seni
Yerepe o o seniyan
Igbati won fi o ledu oye
Lo so gbogbo ile dahoro
ase

Their minds are full of evil
Their characters are devilish
Their divination is malevolent
These were the reasons why they do not enjoy patronage
These are the messages of Ifa to Yerepe
The one who was the offspring of the 16th king of Ika
Yerepe, you are a bad person
Yerepe, you are a wicked person
It was when you were installed
That you decimated the whole household
ase
We need to clean and empty our minds of any negative and destructive thoughts and intentions in order to avoid the calamity that might be the outcome of such an action.
Ase

Verse 2

The meaning of Ose-Meji, as it comes out from the divination that Ose made when coming to the world from heaven to become relevant, Ose was told of having so much enemies both on earth and in heaven, he then asked to make a sacrifice to conquer all these enemies, He did as Awo said, and He conquered in heaven and on earth (Ose segun ni Aye ati Orun) makes him a victor in two places, He was since then called Osegun-Meji which is believed to have been shortened to Ose-Meji today. He then talked of how Ose-Meji came in to Ibadan and met the founder of the city Lagelu, who asked Ose-Meji to make a divination for him to make Ibadan big with high population.

Odu'fa Ose-meji came specifically to Ibadan. In its some of the verses, the one, which deals with its coming to Ibadan reads thus:

Ibere agba bi eni naro lori,
A difa fun Ose.
Ti ns'awoo re ode Ibadan
O ni Ode Ibadan ti oun nlo yii
Oun le rire nibe
Nwon ni ebo ni ki o waa ru
Nwon ni pipo ni rere re
O si ruu.
Osi ni Opolopo aje.
O ni be e gege
Ni Awo oun fenu rere ki Ifa
Ibere agba bi eni naro lori
Adia fun Ose
Ti nsawoo rode Ibadan
Aje de o niso.
O roo mi a da yaya,
Aje je nri o mu so kum
Aje je nri o mu se ide.

Before Lagelu and his people left the hill in the bush to found the present Ibadan he consulted Ifa Oracle.

Upon realizing his folly, which led to the total destruction of his first, Ibadan settlement, because of his rejection of Awo Ateka's prophecy, he did not want to fall into such an error again. He consulted Awo Ateka for help about his proposed new Ibadan settlement. Ateka refused persistently to help, because of the levity with which Lagelu treated his (Ateka's) earlier prophecy. As Lagelu was appealing and persuading Ateka, Ose-meji, a brother to Ateka intervened and it was resolved that Ose-meji should help Lagelu about his proposed settlement.

Then Ose-meji asked Lagelu to leave the hill in the bush for a place called "Oriyangi" (which is at the present Ose-Meji Temple). But before Lagelu could leave for the new Ibadan settlement, certain rituals and sacrifices must be performed at the new site, and that Lagelu should provide all the materials needed for the rituals and sacrifices. The materials were in groups of two hundred each type as enumerated below:

Igba ahun	=	200 tortoise
Igba eku	=	200 rats
Igba eja	=	200 fish
Igba abo adie	=	200 hens
Igba akuko	=	200 cocks
Igba ewure	=	200 goats
Igba agutan	=	200 sheep
Igba Igbin	=	200 snails
Igba ilako	=	200 "
Igba Irere	=	200 water tortoise
Igba Obi	=	200 kola nuts
Igba atare	=	200 Alligator-pepper
Igba Orogbo	=	200 bitter-kola

Plenty of palm oil and a (hunchback man) "Abuke kan" who will accompany the sacrifices to Orun.

All the enumerated materials except "Abuke" were ready at the site for the ritual and sacrifices. Then Lagelu as demanded by Ose-meji could not get "Abuke" and without the necessary rituals and sacrifices at the new site Lagelu could not settle there.

Fortunately at the time and place of the rituals, Ose-meji's Ifa apprentice named "Fabambo" who was a hunchback man (Abuke) was present. Ose-meji's full determination to help Lagelu, made him (Osemeji) to give consent to the use of his Ifa apprentice "Omo awo Fabambo" for the ceremony. So, following a hint from Ose-meji, Fabambo agreed to be used.

All the necessary ceremonies were performed as planned by Ose-meji for Lagelu and his people at Oriyangi.

On completion of the necessary rituals and sacrifices, sixteen people, eight males and eight females were chosen to carry the sacrifices (Ebo). The "Ebo" were in sixteen bits and the people were ordered to carry it in two groups into two different directions. Osemeji said that Ibadan would extend to wherever the carriers of "Ebo" stopped. (The carriers never returned.) Ose-meji then told Lagelu to worship Odu'fa Ose-meji yearly with the same set of materials used except a hunch-back man (Abuke) who was later replaced to a big cow with hunch back. He asked Lagelu to worship Oke'Badan as well, saying "Ibi ti a ba ti gun ni ati te". He further directed that Lagelu should be buried on the hill when he died. He prayed for Lagelu that he would prosper and be famous at his new settlement.

Ose-meji then put the tail end of his "Opa Osun" Osun Staff into the ground and disappeared from the spot.

Around this mound – "Oriyangi" Lagelu and his followers built houses and established a market, which has become very famous in Ibadan. It is now called Oja-Oba, Ibadan. This settlement prospered and people from other parts of Yorubaland began to settle there permanently.

Lagelu and his people attributed their success to the kindness of Odu'fa Ose-meji and the spirit of the hill, and since then, Lagelu and his people had been worshipping Odu'fa Ose-meji and Oke' Badan. Till today Oke'Badan is being worshipped by the people of Ibadan annually and Lagelu's grave has become a shrine where Ibadan people go to pay homage during Oke'Badan festival every year.

NOTES:

ÒFÚN MÉJI –

Òfún Méji is the last of the Odu Meji. *Òfún Méji* from the elision "O ofun," which means like spirit of whiteness with whiteness being a reference to pure consciousness in its primal form. *Òfún* is the ase or spiritual power that generates consciousness in the Immortals who guide Creation. Ofun creates the manifestation of our prayers. So in Ose Meji we found that Ose creates abundance through prayer. In Ofun, those prayers manifest. Everything we see in the physical world is created by light (and sound). Ofun is the source of phenomena or manifestation in the universe. *Òfún Méji* is a sign denoting greatness and is related to supernatural manifestations. It is also a sign sacred to *Odùdúwà*. In this odu the fundamental principles of earth are born, while in *Ogbè*, mankind is born. However, these two odus are in a special relationship of a mystical nature in that they are the last and first odus, representing the universal cycle as symbolized by the Ouruboros (the snake devouring itself). Ofun means things are flowing well.

The main ire of this odu is the ire of leadership and honor. In its negative manifestation, *Òfún Méji* would be manifestation through invocation that are contrary to harmony, balance and spiritual growth. Patience and compromise are called for and understanding the dynamics of give and take. With hard work and the right sacrifices, success is guaranteed. Ebo to Iyami to avoid unexpected bad fortune. Should receive Ifa for protection from enemies. Must be hygienic and clean. Children of *Òfún Méji* are generous. They are rich in wisdom. They exhibit the traits of Obatala. They can be asthmatic, and frail. For financial prosperity, ebo to Aje and Olokun. They should always be generous and kind especially with family. This person has met with much failure, but hope springs eternal. With proper ebo, success is at hand.

Ofo ase Ofun Meji: "The Universe makes Miracles manifest in my Life at every Moment!"

Ogbe funfun kenewen o
difa fun Orisanla won ni ko rubo
pe gbogbo nkan to n'to ko ni wo
o rubo ojo ti gbogbo
nkan to n'to ko wo mo niyen
ase

Ogbe the stranger cast Ifa for Orisanla
who was told to make ebo so that all he was doing would be sanctioned.
He made ebo, and that was the day he recieved all the blessings that he needed.
Ase

Ifa says this person should worship Obatala. Ifa says that if this person is an Obatala worshipper, they should make ebo to Obatala for abundance. Ifa says the ebo should be made with a recitation of this odu.

Verse 2
Ìpàdé ònà a b'enu símíní
A difa fun iró
Iró mbe laarin òtá
A pa iro pa iro
Iro ò kú mo
Ara ni fi nre, iro di opitan Ife
The converging point of roads
Divined for lying (dishonesty)
Lying was surrounded by enemies
In spite of efforts to kill lying [In spite of attempts to discourage dishonesty
Lying became vicious
Ase

Ifa foresees long life for a client for whom this Odu Ifa is revealed. Ifa says the client will survive any attempt on his or her life. Ifa recommends ebo for him or her.

Itan:

Iro (Lying), personified, did not like the fact that he was always blamed for people's bad choices. In his judgment, people love to divert attention from them when they go wrong. His feeling was that people love to blame him, and even lash out on him, with statements like, a) "You are a liar," or b) "Why did you lie?" Moreover, Lying did not like the negative stigma associated with his name. For that reason, Lying consulted Ifa for his own protection. "Ire aiku" was revealed for Lying, and ebo was recommended by Orunmila. Lying made the ebo. Ever since then, life has become everlasting for Lying as he has survived all and every person who has used his name negatively.

Ifa assures victory for whomever this Odu Ifa is revealed. However, it is essential that the person makes Ifa's recommended ebo.

Ase

Bi igi baku igi niyori
Bi eniyan baku aku awon eniyan sasa nile
Bi eni ori eni baku ,eni ilele asi di eni ori eni
Adifafun araba pataki
Ti yo kayin igi loko
Kowo kowo araba ko wo mon oju ti iroko
Koku koku otosi kokumon
Oju ti oloro
Yoku san awo ,kasai ku san awo
Eniyan ti n bawo lodi yoku san awo
Ase

If a tree falls

Surely another tree will rise
When a human dies,
Another human is born
If the person on the mat dies
Another person will replace him/her on the mat
Cast Ifa for Araba Pataki
Who will remain standing after another tree's death
He was asked to do ebo
He complied
Iroko Tree is waiting for Araba to fall
And he is not falling
Iroko was ashamed ,
And if the expectation of wealthy on poor ones to die are not accomplished
The wealthy people are ashamed.

NOTES:

BOOK OF OGBE

OGBE OYEKU - Ogbe Yeku is the father of all combinations (minor odus). In this odu, the open road in Ogbe leads to a successful completion. This odu speaks of balance between work, play and rest. It tells us to live in the moment. Warns that failure to find balance can lead to attraction of negative entities. Ifa says that there is to be success and happiness for this person, but must always do the prescribed ebo without hesitation. A cycle is coming to an end; time to prepare for the next project, adventure, etc. Must not move or change jobs or anything like that at this time. This person will be succesful and happy. Ebo to Obatala and Ori for success. For enemies, Ifa and Ogun. If going through bad times, this can be remedied with ebo. Odu and Egbe are prominent in this odu. It's a good year for business.

Ogbè Yèku baba àmúlù
Orí Ogbó, Orí ató ni baba edan
Òsòòrò ni Baba òjò
Díá fún Gbàtólá
A bù fún Gbàtówò

Níjó ti àwon méjèèjì nfomi ojú sùngbéré Ire
Wón ní kí wón rúbo
Wón gb'ébo, wón rúbo
Njé ayé ye Gbàtólá
Ayé ye Gbàtówò
Ayé oyin kìí kan
Ase

Ogbe Yeku is the father of all combinations
Longevity is the father of Edan
The torrent is the father of the rain
They were the ones who cast Ifa for Ifa Gbàtólá
They also cast for Ifa Gbàtówò
When both were in need of all the good things in life
They were advised to do ebo
They did the ebo
Therefore, Gbàtólá's life is successful
Gbàtówò's life is successful
The life of honey is never bitter
ase

OYEKU OGBE – The completion of a cycle leads to an open road. Speaks of successfully moving into the next stage of our personal development. Warns of not moving smoothly into the next stage. Warns of a conflict that the person should mediate. In this odu we find the adage, "Ise ti Ori, ran mi ni monje. Ona ti eda; la sile ni mo nto." "I am doing what I am destined to do; I'm following my predestined path." Ifa advises this person to do ebo so as not to lose the good fortune that is close to arriving. The good fortune would appear in his/her home.

Oyeku Ogbe, Oyeku Ogbe
a da fun omo ti ko ku ti o nya l'aye
Nwon ni ibi ti-re ni a yio fi agba dida ti si

Nwon ni aguntan kan ati egbawa ni ebo
Olomo o fi aiku ya l'aye ni oruko ti a pe ona
Ifa ni ki eni-kan rubo ki o ba le di agba
ase

"Oyeku next to Ogbe, Oyeku next to Ogbe"
Was the one who cast Ifa
For "The child that does not die but returns to life"
They said no one would be as old as he
They said one ewe (sheep) and five shillings is the sacrifice
"The child who does not die but returns to life" is the name of Road
Ifa says he should make ebo
So that he may be able to grow old
ase

OGBE IWORI –

An open road leads to the resolution of conflict. This Odu also speaks onbeing on the right path to inner transformation. But there might be emotional confusion. Patience! Speaks of virility and creating children. Will have good succesfull children. Admonishes to take responsibility for your children. Speaks of a troublesome person close to us, but warns not to argue with them. Conversely, speaks of the good fortune coming from a good friend. They should speak well of eachother and be generous with eachother. If having a problem focusing, ebo to Esu. Must not hold bad feelings for anyone. It will bring this person bad fortune. Speaks of success. Speaks of receiving a gift. Obatala is prominent in this odu, The person should do ebo to Obatala including a lit candle at his shrine for 7 days. Warns not to lend what you expect to get back. Must always respect elders. Sango for protection.

Ogbe o o Weyin
B aja re o baa pa Ikun
Dia fun Adimu

Omo atanna ire fun Oosa ri wa
Ko pe ko jinna
Ka wa ba ni ni jebutu aje gbuurugba
Odun odunnii lodun olaa tiwa
Odun odun nii l Oosaa tan na ola f Adimu
Odun odun nii lodun olaa tiwa o
ase

Ogbe, pray, look backwards
 Maybe your dog will kill an Ikun
Was the one who cast Ifa for Adimu
Offspring of he who lights benevolent lamp for Orisa
Because of success
Before long not too far, Behold in the midst of plenty of wealth
This is the year of success
This year is the year that Orisa lights the lamp of success for Adimu
This year is our year of success
Ase

The gist of the commentary states that Obatala was responsible for the situation. It states that an Obatala worshipper has neglected Obatala. The possible ebo is, two native lamps, two pangolins, shea butter, four guinea fowls, four white pigeons and money. The lamp should be dressed with Shea butter and Sefusefun leaves that are ground. The odu is then to be imprinted using the sefunsefun powder which should also dress the lamp. The lamp should also be lit for seven days.
Ase

IWORI OGBE -- resolution of conflict leads to the open road or conflict leads to instability. Speaks of the need for honesty in resolution of a problem or conflict. Failure to resolve the problem might lead to illness. Wealth comes in trickles; need for ebo. A friend provides good advice or makes a good and trustworthy business partner. Suggests spending more time with the family especially to play with the children. Perhaps a sick child. Sometimes sick children are visited by astral mates. A party for the sick child's regular mates (egbe) might be prescribed. And ebo to Egungun. If considering a business venture with a partner, it is a go. The following verse teaches us about mending a "bad" ori.

Gunnugun ba lonrule
Ojuu re a tole
A dia fun Saniyan
Saniyan ti seru ipin lorun
Won ni o rubo
Onikaluku lo ti yan ipin ti oun o jee nnu
Iya e
Ngba ti n bo latode orun
Ngba o de ile aye
N wa n beere pe bo ni?
Ebo l'Orunmila mo
Gbogbo nnkan tee ba ayan ti o ba daa
Oun ni o moo baa yin fu ebo gbe e soju
Ona
Won ni ko lo obo Ori e
Won lori ni mooo ba won ja
Won o moo pe Ifa ni
Lo ba rubo
Aye ye won
Won booku ona
Won ni bee lawon Babalawo tawon wi
Gunnugun la lorule
Ojuu re a tole
Ojuu re a moo took
A dia fun Saniyan
Saniyan tii seru ipin lorun

Won ni o sa kale o jare
Ebo ni o se
Won a nifa ni
 Saniyan
B'Ori ba n ba woon ja
Won a nifa ni
Saniyan
Ori ni n ba woon ja laye
Ase

The Vulture perches on top of a high wall
Its gaze would cover the city
Its gaze would cover the forest
Cast divination for Saniyan
Saniyan the slave of destiny in Orun
He was asked to offer sacrifice
Everybody had chosen what he or she would become during his or her subliminal stage
When coming from the city of Orun
He was asking for what to do
"Do you know what?" They said
Orunmila is the one that knows no other thing except ebo
All those things which man chooses as destiny that is bad
It is he that would use ebo to mend it
They told Saniyan to go and make ebo to his Ori
It is their Ori that would be against them
They would say it is Ifa
He performed the sacrifice
And life pleased him
They retraced their steps to the right way
They said it was exactly what their Babalawos predicted
The vulture perches on top of a high wall
Its gaze would cover the city
Its gaze would cover the forests

Cast divination for Saniyan
Saniyan the slave of destiny in Orun
He was asked to take care of the ground
And offer ebo
They would say it is Ifa
Saniyan
If their Ori is against them
They would say it is Ifa
Saniyan
So it is their Ori that is against them in the earth
ase

This verse tells us not to blame anyone one else for our shortcomings or bad luck, but to look to our Ori. Our Ori being against us suggests mental illness. Notice that it is Vulture and Orunmila that fix the problem. Vulture represents female power and Orunmila male power. It is when the feminine and masculine are brought into balance within the Ori of the individual that we can fix this Ori that is working against the person. How can our Ori be working against us? forgotten destiny and/or imbalance.

OGBE ODI – the open road leads to rebirth, or leads to senseless change (ire or ibi). This odu speaks of rising from poverty through hard work and a positive attitude. These attributes will attract people to us and expand our personal network thus increasing our opportunities. Ebo to outshine ones competition at work. However, no good deed must go unpunished. Ifa says that every positive creates its balancing negative, so the warning is to watch out for jealous people disrupting our progress, or the possibility of ridicule. Speaks of a relative abroad who will be coming back and bringing something good for the person. Also speaks of this person having many children. Warns of wandering aimlessly. Ebo for peace of mind. Children of this Odu have the gift of seeing through dreams. Shouldn't loan or borrow money at this time. Ifa says it expects the ire (good fortune) of long life for the person for whom Ogbe Odi is revealed. Ifa says that this person is feeling weak and diminutive in stature but he or she will live a long time. He or she must offer proper sacrifice and ritual to make Osun. He or she will be respected and protected by the deities. Because of his or her condition, he or she should protect themselves from rain or too much sun.

Ogbe di Kaka
Ogbe di KoKo
Ogbe di ganmuganmu Ire ma han
Dia fun Esu Odara
O n lo fara sofa lodo oba meta
Eni to ni oun o f'Awo sesin
Ara re lo n se
Ekun araa won lawon n sun
Aiwe araa won lawon n gba
Ogbe di Kaka
Ogbe di Koko
Ogbe di ganmuganmu ire ma han

They were the ones who cast Ifa for Esu Odara
When going to make himself a pawn for three kings
Those who planned to humiliate an Awo
Will only undo themselves
It is themselves they are crying for
It is their misfortune they are mourning
Ase

ODI OGBE – rebirth leads to an open road. A threat from enemies is eliminated. Warns of serious consequences if a threat is ignored. In this odu we are implored not to lie. Ebo to Sango for victory. Ifa says if the client is a man, he will be blessed with lots of women; but be careful, his enemies might send him a woman who will cause him many problems. Don't get into it with anyone talking badly. Don't disagree with parents. Ebo for long life. Possible initiation into Orisa.

Idin gbere a rin nako
adifa fun lajon bala
ti n lo re se oko arugbo
won ni ebo
ni ko mase nitori omo
nje omo n be ninu arugbo ayamo
bi a ba si fetu fun ifa
idingbere a rin nako
Kee pe o
Kee jinna,
E waa wo'fa awo ki,
B'o ti nse
Ifa de, alase
Ope, abise wara
ase

Idin gbere a rin nako
cast divination for lajon bala
that was going to be a husband for the old woman
he was asked to offer sacrifice
for a blessing of children
he complied
the old woman recieved the blessing of children
Very soon
At no distant date
Come and see the Babalawo's prediction
Coming to pass
Ifa has come, the great authority
Palm-tree, whose predictions come true speedily
ase

OGBE IROSUN – The ancestors open the road. This person must lean on their ancestors for stability. Ogbe Irosun tells us that every small bush wants to be as grand as an Iroko tree but when a storm hits, the bush is glad for the tree's protection (ancestors protect us). The importance of ancestor reverence is stressed. This odu says it is bit by bit we fulfill our destiny. Speaks of loss – death, illness, court cases, etc. – and provides the fix. Admonishes us to behave ethically and observe taboos. Relationship is central concern at this time. No cheating! Treat those under you with respect. Speaks of the blessing of children. Ebo for pregnancy (sixteen eggs) or for wealth (eggs and snails) to Odu. If in business, this year will be profitable with ebo to Ogun (two pigeons). Ebo to Egungun for protection of children.

Ogbe dawo osun tile ko ro jinginni
adifa fun odukeke
to n lo re ko ire aje wole
won ni ebo
ni ko ma senje
ki lo n ko ire bo wa fun alawo
odukeke ifa lo n ko ire bo wa fun alawo
odu keke
Ero Ipo
Ero Ofa
E waa ba ni ni jebutu ire
ase

Ogbe stepped down with Osun staff and made a mysterious noise
cast divination for odukeke
who was going to bring wealth
he was asked to offer ebo
he complied
thus who is bringing wealth for a priest?

it is odukeke that is bringing wealth
it is odukeke
Travellers to Ipo
Travellers to Ofa,
Come and join us where there's plenty of good fortune
Ase

IROSUN OGBE – Following the guidance of Egun leads to fulfillment of destiny. Warns us to follow taboos and do ebo. Abori is also recommended. This person is destined to become rich, but destiny is not assured to anyone. This person will face much adversity. It is how the adversity is handled that assures victory. Ifa says that this person should be careful not to be greedy in order to avoid trouble. This person should not say that he will do things that he cannot do. She will create trouble in so doing. She might say, "So and so is doing something, I want to do that too." He will meet trouble there. He should be careful and offer a sacrifice so that he doesn't meet trouble. Ifa says that this person should also offer a sacrifice so that when a blessing comes, she may live long enough to enjoy the blessing. He must make an offering for a long life in order to enjoy the blessings. Ebo and spiritual discipline through daily prayer are the road to the good fortune in this verse.

Idawo lọna
Idawo ni papa
a dia fun gunugun eyi ti ṣọmọ olore
abufun Elulu eyi ti ṣọmọ olore
Ẹbọ ni wọn ni ko ṣe
Igun nikan lo gbe ẹbọ nbẹ to rubọ
Ẹru Ẹpo, ẹru Ọffa
ẹyin a wa wofa awo ki bi ti n ṣẹ
Oun ṣe wa wofa awo ki bi ti n ṣẹ
ẹ wofa awo ki bi ti n ṣẹ
Ẹru Ẹpo, ẹru Ọffa

THE HOLY ODU

ẹ wa wofa awo ki bi ti n ṣẹ
ase

Idawo can show the way
or not at all
It's value depends on the person who is using it
This helps us to understand the case of
 Vulture, the daughter of Olore
This helps us to understand the case of Elulu
the son of Olore
The sacrifice that was prescribed
Vulture was the only one who prepared it
People of Ẹpo, people of Ọffa (everyone)
come see how what the priest said has come to pass
He said, come see how what the priest said has come to pass
come see how what the priest said has come to pass
People of Ẹpo, people of Ọffa
come see how what the priest said has come to pass
ase

    Vulture (Igun) and Olore were told to offer a sacrifice. They were both the children of Olore. Elulu was the elder, Vulture the younger. Both of them were told to offer a sacrifice because of a coming day when their blessings would arrive, so that they might live a long time. They were told not to be greedy. If something does not belong to them, they should not say that they are the owners. If they want to take something that they should not have by force, that thing that doesn't belong to them, this will result in disgrace. Ifa told them the very same day. Elulu rejected the advice, he didn't offer the sacrifice. He understood, but didn't offer the sacrifice, he didn't prepare the offering. He called the Babalawo a liar, he called Eṣu a thief. He looked up at the sky as if it were never to become dark again (arrogant). He said, "Ha! what sacrifice do I need to make. You are just trying to rip me off." Vulture understood her role better. She offered the sacrifice. Her sacrifice was acceptable.

Then the prescribed day came, and a blessing came to their house, to their neighborhood. A title had become available inside their father's household. The people of the town said, the title that is in this neighborhood, come take it for us. When the people held a meeting they decided that Vulture and Elulu were the rightful holders of the title. Elulu was the eldest in the house. Elulu jumped on the opportunity and said the title belonged to him because he was the eldest. Vulture didn't want to start a fight, so she let her brother have it. They took Elulu and made him the title-holder. When Elulu became the chief, the people took care of the palace for him. They gave him everything he wanted to eat or drink. Then one day, he saw a butterfly flying in the middle of some thorn bushes. He said, Ah! A fine meal is passing by there. His courtiers said, Chief, can't you be happy with what you have before you? He said, That thing flying there is a great meal, come let's catch it. Ah! They offered him good advice, but he didn't take it. Then he flew out of the palace. He chased after the butterfly and his clothes got entangled in the thorns. That is where he died. Greed killed him. When he had the chance to offer the sacrifice before, if he had done it, he would have had a long life and kept the title for a long time. They said, alright the way things are now, when they finished announcing his death, when they finished burying him, his younger brother, the one who offered the sacrifice at the beginning, they unanimously decided, Ah! Let's make the younger sister the chief. This is why we say, the person who will benefit from the inheritance won't allow a dying person to get well again. They took Vulture and made her the new chief, and she was well-received. Everyone liked her. The town experienced peace and prosperity and everything worked as it should in the town.

OGBE OWONRIN – Our progress encounters unexpected problems. Provides solution to turn bad luck into good luck. Advises patience and ethical behavior. "Unnecessary haste for success can make one engage in criminal activity." Warns of serious accident if going to travel. No alcohol.

Elamosin ki owori babalawo
Nugbuke muro yajoye abore Oni oo
Orunmilo dafa fun Nugbuke
Ogboo oni
oru lutu Esu
Orere domi dami dami o
Orere
Dami lowo uku
Orere dami dami looni
orere
Dami lowo ajojo
Orere dami dami dami o, orere
Dami lowo 'ota o
Orere dami dami loni o
orere
Dami lowo osika
Orere dami dami loni o
orere
Dami lowo Ogun baleje
Orere dami dami lonio ore e
Ugbogbo kpaa o amoren kpaa
Ejiirin Omoren lale
Ejirln jin o
Irete mote omorenla le itete tee o
Ase

Elamosin ki awari babalawo
Nugbuke mura yajoye abare Oni oo
Orunmila divined for Nugbuke hen
Who was to be crowned
Ebo manifests
For those who make it

Nugbuke, the crown prince
Is today beginning
His coronation ceremonies
All dangers ahead and behind
On the right and on the left
Of the rood to the coronation conclave
Should melt and evaporate
Because from sun rise to sun set
No danger befalls the sun
I have neutralised
All dangers and poisons
On the route
To the coronation conclave
Death. sickness and misfortune
Should all clear from the way
Ase

When the Oba of Oboa in Akoko died. it was the turn of his eldest son Nugbuke to succeed to the throne. The people of Oboa were however not disposed to accepting Nugbuke as their ruler. Tradition, however, was on the side of Nugbuke because all the other children of the Oba were women. The other male children were still very much in their infancy. When the king makers discovered that there was little they could do to stop Nugbuke from taking the crown, they contrived other diabolical means of stopping him·. It was at that stage that Nugbuke invited a surrogate of Ogbe-Owonrin to make divination for him on what to do to ascend to his father's throne without let or hindrance. The name of the owo was called Oklkl bababa nimeru okpokpo. There was a secret shrine in the town called Otu-Ife which was the secret conclave at which the coronation ceremonies traditionally began. The prospective Oba had to walk blind-folded from his house to the shrine.

Unknown to Nugbuke however, the conspirators who were determined to stand between him and the crown had plotted to line the route with all kinds of harmful installations. They planted charms, dangerous Insects and animals, serpents and scorpions through the route, from the town to the shrine. The dangerous things were concealed and planted on the foot-path ali along the way. ·

At divination, Oklkl bababa advised Nugbuke to offer a he-goat to Esu and to prepare ebo with three palm branches like the ones used for reinforcing the floor of a new building or a well during construction and called (Ugbogbo egho In Yoruba). The awo prepared a special pot with a hen, a cock and the relevant leaves used as antedote for poisoned or spoilt ground. The three palm branches were painted with chalk and camwood. OgbeOwanrin and Oklki bababa volunteered to accompany Nugbuke to the shrine. It was the tradition for the kingmakers and the chief priests to go to the shrine before the crown prince. The crown prince would traditionally leave the town for the shrine after Oro or the secret herald had declared a curfew throughout the whole town from the direction of the shrine. As soon as the curfew was declared by Oro. it was the call-tune for the crown prince to commence his journey to the shrine, whlch was after dark. Nugbuke and one of his escorts held a palm branch each while Okiki bababa held the antedote pot. It is important to emphasise that although tradition demanded that no one should accompany the crown prince to the shrine, the two awos defied the custom because no secret chronicle (Oro) can stop any lfa priest.

As they began the march to the shrine, the awo holding the pot was sprinkling the liquid from the pot with a special palm frond as the others were hitting the ground with the palm branches. The exercise was accompanied throughout the route with the following song:

Elamosin ki owori babalawo,
Nugbuke muro yajoye abore Oni oo.
Orunmilo dafa fun Nugbuke.
Ogboo oni. oru lutu Esu,

Orere domi dami dami o, Orere
Dami lowo uku
Orere dami dami looni orere,
Dami lowo ajojo
Orere dami dami dami o, orere.
Dami lowo 'otao
Orere dami dami lonio orere.
Dami lowo osika
Orere dami dami lonio orere,
Dami lowo Ogun baleje,
Orere dami dami lonio ore e
Ugbogbo kpaa o amoren kpaa
Ejiirin Omoren lale.
Ejirln jin o,
Irete mote omorenla le itete tee o

With these operations they succeeded in neutralizing all the dangers on the route to the shrine. As the trip got to the gate of the shrine, Nugbuke was told to lead the procession. When the kingmakers and the priests saw him at the gate they instantaneously stood up and gave him a standing ovation, amazed that he was able to survive the ordeal. They had no choice but to begin the coronation ceremonies. After concluding the ceremonies at the shrlne, all the elders led him in procession to complete the installation at the palace. He was successfully crowned the next Oba of Oboa-Akoko.

When this Odu comes out divination, the person should be told that the ground of his house has been spoilt for him/her and that he should offer a he-goat to Esu. The same operation that was done for Nugbuke should be done for the person by anointing the ground from the lfa shrine to the Esu shrine. The water from the pot should be sprinkled around the house.

Ase

OWONRIN OGBE – Chaos leads to ire (good fortune) or lack of humility (arrogance) blocks ire. Ori tutu is the main thing with this odu. A cool head. The person needs to keep a cool head, calm the mind and minimize confusion so to better analyze and solve any problems and avoid a possible accident. Divination will reveal the impending issue. Head cleaning and house cleaning a must, and probable ebo to Esu and/or Obatala. Owonrin S'ogbe is one of the Odus invoked when doing ebo:
"Owonrin Sogbe, k'Esu o waa gba a"
"Owonrin Sogbe, the one that calls on Esu to quickly accept it (the ebo)"

The person needs to follow the guidance of their parents, and develop iwa pele. Possible adimu to person's Egun. Dried okra soup and pounded yam pudding. Also admonishes the person to not lend anything to anyone for a time determined by the diviner. If the person has things loaned out or someone owes money, let it go; do not get into confrontation. Take what you can get and leave it at that. Greed is very much thought to cause one problems. Owonrin Sogbe says,

Ohun ti a ba fi eso mu, ki I baje
Ohun ti a ba fi agbara mu ni nni 'ni l'ara

An honest acquisition lasts longer; an honest approach brings positive results
A dishonest approach leads to difficulties
Owonrin S'ogbe tells us to receive with gratitude and contentment, and give with no strings attached.

This odu speaks of a confused mind, which in this case is being caused by Esu, but could also be from other negative forces. Either way, the problem isn't Esu it's the person who by their resistance to growth have brought Esu into their lives or by negative thinking are attracting negative energies. Head cleaning and ebo to Esu (maybe 3 roosters and money). In addition, Ifa medicine of bitter Jogbo leaf (the person is bitter) crushed in water and the iyerosun from the opon sprinkeld in it. The person must drink it while the awo chants the incantation. Most important changing the way they think or releasing from dogma. Doing this will bring the blessings of Ogbe. Abori at the river to calm the mind and dispel confusion. This change can lead to transformation as we examine our past lessons and apply the wisdom gained in new ways. The ancestors speak in this odu and it is through dreams that they communicate. Ifa says pay attention to your dreams. Ebo to Esu to close the door to misfortune. By constant head cleanings (abori) we will increase our intuition and ability to handle the chaos with a cool head. Our intuition is keen. Ebo to Obatala for clarity and wisdom and patience, and Egbe for support. Our suffering will only come from our own lack of confidence. Ifa warns us not to rely heavily on the advice of friends. Daily prayers to Ori and ebo to Ogun. It will be Ogun and Ori who will restore all that Olodumare has given. Ifa says to work very closely with an Ogun priest and do not discard any gifts that are received in mysterious circumstances. Ifa says to feed Ogun often as you pray for blockages to be removed from emotional and financial difficulties.

Esu kuori
Egba kuori
A difa fun won Nireesa jekujeja
Esu kuro lori mi
Kuro lori awon ore mi
... O dori Odi
O dori ota
O dori agbebo momo rubo
Esu moo ba Oluwa re rele
Bi n roko
Esu moo tele
Bi n rodo

Esu moo tele
Ase

Esu don't revolve around my Ori
Sickness dont revolve around my Ori
Cast Ifa for them in Iresa jekujeja
Esu please stay away from my Ori
Leave the Ori of all my friends
Go unto the Ori of malevolent enemies
go unto the Ori of my defiant enemies
Esu follow them to their homes
When they go to their farms
Esu follow them
When going to the stream
Esu follow them
Ase

OGBE OBARA – the open road leads to self discovery. This odu speaks on the necessity to watch our health closely and exercise. This person needs to keep his/her mind calm. Speaks of our iponri protecting us on earth and prayers to Olorun. Ifa predicts lots of money coming to this person but they need to prepare their ori lest the opportunity pass by. Take leaf of Ela, palm leaf and blood from a pigeon and grind and rub into incisions on the head. Ifa says to be kind and generous with our spouse because they will bring peace of mind to the home. Ifa says, the person has a close friend who is not really the person's friend and will bring misfortune. This odu speaks on protecting our children. Adimu to Esu and Yemoja for protection of our children. Ifa says he foresees victory over our enemies. We must appease Sango to lighten any attacks against us, and appeal to Orunmila for total victory over all our enemies. Ifa says that abundance and prosperity will come to groups easier than individuals. We should make ebo so that the groups are in harmony, or that any group formed will be in harmony. Ifa says take good care of our spouse. He or she will bring good fortune. This person has an enemy close to him/her. This person's child will one day rise above all this person's enemies.

ogbe gbarada telegan loku
ifa se oun tan o ku ti elenu
adifa fun olomo ara adie funfun sepile ola won ni ebo ni kose
o rubo ni o ba la
Kee pe o
Kee jinna
E tete waa ba wa ni jebutu aje suuru
Ase

Ogbe does things wonderfully
Cast divination
For he who was asked to offer a white chicken to his Ori to receive blessings
He did the ebo
And became blessed
Very soon,
At no distant date
Come and join us where there's plenty of money and peace of mind
Ase

OBARA OGBE – self transformation leads to the open road. This odu is central in Ifa. It embodies the reason for everything we do in our tradition. This Odu speaks of the person becoming very rich. Also says the person will become famous based on the power of speech and the ability to resolve conflicts. It brings such great blessing because, again, the whole point of what we do is to engage in continous self transformation, being reborn everyday. When we do this, the door opens to Ogbe, which is perfect alignment with destiny. However, every odu is perfectly balanced. Positive and negative come in equal amounts. So, this odu has the ase to bring great blessings and great misfortune. In this Odu the misfortune usually is coming from ajogun. So it recommends Ebo to Esu for protection from ajoguns if indeed it is found in divination that the odu comes in ibi and the source of the ibi is ajogun.

Aworan o loju ekun
A difa fun Latoose tii somo Arole
Sigidi o yirun pada A difa fun
Siinrinkusin tii somo osin
Ope eluju abimo gudugudu
A difa fun Soorowo tii somo iyami aje
Oju wonu ibu o jokoo
A difa fun Karubo ko da tii somo Elegbara
Nje baa ba feku rubo Ifa je o moo fin
Siinrinkusin
Ifa jebo o da felebo
Siinrinkusin
Nje baa ba feja rubo
Ifa je o moo fin
Siinrinkusin
Ifa jebo o da felebo
Siinrinkusin
Nje baa ba feran rubo
Ifa je o moo fin
Siinrinkusin
Ifa jebo o da felebo
Siinrinkusin
Ase

A portrait has no eye to shed tears
Cast Ifa for Latoose the child of Arole
Wood icon cannot turn its neck
Cast Ifa for Siinrinkusin the child of Osun
The magnanimous Ope tree with flambuoyant fronds

Cast Ifa for Soorowo the child of Iyami Aje
Oju wonu ibu o jokoo
Cast Ifa for Ka rubo ko da the child of Elegbara
If you use rats for sacrifice let it be accepted
Siirinkusin
Ifa let the sacrifice be accepted for the one who offered it
Siirinkusin
If you use fish for sacrifice let it be accepted
Siirinkusin
Ifa let the sacrifice be accepted for the one who offered it
Siirinkusin
If you use meat for sacrifice let it be accepted
Siirinkusin
Ifa let the sacrifice be accepted for the one who offered it
Siirinkusin
Ase

OGBE OKANRAN – the open road leads to new directions. This odu says we need to try something different to achieve our goals easier. Time to brainstorm new ideas, new methods. Warns us to take responsibility for our actions or experience the consequences. Speaks of losses due to half-measures. Person needs to slow down and make sure each step is complete before going to the next step. The person needs to do the entire ebo. Ebo to Ori for success. Ebo to Ogun to lessen the difficulties brought by half measures. This person will surprise even her/himself regarding a wonderful accomplishment. If a child is expected, the child will accomplish great things. Ifa predicts long life for this person. Unexpected good fortune is coming; must do ebo to secure it. The good fortune is coming from the person's Ori. The person must propitiate their Ori. This odu says that if we maintain good character and not think bad things about others, we will be protected from any evil done against us.

Ogbe n kànràn

THE HOLY ODU

A sese ileke
Diá fún Orí omo atèté n'íran
Omo atètè gbeni kù f'Óòsà
Wón ní kó sákáalè, ebo ní síse
Ó gbé'bo, Ó rúbo
Ori níí ró'ní táàá fíí j'oba
Riru ebo ni i gbe ni
Airu ki i gb'eeyan.
E waa ba ni ni wowo omo
Ase

Ogbe touched the material firmly
Like the sound of a suitcase tied shut with rope
They were the ones who cast Ifa for Ori
the principal initiator
of all achievements
Who supports one well ahead of any Òrìsà
He was advised to offer ebo
He fulfilled
It is doing ebo that brings blessings
Neglect of ebo pays no man
Come and join us where there are plenty of children
Ase

Ori went to the above mentioned awos for consultation to see if it was possible to help all humans during their time on earth. Ori was told to do ebo of money in order to accomplish its mission. In short time, there was no Òrìsà or Irúnmolè that could help anyone, nor was there any that could hurt anyone who was propitiating their Ori. Since that day, Ori became the extension of Olodumare whom resides in each human. So anyone who receives the help of his/her Ori receives all the good things in life.

OKANRAN OGBE – taking a new direction leads to the open road. Good fortune comes from assuming new responsibilities. Speaks of overcoming enemies or competition at work to rise to a new position. This odu tells us to act like Orunmila (Ifa ethics) in order to receive blessings. Ebo to Ifa for blessings. Ebo to Ogun for victory over enemies. Good time if planning a new business venture.

A kii s' omo Babalawo ka binu
A kii omo Onisegun ka saigboran
A kii omo Baale ka ba lu je
Dia fun Adekanmbi
Tii omo Okanran Sode
Mo gbo wipe Awo N sode
Mo awon so o
Kee pe o
Kee jinna
E waa wo'fa awo ki
B'o ti nse
Ifa de, alase
Ope, abise wara
Ase

A Babalawo's child must not display anger
An herbalist's child must not be recalcitrant
The child of the community head must not create chaos in the community.
These were the declarations of Ifa to Adekanmbi
Who is a child of Okanran Sode?
When I hear that Awo is being initiated
I joined them and got myself initiated
Very soon
At no distant date
Come and see the Babalawo's prediction
Coming to pass

Ifa has come, the great authority
Palm-tree, whose predictions come true speedily
Ase

OGBE OGUNDA – a.k.a. Ogbe Yonu (Ogbe calms our anger) an open road requires the removal of obstacles or the open road encounters conflict. "Anger does us no good, patience is the Father of Good Character." Ifa will bring us victory over our enemies. This odu speaks of receiving wealth from prior efforts. Ebo to Ifa; fish, rat and kola. Success is imminent. Warns us to be generous with what we have. Warns not to turn down a gift or an opportunity that at first glance doesn't look good. In this odu is also found the itan (story) of How Orunmila calmed the anger of the Mothers (Iyami). The man should avoid confrontation at this time, cool head prevails. Fighting could lead to prison time. The woman should be very careful with her credit. Tells the story of the guy (awuretete) who does his job very well, but quietly. He is overlooked and even ridiculed, but in the end, receives recognition and a pay raise. Warns not to disrespect our superiors at work and to not forget our elders who taught us the ways of the religion. Ori tutu – a cool head, and suuru – patience and compassion, are the keys to victory in this Odu. This person is experience tough times, but Ifa says don't give up because we will overcome with ebo and suuru. Ebo with two pigeons, two hens, two guinea-fowls, two roosters, two rats, two fish and money. River bath and abori for a cool head. Ifa says this person will receive the promotion above her/his competitors, but must act with patience and take whatever abuse his competitors throw at him/her. It will be noticed by the bosses and this person shall triumph.

Inú bíbí níí so ibi ti wón ti wá
Alájàngbulà níí fiira rèé hàn
O tún kó'seè rè dé, orúko níí so'ni
Diá fún Òjòlá
Diá fún Sèbé

Díá fún Oká
Díá fún Nìnì
Tíí s'omo ìkeyìn-i won
Tí yóó je Alápà-Níràwé
Nílé Oníyanja
Wón ní kó sákáalè, ebo ní síse
Riru ebo ni i gbe ni
Airu ki i gb'eeyan.
E waa ba ni ni wowo omo
ase

Uncontrollable temper often reveals one's experience
He who fights without paying attention pleads for never ending conflict
And exposing him/herself (in bad light)
"You-have-come-again-with-your-attitude" has only one (bad) name
They were the ones who cast Ifa for Òjòlá (boa constrictor)
And did the same for Sèbé (viper)
They also divined for Oká (cobra)
And projecting the same for Níní (a non-poisonous viper with beautiful colors)
Who was the last to be born
When competing for position of Niràwé Alapa
In the land of Oniyanja
They were advised to do ebo
It is doing ebo that brings blessings
Neglect of ebo pays no man
Come and join us where there are plenty of children
Ase

Alápà-Niràwé was the title of the King of Àpá. When he was king the community was quiet and prosperous. Everybody was happy. After many years he passed to the realm of the ancestors. He had four sons: Òjòlá (boa constrictor), the oldest; then Sèbé (viper);

after Sèbé came Oká (cobra); and the youngest was Níní (a non-poisonous viper with beautiful colors). The Elders who would crown the new King in Àpá were aware that the attitudes of the first three sons were of bad character; jealous, vengeful, etc. So they had the four brothers come for divination to see who would be crowned the new Àlapá- Niràwé of Àpá. They also invited the three Babalawos mentione in the divination session, Ogbè-Ògúndán (Ogbe-Ìyònú) was revealed.

They advised all four brothers to do ebo of 2 hens, 2 guinea fowl, palm oil and money. They were also advised to exercise patience, absorb insults, show magnanimity, never get angry when bullied and make sure that they would never be provoked to anger. Only Níní obeyed the advice of the Awos and offered the ebo.

Òjòlá, Sèbé y Oká considered the advice of the Awos as a plan to undermine their authority and belittle them in the presence of their subjects. Anyone who crossed the road, Òjòlá swallowed. Sèbé would bite anyone who he saw . Anyone who stepped on the tail of Oká was bitten mercilessly . Those who came across Níní were usually surprised to see how submissive, tolerant and gentle he was. They would step on him or kick him but he would not retaliate. A few months later, all citizens of Àpá converged on the market and organized a gathering in front of the house of the director of the kingmakers. They sang songs relating that the people preferred to have Níní as the next Niràwé Alapa. The director organized a meeting with the council of kingmakers (Ogboni members), to do divination and Ogbe - Ìyònú was revealed . Ifa confirmed Níní as the future king. Òjòlá, Sèbé y Oká protested the decision, but the entire community said they lost their chances as a result of their malicious behavior. Nini was so happy he again offered the ebo but was told that he cannot offer the same ebo twice on the same subject in the same Odu.

Ase

OGUNDA OGBE - removing obstacles leads to an open road, or conflict leads to arrogance. Speaks of the need to always tell the truth and avoid lying and self-deception. Honesty and integrity are prevalent energies of this odu. This person must avoid feelings or thoughts of jealousy. Jealousy is a result of not being in tune with Nature's truth; that we live in an abundant universe in which there is enough for everyone. This Odu speaks strongly regarding Ori; that this person's Ori is with her/him. Adimu (food offering), and head cleaning (abori) ensures ire. So the most important message of this odu is that the person must act according to Ifa ethics at all times, which brings blessings through the person's Ori. This brings us back to the metaphysical principle of Ogundabede; removing obstacles leads to an open road. Ogun is the orisa we turn to to remove obstacles, but in Ogundabede we see what that really means. It isn't so much about removing physical obstacles; It's about obstacles to our spiritual growth. Dishonesty, jealousy, etc. are obstacles that have to do with ego. It is Ogun who will remove the obstacles to self-reflection and the courage to admit our faults and expand our consciousness of self and world. When we do this difficult work, we are reborn with a new consciousness, a new outlook and a larger commitment to iwa pele which brings our ori in alignment with our iponri which in turn allows ire - blessings - to be released in Orun. That is why Ori is the central character here with Ogun as the orisa clearing the way and Obatala as the source of consciousness, ori and ethical behavior.

Alagba lugbu omi ko ko eja l'omo
Odo abata segi-segi ko ba akan l'eru
Alakan gbe nu okun jugbada-jugbudu
D'ifa fun oni awaaka
Won ni won ma le kuroni ile baba re
Oni awaaka, iwo lo ni odo, iwo lo ni ibu
Ko si eni ti yo gba odo l'owo oni
Ko si eni to ma gbaodo l'owo oni

Oni awaaka, iwo lo l'odo, iwo lo n'ibu
Ko si eni to maa gba odo l'owo oni
Ase

The sea does not harm baby fish
The swamp doesn't scare the crab
Crab lives in the ocean with relish
Divined for the mighty crocodile
They threatened to drive him away from his father's house
Mighty Crocodile, the water and its surroundings are your home
Alligator, the river water and its surroundings are your home
Mighty Crocodile, No one will run you out of your habitat
No fish can take the sea from the crocodile
Alligator, you own the river and its surroundings
No one can take the sea from the crocodile
Ase

OGBE OSA - open road leads to abundance or to self deception. This odu speaks of traveling to find abundance. This person must speak truthfully and act with good intentions. This will be rewarded by their Ori with success and protection. Also the need to watch out for traitorous friends. In this odu we find the story of the founding of Egungun. Also how Iyami can create and destroy. Ebo to Ibeji. Speaks of the need to stand one's ground in the face of the urge to run. Speaks of the need for ebo to receive wealth. Ebo to Ori for positive changes. Must do periodic Ori ritual (B'Ori). Ifa asks this person to do ebo to always receive his/her blessings and fortunes, or the ire will pass right by this person. This odu warns of possible incarceration. This person must not lie or cheat. Those who lie and cheat against this person will be exposed. Ifa says no matter what unbearable hardship the person is going through, he/she should never resort to stealing, cheating or dishonesty. This Odu comes with strong protection "you can't touch this!"

Ogbe' sa gun'gi
Ogbe's g'aja
A d'ifa fun gbogbo eleiye
ti nwon nti'kole Orun bo wa'le aiye
Nigbati nwon de'le aiye, nwon ni awon fe ni ibudo
Nwon ni, ibodo meje ni opo ile aiye
Nwon ni, meje naa ni ibi ti awon yio ni ibudo si
Nwon ni
akoko ti awon o koko ni ibudo
Ase

Ogbè Òsá climbed to a tree
Ogbè Òsá climbed to the roof
Ifa was consulted to all the birds serum
that came from heaven to connect to earth
When they came to earth they said, that they desire to find a place to live in
They said that seven residencies where seven anchors on earth
As said, these seven places (egbe Ìyáàmi) will be where you will live there are three qualities of birds and the spirits there are seven
They said that they would sit in the Iwo tree called Orogbo (the Orogbos herbal quality is to compel a person to tell the truth)
They said that they would live in a Arere tree (Arere means fountain of good fortune)
They said that they would live in the Ìrókò tree (this tree is connection to Egun)
They said that they would live in the Iya tree (this is home of the ancestral mothers)
They said that they would live in the Asurin tree (this refers to a manifestation of good fortune)
They said that they would live in the Obobo tree (the main tree from the forest that represents the elemental and main Asé)
They said that they would stay in each of these trees and that their will had to be done in each one of this trees.

They said that if one flies to the Iwo tree it would bring good fortune
They said that if one flies to the Arere tree, nothing would destroy the good fortune of human beings.
They said that if one flies to the Ìrókò tree they will meditate and they would provoke an accident to a human being
They said that if one flies to the Iya tree they will let go of his life
They said that if one flies to the Asurin tree all the people will manifest their dreams
They said that if one flies to the Obobo tree they will have access to the energy and the birds
It is in the Asurin tree that you will make your domestic beginning and you will chant the following song:

Gbogbo eleiye, igi asurin l'e, igi asurin l'egun o
(All birds were placed in the Asurin tree)

When you have sung this song, if you wish to go to the sea, you will go to the sea, if you wish to go to the lake, you go to the lake, and you get in a blink of an eye. If you say you will circle the earth, you will quickly circle the earth. If you say you will go to heaven you will go even faster. The Asurin is the place where the birds find their energy.
Ase

OSA OGBE – (Osa Esu) Abundance creates an open road or self deception leads to arrogance. Person might need initiation or at least some form of spiritual elevation. Most likely ebo to Esu (razor blades and palm oil perhaps?), who will definitely show up to block the ire if the person is in self deception mode. However, before the ebo, the person best get their head straight, admit they know nothing and spend a day in a very dark closet with themselves. Ebo for the courage to do what is needed. This Odu also speaks of wealth coming to this person, so it's not all bad. Ebo to Aje of money for success. Person can't be feeling sorry for those who lost out in the competition for this money they got coming. Maybe like competing for a contract and the person knows some of the other competitors and knows they are struggling. "No one knows the end; we can only see the mirage, who can tell?"

Osa nlu Ogbe njo oro mon jo gbo, olomo oyan
Okara k'esu
D'Ifa fun Orunmila
Ifa ntomi oju Sogbere ire gbogbo
Ebo ni won ni ko se
Nje igba timoyan akara kese ni mo alaje
Da lagya d'olomo d'onire gbogbo oro mon jo
Gbo olomo ayan akara Kesu
Ero Ipo
Ero Ofa
E waa ba ni ni jebutu ire
Ase

Osa is drumming and Ogbe is dancing, oro mo njo gbo
The giver of bean fritters to Esu
Cast Ifa for Orunmila
Ifa was crying for lack of all ire
He was asked to do ebo
Now that I have made an offering of bean cakes to Esu
I have become wealthy
I have gotten married and had children
And was blessed with all ire
Oro monjogbo, the giver of bean cakes to Esu
Travellers to Ipo
Travellers to Ofa,
Come and join us where there's plenty of good fortune
ase

OGBE IKA – open road leads to a time of contemplation. This odu tells us to follow the guidance of spirit and follow taboo as the foundation to new possibilities. It tells us to step back and contemplate things before acting. In this odu is the story of why the Osun staff must stand up straight. This odu predicts Ire of unprecedented prosperity for the person to whom this Odu is revealed. Ifa says that when the person receives the prosperity, no one would be able to go up against him or her using their money or influence; they won't be able to match his or hers. The odu speaks on overcoming jealousy and envy in order to achieve success and respect. This person is in opposition to the tenets of Ifa and needs to receive a hand of ikin to care for so that Orunmila will stop blocking his/her progress. If going through tough times, ebo will rectify. Ifa says if this person is traveling to make ebo to Orishanla so that the trip would be successful. Ifa says this person lost something but with ebo the good fortune will come back to the home. Warns of losses from problems with Aje (witches).

ogbe kare ile
omo osin,omo ora
omo ogun lele lalade
adifa fun etiponla ti n se aya aworo
won ni o kara nle ebo ni ko ma se
nje etiponla se o de o
aya aworo o tun pade sile oko owuro
etiponla   se   o
de o aya aworo
Ero Ipo
Ero Ofa
E waa ba ni ni jebutu ire
ase

ogbe lets go home
the son of osin and ora
the son of ogun at the opening space

cast divination for etiponla the wife of aworo
he was asked to offer sacrifice for blessing of relationship
thus etiponla welcomed the wife of aworo
now you are back to your husband's abode
Travellers to Ipo
Travellers to Ofa,
Come and join us where there's plenty of good fortune
ase

IKA OGBE – contemplation leads to the open road. Ifa says patience is the foundation of good fortune. This odu speaks on infertility. Speaks of standing up for our rights and demanding basic respect. Warns us to watch our words. Ika represents the power of the word and negative words are just as powerful. Proper ebo brings good fortune. Must be careful at work. Speaks of frenemies all around. Ebo to Esu for ire.

Ika gbemi n'o joba
Ika o gbemi n'o joba
T'ika gbemi t'ika o gbemi, n'o joba Alagbe
D'Ifa fun Esu Odara ti n torun bo w'aye
Omode ilu tala o gbe
Ika Ogbe
Agbaagba ilu tami e o gbe
Ika Ogbe
Esu Odara jeki nla kindoba
Odundun l'oniki won o maa dunwa s'odo mi towotowo
Esu Odara jeki nla kindoba
Tete l'oniki won o maa fi owo nla nla temi l'owo
Esu Odara jeki nla kindoba
Kijikiji rinrin kimule ti
Esu Odara jeki nla kindoba
Ara gbogbo ni sefunsefun firi s'aje

THE HOLY ODU

Bi akuko adie ba ko o f'ona ilu an eni to o sina
Esu Odara jeki nla kindoba
Epo ko loree pea won olowo'nla nla wa
Esu Odara jeki nla kindoba
Ika Ogbe Esu Odara ol'owo nla nla wa
Iyeresun manje ki ire'temi osuna
Ase

If Ika favors me, I will become king
If Ika does not favor me, I will also become king
Whether Ika favors me or not, I will become king at Alagbe
Cast Ifa for Esu Odara
On the day He was coming from Orun
Young ones, who is it we will worship
Ika Ogbe
Elders, who will we worship?
Ika Ogbe
Esu Odara, let me become rich in order to become king
The leaves of Odundun will cause the rich people to come to me with their money
Esu Odara, let me become rich in order to become king
The leaves of Tete will bring the rich people's money to me
Esu Odara, let me become rich in order to become king
The leaves of Rinrin bring me the easy life
Esu Odara, let me become rich in order to become king
The leaves of sefunsefun are full of riches
Esu Odara, let me become rich in order to become king
The palm oil will call the rich people
Esu Odara, let me become rich in order to become king
Ika Ogbe and Esu Odara will bring the rich people to me
The iyereosun will not allow (name of person) my luck to sleep
ase

OGBE OTURUPON – the open road leads to good health. This odu comes with protection from any death caused by evil machinations of others or negative entities. Ifa predicts a long life for this person. This is accomplished through the development of good character. Warns us of possible illness blocking our progress. Must protect against spoiled plans or health. If this is a man, warns him to tell his wife to avoid any arguments with anyone. Speaks of the person falling behind in a competition of some sort. Ebo will lead to victory. Ebo of money to Ifa for ire. Warns this person to protect the legacy of his/her ancestors. Ebo and head washing (abori) to Ori for ire. Ori wash with the leaves of Ela to end tough times.

ogbetomopon
to mo sun a gba pon omo ko ni ere
bi omo ba n ke iya la kesi
adifa fun orunmila
baba n tikole orun bo waye
won ni okara n le
ebo ni ko se
Riru ebo ni i gbe ni
Airu ki i gb'eeyan.
E waa ba ni ni wowo omo
ase

Ogbe restrap your child
Ogbe restrap your child
Strapping to your back someone elses child does not have gain
Cast divination for Orunmila
When he was embarking on journey from Orun to earth
He was asked to offer sacrifice
He complied and all his children lived long
It is doing ebo that brings blessings
Neglect of ebo pays no man
Come and join us where there are plenty of children

ase

OTURUPON OGBE - This odu provides the cure to illness. It brings a blessing of prosperity. This person might be about to receive good news at work. One of the main themes in this odu is the blessing of children. It has the ase of conception. Warns to provide spiritual protection for one's children. This odu also brings the blessing of long life. This person needs to be more organized and must be more careful of the people around him/her. This odu speaks of people wishing for this person's failure. It speaks of possible trouble either at work or in the home. Ori, ifa and egbe are prominent in this odu. Ebo to ori and ifa for long life and protection. Egbe for prosperity and ifa and esu to open the way for ire.

Ki o sedi bi da
Ki o sedi bi da
Ki o sed iba baba kuno luna kebo o ribi lo
Emi beere ni n se igba obeere
Eyin odi loko n bale
Oko asa kii bale ko sawo
Adifa fun Esu Odara toni
Oun yio se oko ayegun
Ebo ni won ni kose
Won si gbebo nbe won rubo
Nje ti n k'oba l'owo l'owo o dorun re
Ti n ko bani ire gbogbo nko
Odi orun re
Esu Odara o dorun re
ase

Ki o sedi bi da
Ki o sedi bi da
Ki o sed iba baba kuno luna kebo o ribi lo

Emi beere ni n se igba obeere
Eyin odi loko n bale
Oko asa kii bale ko sawo
Divined for Esu Odara
On the day he wanted to become Ayeyun's husband
He was asked to do ebo
He complied
Even though I am poor, Esu Odara
I will remain the same
Even though I am rich, Esu Odara
I will remain unchanged
Esu Odara bring me riches
Esu Odara let all ire flow from Orun
ase

OGBE OTURA – Open road leads to mystic vision. This Odu brings plenty of ire, but warns us we must work hard to be successful. Person has a lot of haters, but will come out unscathed. Must not wear dark colors and only white sheets. Obatala and Esu are prominent. This person will get more success as they get older, but must remember those who helped him/her. Ebo to Orunmila for protection. Ebo to the Iyami to prevent illness. Must respect women. Ebo to Obatala to end tough times. If planning a new venture, must do ebo to ensure success. Better to go it alone than with a partner.

olala awo obe
lo difa fun obe
obe ma se odun oni yi o tun se temi towo tomo
ebo ni won ni kose
Kee pe o
Kee jinna,
E waa wo'fa awo ki,
B'o ti nse

Ifa de, alase
Ope, abise wara
ase

olala the priest of knife
cast divination for knife
when he was celebrating this year and requesting for next year
they asked him to offer ebo
he complied
since then knife has been living long
Very soon,
At no distant date,
Come and see the Babalawo's prediction
Coming to pass
Ifa has come, the great authority
Palm-tree, whose predictions come true speedily
ase

OTURA OGBE - Otura Ogbe (Ori Ire) Mystic vision leads to a clear sense of destiny. This is the whole point of mystic vision. Otura Ogbe from the elision o tutu ra o egbe meaning the spirit of coolness spreads divine consciousness. For the Yoruba, coolness is a reference to mystic vision so the words otura ogbe is saying mystic vision is a portal to accessioning the consciousness of the Immortals. As is always the case with Ogbe, we gotta be careful of becoming arrogant. This is a powerful odu. The person, if it comes in ire, should rejoice. As we can see from one of its nicknames - Ori Ire. This odu has a lot to say about Ori and both Ogbe and Otura are Obatala's odus; Obatala being the source of consciousness or Ori. It speaks of suffering losses. Speaks of the need to rise above our past problems. Warns of angering the Mothers. In this odu is the story of Olokun and the Segi beads. Ori work is most probably to be recommended. Ebo to family egungun is recommended for wealth. This person might be too nice. Lol. that is, should not assume others are also nice. Ebo for victory over the haters. Here we find the story of how Orunmila had been losing many things on earth, so he went for divination and did the ebo. In the end all ire came back to Orunmila.

Ogbologboo alangba amu
Nii sare geerege lori apata
a dia fun Oninu rere
Eyi tii won o moo gbeebu ika sile de
Won ni ko rubo
Oninuu re ba rubo
Lako lako lo rubo e
O ru igirapa oruko
 opolopo owo
o rubo tan
Eboo re ba da
Aye ye e
N ni wa n jo ni wa n yo
Kee pe o
Kee jinna
E tete waa ba wa ni jebutu aje suuru
Ase

It is the old and experienced lizard
That runs quickly over rocks
Cast divination for the Nice Man
The one for whom they would sow the seed of discord pending his arrival
He was asked to do ebo
the Nice Man did the ebo
he did it in full
He offered a mature he goat and a lot of money
He finished the ebo ritual
the ebo was accepted

Life pleased him
Very soon,
At no distant date
Come and join us where there's plenty of money and peace of mind
ase

OGBE IRETE – the open road requires determination or leads to stubborness. There is a fine line between determination and stubborness. Humility is the medicine to avoid crossing the line. Odu warns against unecessary travel; possible loss. Protection from Orunmila from Ajogun. Speaks of teamwork leading to success in business. Person is going through rough patch, but with faith in Orunmila and perseverence, she/he will encounter wealth. Ebo of fish and rat to Ifa. Warns of trouble in relationship especially if the relationship is with someone who already has a current significant other. Honey to Ifa for long life and good things. If pregnancy is wanted, hen that is nesting should be offered to Oshun. Speaks of the need for initiation into Ifa. This person needs to be close to Ifa, but very careful what they ask for. This person will be successful and it will spread to those around him/her.

mo gba mo te ni iregun ifa
iregun ifa ko tan iregun ifa kuseyin bi owo aso
adifa fun aje osina omo aso ebi dare
o n tikole orun bo waye
won ni ebo ni kose
nje eniyan sanko sanko ni aje ma n wa kiri
Kee pe o
Kee jinna
E tete waa ba wa ni jebutu aje suuru
Ase

mo gba mo te ni iregun ifa
iregun ifa ko tan

iregun ifa ku seyin bi owo aso
cast divination for money
when he was coming from orun to earth
he was asked to offer ebo
he complied
thus it is wealth in the form of money we keep on looking for
Very soon,
At no distant date
Come and join us where there's plenty of money and peace of mind
ase

IRETE OGBE – Irete Ogbe determination leads to an open road (ire), or stubbornness leads to arrogance. This person needs to worship Olokun as the way to abundance. Warns of the need for humility and to take care of one's health. The determination to achieve one's destiny, to apply spiritual discipline and iwa pele to the task, is the road to abundance. However, those born under this sign need to keep their feet firmly placed on the earth, and not get tunnel vision and spend all their energies on spiritual matters in order to avoid earthly challenges. This odu also comes with an admonition regarding a man's relationship with his wife, and the need for teamwork to achieve success. If the wife doesn't support the man's efforts, and vice versa, they will fail. He must appease his wife and gain her confidence. In this odu we learn that even before birth we do ebo in order to assure that those things that were given to us by Olodumare, those things that will help us achieve our destiny, are not taken from us. The trip from Orun to Aye (heaven to earth) is a perilous one. We can have our "things" "stolen" by ajoogun, etc. on the way. This person, with hard work, faith and determination will be an important person one day.

Ifá pe ka sora ki oran arun o kuro lorun eni
Apapa n subu

Apapa n dide
Apapa n yimo lorun ese kororyin koroyin koroyin
A difa fun Aranimogija
Eyi ti yoo gbo gboo gbo
Eyi ti yoo to too to
Ti o lole aye Karin kese
Ebo n won ni o se
Nje iku ti I ba pa mi mo fi ro sorun enikeni
Mo di aranimogija
Mo dolomo jeeje
Arun ti I ba se mi mo fir o sorun enikeni
Mo daranimogija
Mo ti dolomo jeeje
  ase

Apapa n subu
Apapa n dide
Apapa n yimo lorun ese koroyin koroyin koroyin
Cast Ifa for Arannimogija
The one that would live for soooo long
And would be very upright at old age
And would be on earth for a very long time
He was asked to do ebo
Therefore, the death that would have killed me
I have shifted to another person
I have become Arannimogija
I have become olomo jeeje
The sickness that would have inflicted me
I shifted to the neck of the wicked
I have become Arannimogija
I have become olomo jeeje
All the evil that woud have befell me
I shifted to the neck of my enemies
I have become Arannimogija

I have become Olomo jeeje

Ase

OGBE OSE - open road leads to ire (good fortune), or to greed. Ifa, Obatala, Oshun and Ogun speak in this odu. Offerings to Oshun for peace of mind and abundance, and avoiding greed by honoring Ogun. This is a great Odu, it brings good news, success and happiness. Ifa says Orunmila and the Orisa are behind this person 100%. Do not worry; just take care of your Ifa and or Orisa and ire will be yours. Ifa says to walk in iwa pele and this person will have a content and happy life. If it comes in ibi, most likely it is a head cleaning and ebo to Ogun that will bring the ire. It is Ogun who will repair the Ori of this person. If the situation is that the person has tried to be successful at many pursuits with no luck, A bowl of spring water for Esu might be recommended. In this Odu we find a story about the Iyami in bird form (Aje), celebrating a marriage proposal. If the person whom this odu is cast is considering marriage, Ifa says yes (in the story, Oloide (odidere, african grey parrot) introduces Ami, his fiancee (the red feather on its tail), to the Aje at the celebration). If this person has made a recent investment that looks like it was a bad investment, hang in there: it will pay off. Ifa says that this person will enjoy his or her life completely. He or she will be wealthy and wealth must come in the form of gifts and signs of appreciation. Calls for initiation.

Bí a da Ogbè-Sé, á je
Bi a da Ogbè-Sé, á mu
Osiká-leeeéká eeyán ní n perí Ogbè-Sé níbi
Diá fún Òrúnmilá
Ifá n sunkún oun o lájé
Wón ní kó sákáalé ebo ní síse
O gbé'bo, ó rúbo

If you know we cast Ogbè-Sé, we eat
If you know we cast Ogbè-Sé, we will drink
Only bad people speak ill of Ogbè-Sé
These were the declarations of Ifá to Orunmila
who was crying because he lacked wealth
He was advised to do ebo
He complied

Orunmila was working frantically to become a wealthy person. All his efforts went for naught. He was poor and unable to make ends meet. Accordingly, he went to his students for consultation of Ifa. He was sure he would be very wealthy in his life. He was also sure that he would get everything he needs in his life cheaply and easily. He did not need to work too hard in order to be successful in life. The Awo advised him to offer ebo with plenty of snails, food and drinks. Everything would be cooked and he should invite some people to share at the party. After this, he went to perform ebo to Ifa with two doves, two guinea-fowl and money. He completed the ritual. Before the year ended, Orunmila had become a very successful man. He was very wealthy. Most of his wealth came to him as gifts without having to do anything. He was full of happiness and gratitude to Olodumare for crowning his efforts with such resounding success.

Bía bá OgbèSé, a je
Bí a Bá da OgbèSé, a mu
Osika-léka eeyan ló n perí Ogbè-sé níbi
Diá fún Orúnmila
Ifá n sunkún oun o lájé
Wón ni kó sákáále, ebo ní síse
Ó gbé'bo, ó rúbo
Njé iyán Ogbè-Sé kíí dí kókó
Sunmunu
E jé ká fayé Ifá sofé je o

Sunmunu
Otí Ogbè-Sé kíí da
Sunmunu
E jé ká fayé Ifá sofé je o
Sunmunu
Eran Ogbè-Sé Kíí léegun
Sunmunu
E jé ká fayé Ifá sofé je o
Sunmunu
ase

If you know we cast Ogbè-Sé, we eat
If you know we cast Ogbè-Sé, we will drink
Only bad people speak ill of Ogbè-Sé
These were the declarations of Ifá to Orunmila
who was crying because he lacked wealth
He was advised to do ebo
He complied
The Pounded Yam prepared by Ogbè-Sé is without lumps
but with seasoning (riches)
Let us enjoy free gifts from Ifá
with seasoning
The liquor prepared by Ogbè-Sé is never sour
with seasoning
Let us enjoy free gifts from Ifá
with seasoning
Meat prepared by Ogbè-Sé is without bones
with seasoning
Let us enjoy free gifts from Ifá
with seasoning
   ase

OSE OGBE – abundance leads to an open road. This odu says this person needs to collect any monies owed and be paid fully for any work. Be careful about doing any work without a contract. Speaks of this person and a friend being succesful in business. Kola nuts to their Oris to become rich. Warns to not let the abundance lead one to greed. Warns us not to associate with bad people. If this person is suffering, it will turn into prosperity with proper ebo. A head washing at the river to lessen the troubles. Says possibly confiding in someone who is an enemy. Ebo for protection from Aje (witches). Ebo for long life of white cloth, white beans, calabash of efun and four white pigeons. If pregnant, ebo for the child's health. For children, offering of okra leaf soup (ilasa soup). Throw a party and serve the soup and drinks, etc.

Mo wá o délé
N ò bá o nílé
Ònà ni mo pàdé Èsù Òdàrà
Èsù Òdàrà ló júweè re hàn mí
Pèlé omo òòkùn méjì tíí mì ragbada ragbada lórí ewé
A díá fún Àwòròkònjobì
Níjó ti òun àti Àwòko jó n sòré
Wón ní wón ó rúbo
Wón ní babaa wón ó dùúró tì wón
Wón bá rúbo
Ayé ye Àwòròkònjobì
Ayé sì ye Àwòko
Inúu Wón dùn
N ní wón wá n jó ní wón wá n yò
Wón n yon àwon Babaláwo
Àwon Babaláwo n yin ifá
Wón ní bèè làwon Babaláwo tàwón wí
Mo wá o délé
N ò bá o nílé
Òna ni mo pàdé Èsù Òdàrà
Èsù Òdàrà ló júweè re hàn mí
Pèlé omo òòkùn méjì tíí mì ragbada ragbada lórí ewé

A díá fún Àwòròkònjobì
Níjó ti òun àti Àwòko jó n sòré
Orí Oyè ni ò
Orí Oyè ni
Àwòròkònjobì
Èyin ò mò pÓrí oyè lórí Awo?
Àwòròkònjobì
Ase

I came looking for you at home
I met your absence
I met Èsù Òdàrà along the way
It was Èsù Òdàrà whom described you to me
I greet you, the child of òòkùn méjì tíí mì ragbada ragbada lórí ewé
Cast divination for Àwòròkònjobì
On the day he and Awoko were good friends
They were asked to do ebo
They were told the spirit of their fathers would be with them
Awoko and Àwòròkònjobì did the ebo
Life pleased Àwòròkònjobì
Life pleased Awoko
They were very happy
They started to dance and sing
They praised the babalawos
The babalawos praised Ifa
They said it was just as the babalawos had predicted
I came looking for you at home
I met your absence
I met Èsù Òdàrà along the way
It was Èsù Òdàrà whom described you to me
I greet you, the child of òòkùn méjì tíí mì ragbada ragbada lórí ewé
Cast divination for Àwòròkònjobì
The close friend of Awoko
Please, it is a Crowned Ori

It is the Ori of a chief
Àwòròkònjobì
Do not you all know that the Ori of a priest is a crowned Ori?
Àwòròkònjobì
Ase

OGBE OFUN - Open road leads to fullfilment of destiny or open road leads to false sense of fulfillment. Speaks of overcoming a potentially deadly disease. In this odu is the itan of when Obatala gave up wearing dark clothes. Speaks of loss. This Odu Ifa talks of marriage. It talks of a relationship that would be riddled with many challenges at the beginning. The Odu talks of a difficult father in-law. With patience, perseverance, and ebo, Ifa foresees success for the marriage. Orisa Nla (Obatala) is an adimu (one of the energies to hang on) as a safety net in regard to the problem foreseen in this Odu Ifa. Esu is also an adimu in this Odu. Ifa also needs to be fed. Be very careful who you let into your home at this time. Ifa says this person will be good in small business, as a merchant or salesperson. Ifa says that although things might look bleak, this person can acquire everything they are looking for in life with hard work, the proper ebo and spiritual discipline (daily prayer). This odu portends ire for the person, but the person must be fearless and bold.

ogbe fohun folohun ki orun o ba mo
bi a ba fi ohun folohu ija ni da
adifa fun orisa nla oseremagbo
to ma gba aso iya oga pamo
won o kara nle ebo ni ki won se
oga rubo gbogbo ire re pada si lowo
Ero Ipo
Ero Ofa
E waa ba ni ni jebutu ire
ase

Ogbe give what belongs to the owner
So you can be free of debt
Cast divination for orisa nla oseremagbo
Who was going to keep the cloth of chameleon's mother
He was asked to offer sacrifice
He complied
And all his fortune was return to him
Travellers to Ipo
Travellers to Ofa,
Come and join us where there's plenty of good fortune
Ase

OFUN OGBE - This odu is represented by the snake eating its tail. The cycle ends and begins anew; a renewal of faith. We need protection as well as spiritual growth, the left and right hand of Ifa. We must avoid arguments, especially with our brothers; and not keep any guns in our house. Avoid getting drunk. The person possibly has a powerful enemy. Protection from jealousy, enemies. Must heed taboos. Need to follow spiritual guidance if we are having problems or confrontation with someone. Conflict with the law or the government. Our Ori is vulnerable and must be protected. This odu represents the alignment of ori and iponri. Our Iponri will help us accomplish the task at hand. Ebo for long life. Keep an extra vigilant eye on the children lest they have a serious accident. Ifa says a fight is imminent.

Igi-rere, Igi-igbo, Igi-rere, igiodan
Peregun nwanini awo Esumeri
Li o difa f'Ofun
Ofun nlo na Ogbe pa
Won niki Ofun rubo ki Ogbe le nde
Agbo kan li ebo
O gbo o ru
Ifa yi fihan'ni pe: Ija kana ti beebee mbo

THE HOLY ODU

Kee pe o
Kee jinna,
E waa wo'fa awo ki,
B'o ti nse
Ifa de, alase
Ope, abise wara
ase

Igi-rere, Igi-igbo, Igi-rere, Igi-odan
Peregun nwanini, the diviner of Esumeri,
cast Ifa for Ofun
when Ofun was going to beat Ogbe to death
Ofun was advised to make ebo (ram)
so that Ogbe might survive the beating
He performed the ebo
Very soon,
At no distant date,
Come and see the Babalawo's prediction
Coming to pass
Ifa has come, the great authority
Palm-tree, whose predictions come true speedily
Ase

NOTES:

BOOK OF OYEKU

OYEKU IWORI –
End of cycle leads to transformation or to conflict. Speaks of infertility or impotence. Speaks of the need to take care of someone. This odu reminds us that it is through sacrifice that we come to have a life that is pleasing to us. Warns of someone being treating this person with contempt. This odu, if the client is a woman who wants children, will provide children aplenty with the proper ebo. The first child should be named Ekundayo –weeping has turned to joy. Ebo against premature birth. Speaks of ire in the form of wealth. Ebo to Egungun and/or Obatala for this. This person needs to worship Ogun. Warns of someone using juju against this person.

Eleku nmu eku pe mi l'aiya
Aiya mi ko ni gba eku
Aiya Oyeku-gbiri l'agba eleja
Nmu eja pe mi l'aiya
Aiya mi ko no gba eja
Aiya Oyeku-biri l'agba
Edi ponripon
Omi di Edi nana iloro

Owo ati omo ni aiya mi nwa o
Riru ebo ni i gbe ni
Airu ki i gb'eeyan.
E waa ba ni ni wowo omo
Ase

Someone who owns rats sends rats at my chest to call me
My chest will not accept them
The chest of reverberating Oyeku is the elder
Someone who owns fish sends fish at my chest to call me
my chest will not accept them
The chest of reverberating Oyeku is the elder
Thick Edi, the water starts to vibrate
Edi of the town where rituals are held
My chest is seeking money and children ooo
It is doing ebo that brings blessings
Neglect of ebo pays no man
Come and join us where there are plenty of children
Ase

IWORI OYEKU – transformation leads to peace of mind or conflict leads to a bad ending. This odu speaks if peace. However, it also warns of potential serious conflict. Warns to not get into any confrontation especially physical (this odu contains the story of the fight between babalawos and egunguns). Ebo to Esu for this. Ifa says to stop doing things in a negative manner. Warns of possible witchcraft against a man. We should go to our Eguns for guidance to avoid any impending danger. Warns a husband and wife to keep their business to themselves. Possible trouble at work. No alcohol. This odu says, "a stream that loses contact with its source will surely dry up." Must propitiate the ancestors. This odu provides wisdom on the idea of having our head and heart in alignment, so that our feet are pointing in the same direction as our eyes.

Oko n lo soko, oko koju sile
Oko nbo nile, oko koju soko
Eyin o mo pe lodi, lodi loko n se
Adia fun won ni ilolodi
Omo Aserubobatan,
Ego, ego lo para ilolodi
Omo Aserubobatan
Ase

Hoe was going to the farm
It faced home
Hoe was returning home
It faced the farm
Don't you all know that Hoe is behaving in contradicting manners?
Cast the divination for them in the city of ilolodi
The child of Aserubobatan
Stupidity was what killed the people of Ilolodi
The child of Aserubobatan
ase

OYEKU ODI – end of cycle leads to rebirth, or to moving forward without a plan. This odu speaks of a person who is poor but that they will reach success with a good plan and hard work; and it will be through women that the success comes, or with the help of the women (Iyami). This person will be successful, but must be honest. Warns us to not be argumentative, because for one, it could lead to illness. Speaks of sexual impotence or disease; warns against a man having too much casual sex with different women. Ebo for pregnancy. Ebo against death. Ifa says there is a person who is showing contempt for this person. This person might be too kind, thus others take advantage of this person and are not afraid of her/him.

Oyeku-Di a da fun Igbin
Nwon ni ki o rubo Alasire:
Akiko adie meta ati egbata
Igbin ko rubo
Lati igba-na ni gbogbo
Aiye ti ma nfi Igbin
Se Alasire
Agbonniregun ni rin-owo-rin-owo
Ni a yio ma he Igbin
Ifa ni ki enikan rubo Alasere
Alasire de
Riru ebo ni i gbe ni
Airu ki i gb'eeyan
Ase

Oyeku-Di was the one who cast Ifa for Snail
They said he should do ebo of three roosters and money
Against one who showed contempt for him (Alasire, A li ase ire)
Snail did not do the ebo
Since then, the whole world has held Snail in contempt
Agbonniregun (Orunmila) says,
bare handed, bare handed, we will catch the snail
It is doing ebo that brings blessings
Neglect of ebo pays no man
Ase

ODI OYEKU – rebirth leads to completion of cycle, or to premature completion. Ebo to Yemoja for healthy children. The client is stuck at this time. Patience and courage to make the right move to break out. This odu, with the proper ebo, brings the blessing of children. Ifa says ebo against earthly enemies. Ebo to Ogun to remove the blockages this person has and Ori for financial success. Ifa says communication with Egun brings relief of daily stresses.

Attention and discipline of prayer and study will procure Orunmila's help.

Sakasaka l' omode Kekere n ko Fa
Omode kekere kii ba agbalagba jija gudu eru
Ko le baa rile Ifa tan ni o
Dia fun won ni Idin-yeku
Nijo ire e won ti si l o
Iya owo ti Omo-Awo ti je
Ifa n padaa bo waa s'eesan o
asilu asilu ni t' eesan Ifa
Iya aya to Omo-Awo ti je
Ifa n padaa bo waa s' eesan o
Asilu asilu ni t' eesan Ifa
Iya owo ti Omo-Awo ti je
Ifa n padaa bo waa s' eesan o
Asilu asilu ni t eesan Ifa
Iya ire gbogbo ti Omo-Awo ti je
Ifa n padaa bo waa s' eesan o
Asilu asilu ni t' eesan Ifa
ase

A child must study Ifa with seriousness and dedication
A child must not struggle about proceeds with elders
It is in order to enable him to get to the root of Ifa
These were the declarations of Ifa to them at Idin-yeku
When all good things of life had left their home
The lack of money which Omo-Awo had suffered from
Ifa is coming to repay him
Ifa repays all it's followers in fold
The lack of spouse which the Omo-Awo had suffered from
Ifa is coming to repay him
Ifa repays all it's followers in fold
The childlessness which the omo-Awo had suffered from

Ifa is coming back to repay him
Ifa repays all it's followers in fold
The lack of all good things of life which the Omo-Awo had suffered from
Ifa is coming back to repay him
Ifa repays all its followers in fold
Ase

OYEKU IROSUN – end of cycle leads to fulfillment of destiny or premature end leads to lost opportunity. This odu reminds us to obey Ifa for success and avoid bad fortune. This verse establishes Esu – money forming groups. This odu says it will lead to financial success. Oyeku Irosun is heavy with ancestral energy. This person should do ebo to the family's Egungun. We must consult our Eguns at each step in our lives. In this odu is the story of when Sango wrongly killed a group of partiers because he thought they disrespected him because they did not offer him wine upon his late arrival to the party. It turns out, they had drunk all the wine, but because the bottles were upright, Sango assumed there was wine in them. From this day on, when we finish a bottle, we lay it on its side. This odu says to always have wine in your home to offer visitors because a wine loving visitor is coming who will help you.

Òyè rùsùrùsù
A dífá fún wọn lẸ̀gbàá Èésú
Níbi wón gbé ń kórí ajée jọ
Wón ní kí wón ó rúbọ
Wón ní ọpọlọpọ owó lẹ bọ
Òwúùrú ẹyẹlé lẹ bọ
Wón níre fún wọn
Wón bá rúbọ
Ẹ̀gbàá ní wón si ń dá
Ńgbà ó pé wón bá kówó
Wón nísinmì

Ọkàan wón balẹ̀
Ayée wón dáa
N ní wá ń jó ní wá ń yò
Ní ń yin àwọn Babaláwo
Àwọn Babaláwo ń yin Ifá
Ó ní bẹ́ẹ̀ làwọn Babaláwo tòún wí
Òyè rùsùrùsù
A dífá fún wọn lẸ̀gbàá Èésú
Níbi wón gbé ń kórí ajée jọ
Taa ló rúbọ báwònyí bẹẹrẹ?
Òyè rùsùrùsù
Àwọn ló rúbọ báwònyí bẹẹrẹ
Òyè rùsùrùsù
Ase

Òyè rùsùrùsù
Divined for the people of Ẹ̀gbàá Èésú
When they were consolidating the concepts of wealth creation
They were asked to do ebo
They were told a large sum of money was the ebo
As well as a matured pigeon
They wished for them the good fortune of wealth (ire Aje)
They did the ebo
Over time, they only contributed like 5 cents each
After a considerable amount of time had passed
They shared their contributions
They all had peace of mind
Their lives became sweet
It was then they began dancing and singing
They praised their babalawos
The babalawos praised Ifa
The people of Ẹ̀gbàá Èésú said it was exactly as the babalawos said it would be
Òyè rùsùrùsù

Divined for the people of Òyè rùsùrùsù
When they were consolidating the concepts of wealth creation
Who performed ebo this plentiful?
The people of Òyè rùsùrùsù
That's who
The people of Òyè rùsùrùsù
Ase

IROSUN OYEKU – alignment of destiny leads to successful completion, or resistance to destiny leads to loss. This odu implores us to follow our destiny for it is the only road to good fortune. This odu says this person should worship Sango to avoid fatal disease and to worship Ifa and Olokun to receive abundance. Warns this person of possible legal problems, especially if engaged in illegal activities. Warns of envy and seduction. Ifa says to have patience and in time your good fortune will come. Tells us not to make the same mistakes over and over; it is time to change our thinking. Stop looking backwards and move forwards. Light a candle or better a wick in palm oil in clay little plate – oil lamp - and put it with Esu and pray that he close those paths backwards and open new ones. Irosun and Oyeku both have strong ancestral connection. This person should propitiate their ancestors and ask them to help bring death to your old ways of thinking. Warns of person who returns to abusive relationships. Says men should take care of their children, and an inheritance is coming. The person should not sell it.

Itakutali-aita-aso
Irikurili-aira-ofi
Li o d'Ifa f'Orunmila nre'le Olokun-sande
Won ni ile Olokun naa a san an pupopupoju
Nitorina ki o ru
Ogbo o ru
Nigbati o j'eru titi ara la won
O nkorin baye:

"*Awo re'le lo f'iye wa o*
Iye awo ko de ku
Iye awo ko de ku
Awo re'le lo f'iye wa o
Iye awo ko de ku"
Ase

Itakutali-aita-aso
Irikurili-aira-ofi
Li o d'Ifa f'Orunmila who was going to Olokun-sande's house
He was told that Olokun-sande's house would be very promising for him
Therefore, he should do ebo
Because he would be envied when collecting his dues
He heard and did the ebo
He was asked to do more ebo
He did it
He was envied when he collected his dues
He sang the following song:
"awo is going home to replenish his iyerosun powder
Awo's iye-rosu powder has run out
Awo's iye has run out
Awo is going home to replenish his iye powder
Awo's iye powder has run out"
ase

OYEKU OWONRIN – end of cycle leads to proper preparation for unexpected changes or premature end of cycle leads to chaos. Warns against adultery. Warns of trouble if this person is going to travel. Ebo against loss. Ifa says this person will accomplish a great feat but must do ebo to ensure it manifests. Ebo to Esu to avoid confusion. Obatala bath to remove negative energy and bring clarity. Ebo to Oya for protection if traveling.

Jafirijafi, kemkejake, Agadgidiwonu-odo-e'f arabo-omi
Li o difa f'Ode, O difa f'Orunmila
Ode nre igbo Olikorobojo
Won ni ki o rubo kioma baa kus'ohun
Akuko adieye meje ati egaaje owo
Ode rubo
Orunmila nlo s'ajo ti o jin gbungbungbun bi omi
Won ni ki o wa rubo kioma baa Kus'ohun
Ata epo, akuko-adiye mesan, obuko mesan, eku mesan, eja mesan, ati eyele
Orunmila gbo o rubo
Kee pe o
Kee jinna,
E waa wo'fa awo ki,
B'o ti nse
Ifa de, alase
Ope, abise wara
Ase

Jafirijafi, kemkejake, Agadgidiwonu-odo-e'f arabo-omi
Divined for Hunter
And divined for Orunmila
Hunter was going to the forest of Olikorobojo
He was asked to do ebo in order to avoid dying there
Seven roosters and money was the ebo
Hunter did the ebo
Orunmila was going on a journey to a distant place
He also was asked to do ebo in order to avoid dying there
A drum of palm oil, nine roosters, nine he-goats, nine rats, nine fish and pigeons
Orunmila heeded the advice and did the ebo
Very soon,
At no distant date,
Come and see the Babalawo's prediction
Coming to pass

Ifa has come, the great authority
Palm-tree, whose predictions come true speedily
Ase

OWONRIN OYEKU – chaos leads to completion or leads to loss. Advises this person to be cautious. Ebo to stop enemies in their tracks. If courting a woman or man, this odu says it will be a good relationship. If travelling, a dispute will erupt. Ebo must be done to avoid it. If the person is sick, ebo to Iyami. Good fortune is coming. Ebo to ensure its arrival.

Ajalorun I kukuteko awo eba'no
Li o difa fun Kuterunbe
Nlo s'oko Aloro odun
Won ni: Bikobasoose ninu odun
Yi mi irugbin oko re maa paa
Riru ebo ni i gbe ni
Airu ki i gb'eeyan
ase

Ajalorun I kukuteko awo eba'no
Divined for Kuterunbe
Who was going to Aloro's farm for the annual festival
He was warned that if he was not cautious that year
He would be killed by the produce of his farm
He did not do the ebo
It is doing ebo that brings blessings
Neglect of ebo pays no man
Ase

OYEKU OBARA – end of cycle leads to transformation or egotism. This odu implores us to maintain spiritual discipline. Ebo to avoid the consequences of bad decisions. This person will not live alone. This person is looking for good fortune. With ebo he/she will receive it. We should pay attention to our dreams for messages from spirit. If this person is having many problems, they should receive Ifa. The person should not try to be someone or something they are not. Ebo to Esu to avoid being a victim of a crime. This person should handle their own business and not relegate to others. In the same way, this person should not let themselves be used to do other's bidding. This odu speaks of the need for honesty. This odu provides the opportunity to avoid repaying a debt. This could be money debt or karmic.

Oyeku pabala, oyeku palaba,
Li o difa fun f'Awun
Nigba ti o nse olofa
Fun Esi won ni biobaru
Egbejidilogun owo ati ewure li ebo
A je owo ohun gun
O gbo o ru
Ero Ipo
Ero Ofa
E waa ba ni ni jebutu ire
Ase

Oyeku pabala, oyeku palaba,
Divined for tortoise
When he was working off money he owed Esi
They said if he could do ebo
He should offer a she-goat and money
He would avoid the repayment of his loan
He did the ebo
Travellers to Ipo
Travellers to Ofa,
Come and join us where there's plenty of good fortune
Ase

Tortoise (awun) had been repaying a loan to Esi by working on his farm. One day he stayed home and did not show up for 5 days. He wrapped up a bundle of stones with a special bead and left it at esi's house when he wasn't there. So when Esi got home. He thought it was just stones so he threw it away. Then Awun asked him if he got his package. Esi told him he threw it away. Awun told him it was coral beads in payment of his loan. They went to court and Awun won the case. In this way, he got out of paying his debt.

OBARA OYEKU – transformation leads to completion or to loss. This odu speaks of honoring isese tradition, and the consequences of not heeding the advice of elders. This person will be successful in business. But must do ebo to Sango and Esu to ensure success and counter enemies. Speaks of meeting the right partner. This person might be the victim of insubordination in the home or at work. Ifa asks this person to do ebo to prevent enemies from getting this person fired from their job and not being able to take care of their monetary responsibilities.

obara yeku yekete
adifa fun orunmila
o n be laarin osi ri
won ni o kara nle ebo ni kose
eropo
ero ofa e wa ba ni larusegun
arusegun la ba ni lese oba orisa
Ero Ipo
Ero Ofa
E waa ba ni ni jebutu ire
Ase

Obara yeku yekete
Cast divination for orunmila
When he was amidst poverty

He was ask to offer ebo
He did it
Thus since then he has been living well
Travellers to Ipo
Travellers to Ofa,
Come and join us where there's plenty of good fortune
ase

OYEKU OKANRAN – end of cycle leads to new opportunities or unnecessary isolation. Speaks of the need for ebo for health and long life. Warns of loss due to over exertion. Ebo to Ifa to fix this person's life and protect from enemies. Warns to be careful, especially about violating taboos and hanging out with the wrong crowd. Warns against arrogance. Do not get into situations that can lead to confrontations like going to clubs, Do not break any laws. You will get caught.

Atorirorayo-Ilelaba-Iroko-ngbe
Li o dafa fun Irawosasa tiise eru Olodumare
Won ni bikobafiti Oluwa re se Ona I yo pa ola moo lara
Ewure ati egbewa owo li ebo
Irawo ko rubo
Nitorinaa ni ojo ti Olodumare bar o ti Igberaga irawo kan
Liase nrii ti irawo naa sidi lojiji a si wo ookun
Ase

Atorirorayo-Ilelaba-Iroko-ngbe
Divined for Irawosasa (the star), the slave of Olodumare
It was predicted that if he failed to to follow Oluwa's advice
His fame would vanish
A she-goat and money should be offered as ebo
Irawo didn't do the ebo
Therefore, the day Olodumare would reflect on the arrogance of a star, we would see a star fall from the sky into darkness

Ase

OKANRAN OYEKU – new direction leads to completion or to loss. This odu warns us to avoid conflict. Speaks of ebo bringing riches; lack of ebo bringing loss. Speaks of ebo to protect children from sickness or death. Ebo for good fortune.

Okanran'Yeku I oro Mi Aromo
I riro niiro Igba elepo
I riro niiro Igba olori
I riro niiro Igba aladin
Kiide'lede'na ko ni ojuto lara
Gbedegbede niiro'di iponmi
Igbin mejo ati egbaajo owo le ebo Biobarubo
Ifa ni a ro eni-ohun l'orun
Kee pe o
Kee jinna
E tete waa ba wa ni jebutu aje suuru
Ase

Okanran"yeku says, "Riches"
I say more riches
Just as is well for a calabash of palm oil
Just as is well for a calabash of shea butter
Just as is well for a calabash of palm kernel oil
So will the comfort of a house facilitate the wetness of the bathroom
And the surrounding of a water pot
Very soon,
At no distant date
Come and join us where there's plenty of money and peace of mind
Ase

OYEKU OGUNDA – end of cycle leads to the clearing of obstacles or to conflict. Warns to watch our words so they cannot be used against us. This person needs to resolve family issues so the rupture is not exploited by enemies. This person should receive Ifa for protection. Ebo of tortoise to Ogun. Ebo to Esu for prosperity. This person is argumentative and does not listen to advice and needs to change. It has led to someone else in the home being argumentative. This odu provides the solution to avoid death and receive long life.

Okunrun maa mu ohun mi
Adifa fun Ikugbola, oko Atawuro mu ola
Orunmila ni Ojo eni da ni eni nla aje
Orunmila ni ojo eni da
moni ojo eni da
Oni ojo ti eni da, 'pe eni ma gbe iyawo
Orunmila ni ojo eni da, 'pe ani ma bi omo
Oni ojo eni da
mo ni ojo eni da
Om ojo ti eni da, pe oun ma ni ire gbogbo,
ni aiye ni o ma ni
Oni ojo.eni da; mo ni ojo eni da
0 ni ojo ti eni da, 'pe oun yi o ku
0 ni ojo ma ni enia ma ku
A ni Orunmila, a ni ohun ahurin ni yen
ase

Invalid, do not take my medications to Orun
Divined for Ikugbola, the husband of Atawuro mu ola
When he was indisposed
He was told that Death was dancing around him
He should make ebo of a sheep and a bundle of firewood
He did the ebo and buried the head of the sheep in front of his house as instructed
The ebo drove Death away
And Ikugbola lived a long, prosperous life
He will eventually grow up and marry
And to have children

And to be endowed with all material wealth
He will eventually die on the day
He was destined to die
This is the philosophy of life
Orunmila however emphasized that the manifestation
Of these desires depends on
The amount of ebo
Which should consist of a ram and the tuber of Abirishoko
Death does not eat the tuber of Abirishoko,
The big ram with large horns,
Uses them to ward off
The onset of Death
Orunmila, protect me from the wrath of Death
And direct the feet of prosperity to me
Orunmila says, the birth of a person
Marks the beginning of his prosperity
ase

OGUNDA OYEKU – the clearing of obstacles leads to completion or aggression leads to loss. This person needs to worship Olokun for prosperity. Must resolve differences with family or friends. Worship of ancestors helps resolve the problems. This odu brings prosperity through kindness and generosity. Speaks of leaving a job to work for someone else and the previuos employer hating this person for leaving. Ebo to prevent this person from ruining his/her new job. Ebo for long life. This odu warns of leg problems. Ebo to Esu for success and Ogun for protection from the nefarious plans of an enemy. Ifa says with proper ebo this person will have a long life, good health and prosper.

Orunmila lo di ajalu gborangandan
Ifa ni oro Ogunda Aiku de
Olodumare ni ki won so fun awon omo araye pe alejo de
Omo araye ni alejo kini?

Olodumare ni alejo owo
Awon omo araye ni ko maa bo
Orunmila lo di ajalu gborangandan
Ifa ni oro Ogunda Aiku de
Olodumare ni ki won so fun awon omo araye pe alejo de
Omo araye ni alejo kini?
Olodumare ni alejo omo
Awon omo araye ni ko maa bo
Orunmila lo di ajalu gborangandan
Ifa ni oro Ogunda Aiku de
Olodumare ni ki won so fun awon omo araye pe alejo de
Omo araye ni alejo kini?
Olodumare ni alejo ire gbogbo
Awon omo araye ni ko maa bo
Orunmila lo di ajalu gborangandan
Ifa ni oro Ogunda Aiku de
Olodumare ni ki won so fun awon omo araye pe alejo de
Omo araye ni alejo kini?
Olodumare ni alejo iku
Awon omo araye ni won ko fe, ki eleyun-un maa lo
Olodumare ni dandan ni fun-un yin lati gbaa
ase

Orunmila sounded a loud clarion call
Ifa says, here comes the message of Ogunda Aiku
Olodumare says to the earthly people that a visitor has come
The earthly people asked who the visitor was
Olodumare said the visitor was money
The earthly people quickly welcomed it
Orunmila sounded a loud clarion call
Ifa says, here comes the message of Ogunda Aiku
Olodumare says to the earthly people that a visitor has come
The earthly people asked who the visitor was
Olodumare said the visitor was a child

The earthly people quickly welcomed it
Orunmila sounded a loud clarion call
Ifa says, here comes the message of Ogunda Aiku
Olodumare says to the earthly people that a visitor has come
The earthly people asked who the visitor was
Olodumare said the visitor was prosperity
The earthly people quickly welcomed it
Orunmila sounded a loud clarion call
Ifa says, here comes the message of Ogunda Aiku (long life)
Olodumare says to the earthly people that a visitor has come
The earthly people asked who the visitor was
Olodumare said the visitor was Death (Iku)
The earthly people rejected that it was not for them
Olodumare said it is compulsory to accept and welcome it
ase

Ogunda Aiku clears the path for delivery of ire from our Eguns. The verse ends with a message that death is also a form of ire.

OYEKU OSA – end of cycle leads to abundance or instability. This odu advises to worship ancestors as the basis for prosperity. To not worship one's ancestors will lead to poverty. This odu says we must compromise to avoid loss. Ebo for good fortune to enter one's home. Ebo for victory against enemies. Speaks of ebo of he-goat to Esu to avoid problems with authority figures. Ebo to Iyami of rabbit to avoid people providing false witness. If this person is struggling to survive financially, he/she should receive Ifa. If this person is in a heated competition for a promotion or something of this nature, ebo for victory. Ifa says good fortune will enter this person's home with proper ebo.

Atéérété orí àsá
Ẹni ó gun àsá yò
A dífá fún Kúkúnrú
Ọmọ abímọ ní pupa ní pupa

Ó bí gbogbo ọmọ è ti ọn rí bélẹ́ńjé
Wón ní ó rúbọ bí àwọn ọmọ è ó ṣe wọ ilée rere
Kí òna ó là fún wọn
Tí ire ó móọ ṣe gẹgẹẹ wọn
Kí wón ó mó díí òná fún wọn
Kúkúnrú ní "Tóun tí bí ọmọ lọpọ́lọpọ"
"Ó di dandan kí wón ó móọ ráyè wọ́lẹ̀ ńbii wón bá dé"
À á séé mọ Kúkúnrú ọmọ abímọ ní pupa?
N làá pé Àgbàrà
Ẹníkan ò jẹ jẹ ó wọ inú ilé
Bí Àgbàrà bá ti lóun ó kòólé èèyàn báyìí
Wón ó móọ pé kó móọ lọ
Kó móọ lọ
Yóó bá móọ lọ
Àyìn ẹyìn ní Àgbàrà ń yin àwọn Babaláwo è
Ó ní Atéérété orí àsá
Ẹni ó gun àsá yò
A dífá fún Kúkúnrú
Ọmọ abímọ ní pupa ní pupa
Kúkúnrú Ọmọ abímọ ní pupa ní pupa làá pàgbàrà
Mó jẹ́ẹ́ ire ó nù mi dákun
Èlààsòdè
Ifá mó jẹ́ẹ́ ire ó nù mi dákun
Èlààsòdè
Ase

Atéérété orí àsá
Ẹni ó gun àsá yò
Cast divination for Kúkúnrú
The child of abímọ ní pupa ní pupa
All his children were slender and beautiful
He was told to do ebo so his children would have a good home to live in

And so that good things would come to them
So that the way would open for them
And so that no one would deny them access
"Once I have children
They can never be denied admission," Kúkúnrú said arrogantly
How do we know Kúkúnrú?
It is another name for the rain runoff water (from the roof of the house)
No one would allow him entry into their home
Once the runoff water decides to enter a person's home
They would ask the run off water to leave
He should leave immediately
He would then leave the place
Runoff water was praising his babalawos belatedly
With grief, he said, "Atéérété orí àsá
Ẹni ó gun àsá yò
Cast divination for Kúkúnrú
The child of abímọ ní pupa ní pupa
Kúkúnrú, The child of abímọ ní pupa ní pupa
Is what we call rain runoff water
Do not allow good fortune to miss us, please
Elasode
Ifa do not let good fortune miss us, please
Elasode
ase

OSA OYEKU – sudden change leads to end of cycle or to loss. This odu says spiritual discipline is the road to long life and to avoid a shortened life. Ebo to help navigate the disruption caused by Osa. Ifa says this person will find wealth in the form of peace of mind. Possible ebo to Oya or Orisa Oko. Warns to not venture out at night at this time. If this person is planning on doing or starting something it is a good time but needs to do ebo to avoid pitfalls.
Perewú Perewúojú òkòtó

THE HOLY ODU

A dia dún Òkánríngbòngbòòngbòn
Níjó tí n fojúú sògbérè ire gbogbo
Wón ní kó rúbo
À á séé mo Òkánríngbòngbòòngbòn?
N làá pe Òòsà oko
Gbogbo ara è látòkè délè
Ajé ni
Wón ní ire Ajé lópòlopò fún un
Òkánríngbòngbòòngbòn bá rúbo
Ayé è bá dáa
Gbogbo ara è lée sajé
Ní bá n jó ní bá n yò
Ní n yin àwon Babaláwo
Àwon Babaláwo è n yinfá
Ó ni béè làwon Babaláwo tòún wí
Perewú Perewú ojú òkòtó
Adia fún Òkánríngbòngbòòngbòn
Níjó tí n fojúú sògbérè ire gbogbo
Wón ní yóó lópòlopò Ajé láyé
Ebo n wón ní ó se
Òkánríngbòngbòòngbòn
Ó wáá gbébo nbè ó rúbo
Kín làá bo nbè bó bá jáde?
Òrìsà oko
Àgbà ìràwò
N làá bo nbè bó bá jáde
Ase

Perewú Perewúojú òkòtó
Cast Ifa for Òkánríngbòngbòòngbòn
On the day he was crying because of all good things
He was asked to do ebo
How do we know Òkánríngbòngbòòngbòn?
He is the one we call Òrìsà oko

253

His body, from head to toe
Is an embellishment of wealth
They wished him much good fortune (ire)
Òkánríngbòngbòòngbòn did the ebo
His life became a success
He tied money all over his body
He then started to dance and sing
He praised his babalawos
His babalawos praised Ifa
He said it was exactly as they had predicted
Perewú Perewúojú òkòtó
cast Ifa for Òkánríngbòngbòòngbòn
On the day he was crying because of all good things
He was assured he would have abundant good fortune on earth
But he should do ebo
Òkánríngbòngbòòngbòn
You listened and did the ebo
To whom is the ebo done if this odu is cast?
Òrìṣà oko
The biggest star
Is the divinity to whom we should give ebo if it is cast
ase

OYEKU IKA – end of cycle leads to self affirmation or self denigration. This odu speaks of the need to worship and receive guidance from the ancestors. Warns of the need for spiritual protection. Offerings to Ori and head cleaning, bath. This odu tells babalawos to always give Esu his share of any ebo. This person must avoid negative emotions like hatred and envy. This person must not be greedy. If in business, he/she will be prosperous if they do not over charge.

Ayejin, Ayejin Aye gbe Agere
Ude ni non'Okpa Tere ko,
Oji gada godo ninu, Agogo Odee.

Ifa-Oyeku-Be-Eka je Eyi kekere lya
Ki 'o rna ba je Eyi nla
Tete je wo mu womu.
Akpa wo mi Amidi galata
Oke domi amuru golo to
Maa jeri wo shengbe
Egba so wo galata gbami o
Ero Ipo
Ero Ofa
E waa ba ni ni jebutu ire
Ase

Ayejin, Ayejin Aye gbe Agere
Ude ni non'Okpa Tere ko,
Oji gada godo ninu, Agogo Odee.
These were the awos who divined for Oyeku and Ika
When they were coming from heaven to earth
They were advised to do ebo of a he-goat to Esu before leaving
They did the ebo
They were told to take care of business when they got to earth
After arriving, they were going to travel to Esi Ilawo
They went for divination
Ifa-Oyeku-Be-Eka je Eyi kekere lya
Ki 'o rna ba je Eyi nla
Tete je wo mu womu.
Were the diviners
They were told to neither be greedy or extortionate
In order to maximize their gains
Travellers to Ipo
Travellers to Ofa,
Come and join us where there's plenty of good fortune
ase

IKA OYEKU – drawing in leads to completion of cycle or to self denigration. This odu tells us to avoid conflict and watch our words. Tells us of the value of retreat to fight another day. Speaks of the need for protection from gossip. Says this person needs to be more assertive. Has the solution for male sterility. Ebo against death. This person is stressed out trying to make ends meet and lacks time to do things. Ebo will bring peace and a better life. Ebo for a blessing of wealth to Iyami. B'Ori ritual and ebo for prosperity.

Ika yenye, Oye yenye
A difa fun Aje
Aje n t'orun bow a s'aye
A difa fun Ori
Ori n t'orun bow a s'aye
Ebo ni won ni ko se
Nje Otito l'Ori juwon lo
Ori emi mon lagba
ase

Ika yenye, Oye yenye
Cast Ifa for Aje
When she was coming from orun to aiye
Also cast Ifa for Ori
Who was also coming to earth
They were told to do ebo
They complied
Is the head superior or is it Ori?
Ase

Ebo: one giant rat, 2 pigeons, eko, palm oil and money. The intestines of the rat are to be offered to iyami.

OYEKU OTURUPON – end of cycle leads to prevention of illness or to prolonged illness. This odu speaks of helping this person avoid punishment for wrongdoing, but implores him/her to improve their character. Says this person has not been successful and passed over for promotions. Ebo will rectify the situation. Speaks of ebo to Esu to avoid major loss from Ajogun. Speaks of the need to be happy with what we have. Warns if this person is awo, to do ebo to ward off death and the plots of jealous enemies and/or the "Elders of the Night." This person might need to become awo Ifa. This person, with ebo, will be prosperous in the town in which they are living.

Muso muso ni shuwaju ijo
Gbeje gbeje ni gbehin ayo
Adifa fun Ifashemoyin,
Ti abi l'ode, to tun toni ode
Ofun le oko ni ode
Ebo lo maru
Oju shemi kimi wi
Adifa fun moburin burin,
Moye ikin mi wo,
Omo kekere Awo nifi opon ide di ifa
Aha ha hi ri hi ri
Oshi shi shiri shiri
Adifa fun Orunmila
O'nfa ologbe ure le rele
Akopole lowo ati aye ero
Ebo ki asin tun bo ifa
Ifa mo wa l'owo re
Ope maje kimi juya
Ope
Ase

When entering a dance
The dancer
Brings his hands forward in anticipation
After dancing successfully

The dancer
Brings his hands down as a mark of achievement
Before sitting down
These were the awos who did divination for Ifasemoyin
Before she settled down to live in the town of Ode
Although her parents were not from Ode
She was born and raised there
Was married and had children there
She was told to do ebo
She did the ebo
Thus she was happy
And her life was good
She sang:
I had an inclination
To go for divination
I later felt like sounding
The ikin tied to my waist
And using them to do divination
I later met a young Ifa priest
Who used a brass tray for divination
He was full of youthful exuberation and fervor
I finally asked him to do the divination
Before going to befriend prosperity
And cajole him to the homes of my Ifa priests
The ebo is done by serving Orunmila
And telling him
"Ope I'm in your hands
Bring me prosperity
Do not allow me to suffer,
Ope"
ase

OTURUPON OYEKU – Illness leads to end of cycle, in this case recurring illness, or to permanent illness. This person is going to be tested. This person might need ebo to ward off ajogun. This person is in professional competition. It will be their idea that will be implemented. In this odu is the story of Iya Ile (mother earth) and her enemy rainfall. What the story implies is that too much of a good thing can hurt you. Rain is what allows life on earth, while too much rain kills. Perseverence and moderation are qualities of this odu. This person needs to find joy and have more fun in life. Too much focus on making money, not enough on family.

Okeebeebee awo aye li
O d'Ifa f'Aye
O d'Ifa f'Omode
Won ni
Ere li ao ma aba omo-ayo se
Biaba nba omode sere a maa fi ayo inu re ran'ni
A d'Ifa f'Onile-owo ti ko ni idunnu
Won ni ki o wa rubo
O waa gbebo nbe o rubo
Ase

Okeebeebee the diviner of Earth
Did divination for the Ayo game and the children
They were told that they should always play the ayo game
By playing with the children
One can share in their joy
This was the Ifa cast for the rich man
Who was very unhappy
He heard and did the ebo (play with the children)
Ase

OYEKU OTURA – end of cycle leads to mystic vision or egotism. More focus on spirit will improve our relationships. Warns of the possibility of a law suit or imprisonment. Ebo for exoneration. Provides protection from illness. This odu says we need to be generous especially with our spouses. This odu tells us magic and charms are not as powerful as one's own Ori. The worship of one's Ori is the path to good fortune.

oyeku betula
oyeku betusa
oyeku fetu sari o sebi oun r'ogun ire se
igbadi lorun akerengbe
adifa fun ojaja kan nimogun
omo afi kangan mowo tarun
nje ori oloja lo doja ire
Kee pe o
Kee jinna,
E waa wo'fa awo ki,
B'o ti nse
Ifa de, alase
Ope, abise wara

ase

Oyeku stooped to lick a magical powder
Oyeku uses magical powders to invoke powers
Oyeku rubs magical powders (etu) on his head thinking thus
To have found the solution to his problems
 Circular remains the neck of a gourd
This was divined for Ojaja at the shrine of Ogun
The child that uses his elegant hand to plait hair
It is the Ori of the Market woman
That makes her commerce profitable
Very soon,
At no distant date,
Come and see the Babalawo's prediction
Coming to pass
Ifa has come, the great authority

Palm-tree, whose predictions come true speedily
ase

OTURA OYEKU – mystic vision leads to completion or egotism leads to loss. Ebo for long life. This person needs to resist the temptation to get involved in a relationship he/she knows is not healthy. This person may have enemies just waiting for her/him to slip up. Must be smart and aware. Ebo to one's Egun for prosperity. Ebo for alignment with destiny, possibly initiation to Obatala.

Òtúrá yànpín o
Ìyànnyàn yànpín o
Won ò mò pé inú onípìín ò dùn
Won ò mò pé inú onípìín bàjé
A díá fún Òòsà Òsèèrèmògbò
Níjó tí Ojú omoo rè ó nù lo
Òun le rÓjú omo òun bàyìi?
Wòn ní kó rúbo
Ó bá rúbo
Òòsàálá rúbo tán
Wón bá rÓjú omo Òòsà
Inú Òòsà dùn
Wón bá n yò
Wòn bá n jó
Ó ní bèé làwon Babaláwo tòún wí
Òtúrá yàpín o
Ìyànnyàn yànpín o
Won ò mò pé inú pnípìín ò dùn
Won ò mò pé inú onípìín bàjé
A díá fún Òòsàálá Òsèèrèmògbò
íjó ti Ojú omoo rè ó nù lo
Wón ní kÒòsà ó rúbo
Kó lè rÓjú o
Òòsá gbébo nbè
Ó rúbo

Àwá mòmò rójú o
A mòmò ráyè
A ì rÓjú omo Òòsà tó nù o
Ase

Otura chooses a destiny
Human, choose your destiny
They never knew that the person with the destiny is not happy
They never knew that the owner of the destiny is sad
Cast divination for Òòsàálá Òsèèrèmògbò (Obatala)
On the day Oju, his child, went missing
"Would I be able to find Ojú, my child," he asked
He was told to do ebo
He did it
Afterwards
They saw Ojú, Òòsà's child
Òòsà was very happy
They were dancing
They were singing
He said it was exactly as his Babalawos predicted
Otura chooses a destiny
Human, choose your destiny
They never knew that the person with the destiny is not happy
They never knew that the owner of the destiny is sad
Cast Ifa for Òòsàálá Òsèèrèmògbò
On the day his child went missing
They told him to do ebo
So he would find Ojú
Òòsà did the ebo
We have definitely found time
And have definitely found space
We also found Ojú, Òòsà's child that went missing
Ase

THE HOLY ODU

OYEKU IRETE – end of cycle leads to determination or stubbornness. This odu speaks on the need to protect one's health and that of their family to avoid chronic illness. If the person is ill, this odu provides the cure – ebo to Esu. If an older woman, it is not too late to have children. Two people are going to travel. Ebo so things will go smooth. This person will be successful; it denotes wealth. This person might need to worship Olokun for prosperity and wealth. Ebo to Aje (the daughter of Olokun) and a head cleaning with pigeon for the ire of money. Speaks of marrying someone who will bring the person wealth. Ebo to Sango for protection. He-goat to Esu and pigeon to Ori to fulfill this person's destiny as a leader.

poku poku poyokoto
adifa fun oyeku
to n lo re soko irete won ni o kara
nle ebo ni kose
igba oyeku gori irete o
ire gbogbo de bani
Kee pe o
Kee jinna,
E waa wo'fa awo ki,
B'o ti nse
Ifa de, alase
Ope, abise wara
ase

Poku poku poyokoto
Cast divination for oyeku
When he was going to marry irete
He was ask to offer ebo
He complied
When oyeku became irete's husband
They were blessed with all ire
Very soon,

At no distant date,
Come and see the Babalawo's prediction
Coming to pass
Ifa has come, the great authority
Palm-tree, whose predictions come true speedily
ase

IRETE OYEKU – determination leads to the completion of a cycle, or stubbornness leads to loss. This person should worship Ifa for long life (perhaps initiation) and warns of the need to be of good character to avoid loss. A change in behavior is needed. Ifa says if you came for divination because of something you are planning or developing it will be good but need initiation so that more people will help you achieve your plan. If this person is going on a business trip ebo of fish and rat to Orunmila against competitor's plans. Ebo for victory against the plans of enemies. Ebo to the Iyami. If fighting for a promotion, Ifa says wait a little bit. Keep working hard and have perseverance. You will win the promotion with ebo to Olokun. Two roosters, 2 guinea hens, 2 pigeons, lots of vegetables, kola nut, cold corn meal pap, palm oil and money.

Ateyeku o se won biripe
Biripe biripe l'onu oko da
Bee na l'omo aranye se
A d'Ifa fun Olokun atabatubu
eri gbogbo ninu omi
Igba ti n f'omi oju s'ogbere ire gbogbo
Ebo ni won ni ko se
O si gbebo nbe o rubo
Nje Olokun wa ma l'agba
Gbogbo eri e f'agba fun Olokun
Olokun ma l'agba
Kee pe o

Kee jinna,
E waa wo'fa awo ki,
B'o ti nse
Ifa de, alase
Ope, abise wara
Ase

Ateyeku o se won biripe
Biripe biripe l'onu oko da
It is how people do it
These were the ones who cast Ifa for Olokun atabatubu
The one that lives in the ocean
On the day she was crying for blessings
She was asked to make ebo
She did the ebo
Olokun is the greatest
All rivers honor Olokun
Very soon,
At no distant date,
Come and see the Babalawo's prediction
Coming to pass
Ifa has come, the great authority
Palm-tree, whose predictions come true speedily
ase

OYEKU OSE – end of cycle leads to abundance or greed. This odu says the successful completion of a project will pay off well. Ebo for children. Warns to not resist the end of something like a job or relationship. This odu speaks on the power of fear to bring bad fortune. This odu speaks on the necessity of death as part of the cycle of reincarnation, "stagnant water becomes a putrid pond." If this peson has a troublesome child, a head washing is needed. Ebo to Esu and Olokun for prosperity in the name of one's spouse. The client or his wife wants to get pregnant. Ebo of a pregnant sheep. If this person is not able to prosper despite hard work, a hand of Ifa is needed or initiation and this person must not listen to negative advice. If travelling, it will be a good trip. This person can rise to be VIP.

Òyè kúsé kùsè kúsé
A dífá fún Òpòló ti ń fojúú ṣògbérè ọmọ
Wón ní yóó bímọ lọpọlọpọ
Ẹbọ ọmọ ní kó wáá ṣe
Wón ní ribiti ribiti lọmọ rè ó móọ rí
Òpòló bá rúbọ
Ló bá bèrè síí bímọ
Ní ọn ń fò kúsé kùsè
Ayé yẹ Òpòló
N ní wá ń jó ní wá ń yò
Ní ń yin àwọn Babaláwo
Àwọn Babaláwo ń yin Ifá
Ó ní bẹ́ẹ̀ làwọn Babaláwo tòún wí
Òyè kúsé kùsè kúsé
A dífá fún Òpòló ti ń fojúú ṣògbérè ọmọ
Wón ní ó sá káalè jàre
Ẹbọ ọmọ ń wón ní ó ṣe
Taa ló bímọ bágònyí bẹẹrẹ?
Òpòló nikàn
Ló bímọ bágònyí bẹẹrẹ
Òpòló nikàn
Ase

Òyè kúsé kùsè kúsé
Cast dafa for Baobab tree
The one that was going to the savanna to settle
"Would I be big?
In such a way as to overshadow all the other trees?" he asked

Baobab was told to do ebo
He quickly did the ebo
He arrived in the savanna
And became taller than all the other trees
"What kind of tree is this?!" they asked
They were told it was Baobab tree
Ifa says this person will have a great name in life
Òyè kúsé kùsè kúsé
Cast dafa for Baobab tree
The one that was going to the savanna to settle
Ebo is what he was told to do
Baobab chose a piece of land in the savannah
He grew enormous
And overshadowed them all
Ase

OSE OYEKU – abundance leads to the end of cycle or greed leads to loss. This odu speaks of the desire to find a spiritual discipline. In this odu is the story of Igbadu (igba odu). This odu portends the ire of prosperity and popularity. Ebo to Egbe for long life. Ebo to Iyami to stop the women working against this person. Whatever issue the person came to divination for, would come out okay with ebo to the Eguns of cloth, etc. ebo to avoid or end family dispute. Ebo against sterility. Ifa says, do not act out of character when people disrespect you. Maintain good character, good hygiene, and dress well, etc., for good fortune. Ifa will protect your children from impending harm with ebo. Ifa predicts a blessing of wealth but this person has to remove from their lives the negative people around them. Ebo to Obatala.

Ise o se Igunugun
Ko ba lo oru
Osi o ta Akala
Ko ba le le aba Oka

A d'Ifa fun Adina
Nijo ti n s'awo r'ode ooro
Ebo ni won ni ko se
Won ola won ti e
O si gbebo nbe o rubo
Ero Ipo
Ero Ofa
Orisanla Oseeremagbo
Ni yi o gbami l'owo eni to n d'imi l'owo
Ase

The vulture is not poor
And it is always flying in the sky
Alaha cannot be poor
And it is always found near oka
Cast Ifa for Adina
On the day he was going on a trip
He was told to do ebo
For the return of all his wealth
He did the ebo
Pilgrims of Ipo
Pilgrims of Ofa
It is Orisanla Oseeremagbo (Obatala)
Who will rescue me from from those who disturb me
ase

OYEKU OFUN– end of cycle leads to blessings or dysfunction. Warns of illness, not doing what is needed to recuperate. Provides peace of mind through alignment with destiny. This odu says ground yourself in suuru (tranquility). Ebo and B'Ori ritual for peace of mind.

Ifa o to ki abi o ko to ki?
Ifa o to ki

Aye Osupa dun joorun
Ko tani lara
Ko buni lara je
Beeni ko roni lara
Ase

Ifa, do not you deserve praise?
Ifa, you really deserve praise
The life of the Moon is more pleasant than that of the Sun
It does not smart the body
It does not bite the body
Also, it is not painful to the body
May we all live cool and pleasant lives
Ase

OFUN OYEKU – miracles lead to completion or dysfunction leads to loss. This odu says we find good fortune through kindness and generosity. Ebo for long life, respect and healthy relationships. This person needs time alone for introspection. Must maintain ancestral altar for the family. This odu speaks on the power of teamwork to get things done in a mutually beneficial way. Speaks of success in business supported by one's Ori. Ifa forseees long life and success for this person as long as they follow the wisdom and taboos of their odu in order to receive the blessings of their odu.

beyan o bat ii ku
Kamo so e kosi ohun ti oluwa re lese
A d'Ifa fun Orunmila
Aba n lo ree tee ti ikun omo alapa n'ifa
Yio te ajimo omo Oba Orisa
Yio te Abori won ran bedu omo Obatala
Ebo ni won ni ko se
O gbebo ni be o rubo
Nje oosa kan winnin winnin ti n be n'ile

Ebora ti n pa asebi
Ebora ti n gbe omo re
Orisa kan winnin ti n be n'ila
Ebora ti n gbe omo re
Ogbere ni odu ko t'ona
Won n'ifa o tero
Ebora ti n pa asebi Odu mi ni se
Emi ni Odu t'ona
Ifa si t'ero
Oosa ti n gbemo re Odu mi ni se
Oko Aje Ifa d'Orisa
Ewi ado Ifa di Orisa
Gbogbo ogberi
Won n bukin lekuro o
Oko Aje Ifa d'ori sa o
Ase

If someone has to die
There is not much to say
Did d'afa for Orunmila
When he was going to initiate the son of Alapa in Eti Ekun town
He also initiated Ajimo, the son of the King of the Orisa
Also Abori Won Ran Bedu, the son of Obatala
He was told to do ebo
He did the ebo
Hence the Orisa of your home
The ebora that kills
The ebora that brings blessings
The only diety in your home
The one who brings good fortune
Is Ogbere Odu ko tona
They said the spirit of death (iku) would not bother them
The spirit that blesses the children is Odu
The husband of Aje, Orunmila has become Orisa

Ewi Ado has become Orisa
All those who are not initiated priests of Ifa
Are now united with ikin Ifa
The husband of Aje, Orunmila, has become Orisa
ase

NOTES

BOOK OF IWORI

IWORI ODI – transformation leads to rebirth; Or conflict leads to loss. This odu speaks on the Ifa concept of immortality. This odu says to avoid drinking alcohol. Warns us not to give in to fear, as fear is a self fulfilling prophecy. Ifa forsees a good life for this person. Says we should not let our loved ones go hungry. The path to a man's heart is thru his stomach.

Ìwòrì wò mí
Ìdí wò mí
Ẹni táa ni níí wo ni
A dífá fún Ìwòrì
Níjó ti ń lọ rèé wòdí
Wón ní kó rúbọ
Bí Ìwòrì ó bàá wòdí
Oúnjẹ níí kún inú è
Ayé yẹ é
Ìwòrì wò mí
Ìdí wò mí
Ẹni táa ni níí wo ni
A dífá fún Ìwòrì
Níjó ti ń lọ rèé wòdí
Ìwòrì dákun
Ìwòrì dábò
Èèyán ṣéé wòdí lébi
Ìwòrì dákun
Ìwòrì dábò

Ase

Ìwòrì look at me
Ìdí look at me
It is only those that are close to us that see our nakedness
Cast d'afa for Ìwòrì
On the day he was going to see Vagina
He was told to do ebo
Whenever Ìwòrì wants to see Vagina
His stomach would be full
Life pleased him
Ìwòrì look at me
Ìdí look at me
It is only those that are close to us that see our nakedness
Cast d'afa for Ìwòrì
On the day he was going to see Vagina
Ìwòrì please
Ìwòrì we plead
How can someone look at Vagina when he/she is hungry?
Ìwòrì please
Ìwòrì we plead
Ase

ODI IWORI – rebirth leads to transformation or weakness leads to conflict. This odu tells us to follow the wisdom of Ifa. This person is going thru tough times but with ebo will achieve wealth. Ebo to end poverty. Must walk in good character at all times. It warns against laziness, having the wrong friends and ignorance.

Bi a l'ogbon ninu bi a ko loo
Ao d'ogberi
Bi a l'agbara ninu bi a ko loo
Ao d'ole ni
A d'ifa fun awon eniyan mab'ologbon-rin

Mab'asise s'ore ero isale aye
Ifa nba o wi, O ni:
Iwo ko ba eniire rin, iwo ko ba eniire s'ore
Ori buruku niimaamu ba eniyan
Kee pe o
Kee jinna,
E waa wo'fa awo ki,
B'o ti nse
Ifa de, alase
Ope, abise wara

Ase
If we have wisdom and fail to apply it
We become ignorant
If we have power and fail to apply it
We become indolent
Ifa was consulted for the people of the underworld
Who are not associating with the wise and hardworking people
Ifa warns
You are not associating with people of good character
This usually brings bad luck
Very soon,
At no distant date,
Come and see the Babalawo's prediction
Coming to pass
Ifa has come, the great authority
Palm-tree, whose predictions come true speedily
Ase

IWORI IROSUN – transformation leads to fulfillment of potential or conflict leads to lack of progress. Speaks on the need for patience and the need to release shame and guilt. Speaks on the need to think before acting. Speaks of ebo for a pregnant woman to have uneventful labor. This person, if she/he has been through hard times, should initiate to Obatala for at the end of the hard times is wealth.

Iwori gosun se owo odo poroporo
Adifa fun eyele ti n se olopo obinrin
O n ti ikole orun bo waye
Won ni ebo ni kose,
Nje a se mo wipe eeyele n
Se oge,
Eele kun osun sowo,
O kun osun si ese,
A o se mo wipe eyele n
Soge
Kee pe o
Kee jinna,
E waa wo'fa awo ki,
B'o ti nse
Ifa de, alase
Ope, abise wara
Ase

Iwori was pounding osun (camwood powder) in a stylish way
Cast divination for the pigeon
Who had many women
When he was coming from heaven to earth
He was asked to offer ebo
he did the ebo
How do we know
The pigeon is beautiful?
The pigeon painted the hand and the leg red,
How do we know the pigeon is beautiful?
Very soon,
At no distant date,
Come and see the Babalawo's prediction

Coming to pass
Ifa has come, the great authority
Palm-tree, whose predictions come true speedily
ase

IROSUN IWORI – this odu speaks of the blessing that comes when we fulfill our potential, which in this case, leads to a positive transformation. This odu is heavy in Ifa ethics and implores us to act ethically as the road to good fortune. Speaks of difficulties, but that it is through difficulties that we grow. We must be joyful, wise and ethical. This odu also speaks of problems between relatives. Ifa says to finish what we start and to praise our father whether dead or alive. Ebo to our father's Ori.

bi egbin bi egbin ko tan ni isale akitan
adifa fun oyingbegi gbegi ti
yio bi gbogbo omo jo edu
won ni ebo ni kose,
ki a rubo
nitori ire omo
Riru ebo ni i gbe ni
Airu ki i gb'eeyan.
E waa ba ni ni wowo omo
ase

such of dirtiness and irritation
does not desist from the waste bin,
cast divination for oyingbegi gbegi that was going to give
birth to all his children resembling edu,
she was ask to offer ebo
for successful delivery
It is doing ebo that brings blessings
Neglect of ebo pays no one
Come and join us where there are plenty of children

ase

IWORI OWONRIN – This odu says transformation leads to being well prepared for unexpected changes. Implores us to avoid conflict to avoid loss. Ebo to Ori to avoid loss of position or for good fortune to return to the person. Don't speak on things too soon. Might need to receive Egbe for good fortune. If client is a man looking for a woman, now is a good time. Ebo to Ogun for long life.

Elepo o jere adiye ko setan katakata da epo nu
Adifa fun iwori ti n se
Egbon owonrin won ni korubo ki aburo re ma ba ku
Eropo ero ofa e wa ba
Ni laiku kangiri
Aiku kangiri la n ba ni lese obarisa.
Ase

The palm oil seller does not benefit from the hen
And because of that pours away her palm oil
Cast divination for Iwori
Who was asked to perform ebo on Owonrin
His junior brother
So that he will not die
He was told to do ebo
he did ebo
Thus the people of opo and the people of osa come
and meet us at the triumph of longlife.
Ase

OWONRIN IWORI – unexpected change leads to transformation or to conflict. Warns us to plan well for the future and work hard. To be well prepared for contingencies is to be wise and responsible. This odu says something unexpected is on its way but as long as we are prepared we will be fine. Speaks of childbirth and of children leading to wealth, or ebo for the children to be succesfull. If a woman, ebo for long life. Ebo to Esu and/or Ogun for protection from enemies.

Owonrin were
Iwori wara
Adifa fun elemoso itape
Tin sunkun wpe owun ko mo arun ti n se owun
Won ni ebo ni ko se
Nje arun kan arun kan eyi
Ti n se elemosho ko ju ere owo lo
Kee pe o
Kee jinna
E tete waa ba wa ni jebutu aje suuru
Ase

Owonrin were
Iwori wara
Cast divination for elemoso itape
Who was saying he does not know his problem
He was asked to offer ebo
Thus nothing is wrong with him other than a shortage of money
Very soon,
At no distant date
Come and join us where there's plenty of money and peace of mind
Ase

IWORI OBARA – transformation leads to spiritual growth. Speaks of the need for honesty and to avoid illicit behavior. Ifa says we mustn't be hard on ourselves. But that hard headedness will bring us misfortune. The person is going thru difficult times, but is stubborn and wants things his or her way. Must be flexible and humble to achieve success. Generous ebo to bring good fortune and end tough times.

Nijoti ti mo ti dele aye
O bere roko ri
Adifa fun agere ti n se obinrin ogun
O sunkun wipe owun ko bimo
Won ni ebo ni kose
O rubo
Tan o bere si ni bimo
Riru ebo ni i gbe ni
Airu ki i gb'eeyan.
E waa ba ni ni wowo omo
ase

Ever since I was born I never bend down to cut a bush
Cast divination for Agere the wife of Ogun
Who was seeking for fruit of womb
She was ask to offer ebo
She did the ebo
And she started bearing children
It is doing ebo that brings blessings
Neglect of ebo pays no one
Come and join us where there are plenty of children
Ase

OBARA IWORI – spiritual elevation leads to renewed passion. This Odu reminds us that there are things more important than money. Sango speaks a lot in this odu and brings the message of the need for passion in our lives. Also protection from enemies. Might call for ebo of rabbit to the Iyami. Iyami and Oro are prominent.

Kangi kangi lawo ilu kangi
Kangi kangi lawo ilu kangi

Benbe nla wonu
Odo o n kun yunmu yunmu
Adifa fun agbe to n fo jojumo lulu fun orisa
Won ni ebo ni ko mase
Nje ifa ma ma je ki ilu temi o parun
Ilu agbe
Ki parun lese obarisa
Ero Ipo
Ero Ofa
E waa ba ni ni jebutu ire
ase

Kangi kangi is the priest of kangi
Kangi kangi is the priest of kangi
Benbe drum enters the river and sounds mysteriously
Cast divination for Agbe (blue turaco)
Who has been drumming for Orisa everyday
She was asked to offer ebo
She did ebo
Thus Ifa please do not let me
who is praising the drum
Perish along the path of Obarisa
Travellers to Ipo
Travellers to Ofa,
Come and join us where there's plenty of good fortune
ase

IWORI OKANRAN – transformation leads to new opportunities. Ifa says act on good advice. This odu brings an abundance of good fortune. Ifa says we should work with a team; be outward going, build our social network, etc. for success. No man is an island. Must avoid fighting; someone could accidentally or purposefully be killed. Implores the client to be truthful with the diviner. If the person is planning some new venture or something, ebo should be done to ensure success. Ebo to Sango for the thing the person came for divination to come out well, but patience is needed because it would probably fail the first couple of attempts. This person should receive Ifa and be close to Ogun and Osanyin.

Ìwòrì ò rinkàn
Awo Olóreè Agbọn
A dífá fún Olóreè Agbọn tisàlè ọjà
Iré tówó òun báyìí?
Wón ní kó rúbọ
Wón ní kò gbọdò dá rin mó
Wón ní ààrin òpò èèyàn ni kó móọ rin
Ààrin èèyàn nire è é wà
Olóreè Agbọn ò bá dá rin mó
Bó si ti wà tée dòní nùu
Bíre ó bàá tóni lówó
Èèyàn làá mò
Ìwòrì ò rinkàn
Awo Olóreè Agbọn
A dífá fún Olóreè Agbọn tisàlè ọjà
Níjó tí ń fomi ojúú sògbérè ire
Ó tí ń rin lénikan ṣoṣo gíogío
Wón ni ó mó rin lénikan ṣoṣo gíogío
Ìwòrì ò mòmò rinkàn
À á ṣe rin lénikan ṣoṣo gíogío
Ìwòrì ò mòmò rinkàn
Ase

Ìwòrì ò rinkàn
Awo Olóreè Agbọn
Cast divination for Olóreè Agbọn
living down by the market place
'Would I have a lot of good things'? He asked
He was asked to offer sacrifice

And told not to be a lone ranger
'You should try to move close to people'
'Your good fortune is in meeting with people'
Olórèé Agbon refused to be a lone ranger
And that is how it is till date
If anything good would come to anybody
It is going to be through someone
Ìwòrì ò rinkàn
Awo Olórèé Agbon
Casts divination for Olórèé Agbon
living down by the market place
On the day he was crying because of good things
He had been going solo and been lone ranging
He was warned not to be individualistic again
Ìwòrì is not iconoclastic again!
How could one be a lone ranger?
Ìwòrì ò rinkàn
Ase

OKANRAN IWORI – new direction leads to a sense of fulfillment. Must communicate well; be willing to ask for help when needed. Must clearly identify the source of a problem. Ebo to Esu for this. Possible ebo to stop someone from usurping our place at work. Might need to receive Esu Odara.

okanran hihi awo ase lodifa fun ase
Ase n gbogun lo si ilu ilomi won
ni korubo ko le mure bo
Esu aisebo
Esu aisetutu
E o ri ifa ojo ni bi
tin se
Riru ebo ni i gbe ni
Airu ki i gb'eeyan.

E waa ba ni ni ire gbogbo
ase

okanran hihi, the priest of basket
cast divination for basket
when he was embarking on a journey to river
he was ask to make ebo
so that he could come back with blessings
he refused to do the ebo
he returned empty handed
It is doing ebo that brings blessings
Neglect of ebo pays no one
Come and join us where there is plenty of ire
Ase

IWORI OGUNDA – transformation leads to removal of obstacles. Warns us to control our anger. Brings an end to conflict with ebo. Ebo to Sango and Ori for success. Possible conflict with current partner's ex. Warns us to stop doubting or procrastinating and move on the issue at hand. Now is the time for action. Warns to avoid meetings at this time. Head wash needed. This person has been working hard to no avail. Ebo to Esu and Ogun so that hard work leads to better income.

iwori aweda
eda o gbogun ebo ni ifa ni ka ma se
adifa fun ori oloye
to n ti ikole orun bo waye
nje ofule fule ori oloye n ru
Kee pe o
Kee jinna,
E waa wo'fa awo ki,
B'o ti nse
Ifa de, alase

Ope, abise wara
ase

iwori aweda
maintaining oneself clean in proper fashion
One is not affected by charms
it is ebo Ifa orders us to do
cast divination for he whose Ori is of a chief
he was asked to do ebo
so he can be a chief
he did the ebo
and became a chief
Very soon,
At no distant date,
Come and see the Babalawo's prediction
Coming to pass
Ifa has come, the great authority
Palm-tree, whose predictions come true speedily
ase

OGUNDA IWORI – clearing of obstacles lead to transformation. Warns against getting into conflict at this time. If the person is going to travel, they will have a successful trip. Warns of need for protection from illness. If thinking about a woman, should move on it; don't let this one get away. Possibility of Ajoogun or other negative spirits causing problems for this person. Ifa says we must be as powerful as Ogun and as wise as Orunmila to beat the negative energies. Might need to receive Ifa (ikin).

Ogunda ki I'akpo
Iwori ko I'ofa
Ofa kan ofa kaan
t'onshe oju akpo yoro yoro
Odifa fun ori na

okonbi omo Sango
nijo t'oma gba ashe lowo Sango
Oni ko lo gba Ifa
Ase

Ogunda has no bow
Iwori has no arrow
When the arrow is shot, it does not miss
These were the awos who did divination for Ori Ina
The son of Sango
He was advised to receive his own ikin
He followed the advice
It was after that when Sango began to receive authority and dignity
ase

IWORI OSA – transformation leads to abundance. Warns us not to run from our responsibilities. Follow the wisdom of Ifa and have faith in our own abilities. We have the answers but are not acting on them. Possible ebo of pigeon to Ori for ire; ebo to Obatala and Oya for prosperity and peace of mind.
adifase bi ala
adifa fun gbabila ti n se omo olowo eyo
won ni ebo ni kose
nje gbaila olowo eyo
iwori awosa o olowo eyo
gbabila olowo eyo
Ero Ipo
Ero Ofa
E waa ba ni ni jebutu ire
ase

the person whose divinaton comes to pass like a dream
cast divination for Gbabila
the son of Cowries (money)

when he was coming from heaven to earth
he was asked to offer ebo
to receive riches
he did ebo
and became rich
Iwori Osa, the owner of cowries
gbabila the owner of cowries
Travellers to Ipo
Travellers to Ofa,
Come and join us where there's plenty of good fortune
ase

OSA IWORI –

In Osa Iwori, external changes lead to transformation. This odu usually points to external conditions. If we take a negative, fearful stance regarding change, we will encounter conflict. This odu calls for courage. The courage to put our faith in spirit and manage change with a cool head. This odu speaks of change leading to wealth due to our own creativity. Many verses on wealth, but also the possible need for protection from enemies.

Temigbusi
A difa fun Ajetunmobi
Won ni:
Ajetunmobi, ire Okun
Ire-Osa ma de
Aje nwole wa
O wo oju babalawo terinterin
O ni:
"Eyin kompe ohun ti mo ti ntorire sare kiri niyen to mo now'hin-w'ohun?"
Won niki o wa rubo
Ki ara le ro pese
O gbo o ru

Won ko apakan Ogede tiofi rubo fun un pe
Kiojee ati pe bee niki o ma je ogede were
Ase

Temigbusi
The diviner for Ajetunmobi
Predicted she would receive good fortune from the sea (Olokun) and the lagoon (Oya)
Money (aje) would come to her home
Smiling, she looked at the babalawo and said
"Don't you know that's what I've been running after?"
She was asked to do ebo for happiness
She did the ebo
She was given some of the bananas she had offered as ebo and was told to eat them
She was told she should eat bananas frequently
Ase

IWORI IKA – in this odu, the transformation of Iwori, if handled correctly, leads to increased personal ase. Our words have power and we must be careful of what comes out of our mouth. We must be positive, kind and grateful. happiness is the key to this person's success. If the person is not happy, they are causing their own hardship. Change of attitude is essential. This person will find success in business. might need Olokun for material success and Ogun for protection. the protection is from jealous adversaries. This person must not flaunt their success, but remain humble so as to reduce jealousy.

bi a ba da iwori ayoka
erin la n rin
adifa fun won ni ijebu mure ogbonkan muda
omo a o irin yebeyebe yari ogun

won ni ebo ni ki won se
eropo ero ofa e wa ba ni larusegun
arusegun la n ba ni lese obarisa
ase

if we cast Iwori Ayoka
it calls for laughter
cast divination for the people of ijebu mure ogbo nkan muda
those who put varieties of iron on the shrine of Ogun (omo Ogun)
they were asked to offer sacrifice for success
they did
and became successful at the feet of the King of the Orisa
ase

IKA IWORI – increase in personal spiritual power leads to a change in circumstances. This person needs to be more disciplined regarding Ifa/Orisa so as to build their ase. It is their own power that will lead to an improvement in their lot. Concentrate on Ori before Orisa. Must avoid bad behavior. This person might possibly become a healer.

Enu kii je kenu o wo
Adifa fun won no Kawura
Ki won o toyu arugbo ile won
Ebo ni won ose
Won si gbebo
nbe won rubo
Kee pe o kee jinna
Ewa bani ni jebutu ire gbogbo

One does not eat while another is watching
Cast Ifa for the people of Kawura
So they could take care of their elders

They were told to do ebo
They did the ebo
Shortly thereafter
Come and see how they have been blessed with all good fortune (ire gbogbo)
Ase

IWORI OTURUPON – working on one's Ori will prevent illness. Warning of illness if this person does not follow the wisdom of Ifa. If a woman and pregnant, possibility of problems with the baby. Possible ebo to Esu and Ogun. This person should never get involved in other folk's relationships. Ebo to Obatala for wealth.

Kere kere awo ile orunmila
lo sefa fun orunmila
nijo ti on lo re gba
obinrin agbe lagba gbe
won ni ebo ni kose
nje aya ti awo ba gba a gba
gbe ma ni o
Ero Ipo
Ero Ofa
E waa ba ni ni jebutu ire
ase

gradually, gradually the priest of Orunmila
cast divination for Orunmila
when he was going to snatch the wife of the farmer
he was asked to do ebo
Orunmila did the ebo
and finally snatched away the wife of the farmer
Travellers to Ipo
Travellers to Ofa,
Come and join us where there's plenty of good fortune

Ase

OTURUPON IWORI – this odu warns us to protect ourselves and our children from illness. It speaks of conflict between two people after the same thing. This is one of four "hot' or "unstable" odus. Special care is required by the diviner. Ebo should be done at once if it is found this person is under attack by ajoogun (malevolent forces). May need hand of Ifa or full initiation for protection, appease your Orisa if you have Orisa, and of course go to the ancestors. This person needs to behave well and with caution. Any illicit activities will backfire. Iwa pele, as exemplified by Orunmila is the best protection

Agberupon
A difa fun Agbado
Won niki Agbado wa rubo
Kio baa le so omo ti oun yoo pon kale li alaifi ati aiku pelu
O gbo ko ru
Riru ebo ni i gbe ni
Airu ki i gb'eeyan
ase

Agberupon divined Ifa for Corn
Corn was advised to do ebo (a pigeon, money, a girdle and Ifa medicine)
In order to safely deliver her child
She didn't do the ebo
It is doing ebo that brings blessings (ire)
Neglect of ebo pays no one
ase

IWORI OTURA – In this odu, one's hard work with Ori leads to mystic vision, or connection with his/her higher self (iponri). It is connection with iponri that allows for blessings to flow. Warns us to have a positive outlook and appreciate the beauty of Olodumare's creation. This odu possibly denotes this person's need for initiation into Ifa for success. This person is disrespected because they are shy, and passive. The person needs to be more assertive and act like they know. Dress for success. However, this person must be respectful and tolerant regarding their relationship with their spouse.

iwori wo tu pere re
adifa fun olomo ti yio gbe ori awure lo si oja
ti yio fi ra awubi wa sinu ile
won ni ebo ni kose
O gbo ko ru
Riru ebo ni i gbe ni
Airu ki i gb'eeyan
ase

iwori wotu pere re
cast divination for the son of who carries a head of good fortune (ori ire) to the market
and returns with bad fortune
he was asked to offer ebo for his journey
he didn't do the ebo
It is doing ebo that brings blessings (ire)
Neglect of ebo pays no one
ase

OTURA IWORI – in this odu, ifa says the person has achieved connection to source, and this will lead to a transformation of self and surroundings. This odu speaks of *suuru*, the father of *iwa* (character). Suuru is a concept not possible to define with one word, but basically it is patience. In our tradition, patience is at the top of the list of attitudes we must acquire. we cannot run faster than our destiny. this odu also speaks of the need to give in order to receive. The most valuable gift is our time. Otura Iwori requires courage. Transformation instigated by spirit can be difficult. Sometimes it leads to changes we don't want or like. The odu below says, "fear had made one abandon weeding the surroundings of a palm tree." In other words, the fear of the unexpected that comes with true transformation leads one to abandon the effort to "clean up" our Ori.

Ahonranmogangan
Ahonranmogangan
Iberu o je a roko idi agbon
Ko mo ba tibi hore hore bani leru
A d'Ifa fun Oruku Ona Eyo
Tomo araye n pe leru
Bo ba dehiin
Won a peru awon ni
Bo de ohun
Won a peru awon ni
A a see mo Oruku Ona Eyo?
N la ape Sango
Won ni ko rubo
Won ni won o da mo lomo nlee baba e
Sango ba rubo
Lo ba sagbere lo
Titiiti ko de
Ngba ti o pada de
N kuo sanmo
Ile e baba e lo beere
Karararara lo saara
Were won n pe ilee babaa re ree
Ilee babaa re ree
Awon o mo
A ba ti pe o leru
Ni Sango wa n jo n ni n yo

Ni n yin awon Babalawo
Awon Babalawo n yin Ifa
O ni bee Babalawo toun wi
Ahonranmogangan
Ahonranmogangan
Iberu ni o je a rook idi agbon
Ko mo baa tibi hore hore bani leru
A d'Ifa fun Oruku Ona Eyo
Tomo Araye n pe leru
Won ni o sa kale ebo ni o se
O si gbebo nbe
O rubo
Oruku Ona Eyo tomo araye n pe leru
Omo delee baba e
Omo waa domo gidi
Ase

Ahonranmogangan
Ahonranmogangan
Fear had made one to abandon the weeding of the surroundings of the palm tree
Such that the hoe's scraping noise in weeding would not scare one away
Cast Ifa for Oruku Ona Eyo, the one that humans refer to as a slave
When he moves near here
They would say, "He is our slave"
When he moves to the other side
People on the other side would say, "He is our slave"
How do we know Oruku Ona Eyo?
He is the one we call Sango
He was asked to do ebo
They told him that thet would recognize him as a real child in his father's house
Sango performed the ebo

He then went away in search of power
He was not seen for a long time
On his return
He left the skies
He asked for his father's house right away
In a loud crack of thunder
Immediately, they pointed out his father's house
"Here is your father's house," they said
"We were only ignorant all along"
"We would never have called you a slave," they said
Sango then started to dance and sing
He was praising his Babalawos
His Babalawos were praising Ifa
He said, "It is a my Babalawos said"
Ahonranmogangan
Ahonranmogangan
Fear had made one abandon weeding the surroundings of a palm tree
Such that the hoe's scraping noise in weeding would not scare one away
Cast Ifa for Oruku Ona Eyo, the one that humans refer to as a slave
He was asked to take care of the ground and do ebo
He heard about the ebo
He did the ebo
Oruku Ona Eyo whom humans call a slave
The child got his father's house
And became a legal and recognized child
Ase

IWORI IRETE - in this odu, the tangible positive outcomes from our transformation give us the determination to continue on the path of self-realization. This person must avoid all negative behavior because their Ori is open and vulnerable to all energy positive or negative. Possible need to receive Olokun for prosperity.

iwori were we
awo ata lo difa fun ata
won ni korubo nitori awon omo re
esu aisebo
esu aise tutu e o ri ifa ojo ni bi tin se
Riru ebo ni i gbe ni
Airu ki i gb'eeyan
ase

iwori were we
the priest of pepper cast divination for pepper
when he was asked to offer ebo because of his children
he did not offer ebo
and since then people have been eating his children
It is doing ebo that brings blessings (ire)
Neglect of ebo pays no one
ase

IRETE IWORI – this odu speaks of conflict. This person has to tread lightly and avoid conflict. Deal with conflict differently than the usual way. This will also throw off the adversary. This is one of the odus popularly used in ebo process. That means it provides good avenue to communication with Orunmila. Possible ebo to Ifa to deal with the conflict. Possible initiation into Ifa. Calls for iwa pele. Possible ebo to Oso and Aje (witches).

Kijiipa awo won lode igbajo
Ologodo tie mi awo ode Ijesa
Aso ode Ijesa mo e kunle ki t'oro mo lai-lai
L'aso fiija so o lo
A d'Ifa fun Orunmila
Nigba Baba nlo ree ba Aje se ja odun

Won no o saka ale o ja re
Ebo ni won ni ko se
O si gbebo nbe o rubo
Oso ile ejo wo mi
Bi gun ba jebo a ju gba si
Ifa pea won aye o ni binu e leyin
Nti won o ba a gba n ni koru
Ase

Kijiipa the awo of Igbajo city
Ologodo tie the awo of Ijesa
Never use the cloth of of Ijesa to sew the Igbajo cloth for kneeling in prayer to Oro
Some cloth are more valued than others
These were the awos who did divination for Orunmila
When he was being bothered by the Aje and the Oso (witches and sorcerers)
He was told to do ebo
He did it
May all the sorcerers and witches forgive me
When the Vulture eats the offering, she leaves the calabash
Ifa says the Aje and Oso will not bother the person
Who gives them what they want
Ase

IWORI OSE – This odu speaks of our transformation finally leading to abundance. Speaks of doing all things in moderation. Warns us of the need for humility. Humility is the portal to the ire of this odu. This odu speaks to long life as this person's primal concern. This person needs to do ebo and do all those things that lead to long life.

Tifa loba
ti orisa losin

adifa fun oba merin
a dan ro won ti ikole orun bo waye
won ni ebo
ire gbogbo ni ki won ma se
won rubo won bere
si se rere
Kee pe o
Kee jinna,
E waa wo'fa awo ki,
B'o ti nse
Ifa de, alase
Ope, abise wara
Ase

what belongs to Ifa is kingship
what belongs to Orisa is respect
cast divination for the four kings
when they were descending from heaven to earth
they were asked to offer ebo for good fortune
they did ebo
and since then they have always been prosperous
Very soon,
At no distant date,
Come and see the Babalawo's prediction
Coming to pass
Ifa has come, the great authority
Palm-tree, whose predictions come true speedily
Ase

OSE IWORI – this odu says our good fortune will lead to a transformation of circumstances. It says we need to be close to our ancestors for protection and prosperity. This odu speaks on the origins of merindilogun, the divination system ruled by oshun. Possible ebo to Ori for good health and Sango for success. If the client is feeling disturbed, possible ebo to Egbe. Ifa says this odu brings wealth, but the person must always be thankfull and kind and be close to Ifa – ethically.

Ose dudu mo gbe ji o
Iwon pupa n doko ka s'ope s'ope ka b'ope b'ope
Kale baa gbo kange kange
Komo an kole baa nawo gbogbo gbeni sin
A d'Ifa fun Orunmila
Nijo ti n s'awo lo sile ereke lado
Ebo ni won ni ko se
O si gbebo nbe o rubo
Ose dudu ereke lado o erigi a bola
Abo l'aje ni abo n'ire gbogbo ni
Erigi a bola ose dudu ereke lado o
Ase

Ose dudu (play on words for black soap) mo gbe ji o
Iwon pupa n doko ka s'ope s'ope ka b'ope b'ope
Kale baa gbo kange kange
Komo an kole baa nawo gbogbo gbeni sin
Cast divination for Orunmila
On the day he was coming from orun to the land of ereke lado
He was told to do ebo
He did the ebo
The black palm tree from ereke lado o
Erigi a bola
Will make it so all good fortune comes to me
Erigi a bola
The black palm tree is ereke lado o
Ase

IWORI OFUN – This odu speaks of transformation leading to our prayers being fulfilled. Ibori is called for. This odu is used in the consecration of the Ile Ori. Thus, this person might need to receive it. It speaks of relationships and the hard work and compromise needed for a successful one. If the person has ikin, they need to work them consistently. This will, among other things, help this person avoid conflict. This odu brings blessings. It is used in a common greeting, "asure iworiwofun." Which means may you be blessed by iwori ofun.

iwori towofin towo fin
iwori ti ese fin ti ese fin
iwori fi gbogbo ara fin geru geru
adifa fun agbado on ti ikole orun bo waye
won ni ebo omo ni kose
ogbe ebo orubo
ogbe eru o te eru
e wa ba ni bayo e wa wo ire
Ero Ipo
Ero Ofa
E waa ba ni ni jebutu ire
ase

iwori prospers from his hands
iwori prospers from his legs
iwori prospers from every part of his body
cast divination for maize corn
when he was coming from heaven to earth
she was asked to offer ebo
for blessing of many children
she complied
Travellers to Ipo
Travellers to Ofa,
Come and join us where there's plenty of good fortune

ase

OFUN IWORI – The success of our prayers leads to transformation of circumstances. Speaks of counting our blessings and being respectful with all people. Possible ebo to Egungun and Iyami. This odu comes with many blessings, usually from Orisa, so must thank one's Orisa on the regular. Must practice perseverance. Might need to receive Ifa, and always go for divination regarding important matters.

Eke mba ile gbe ile
Eke won o gbo owun ile
Èkùtè. mba àba gbe'le
Won o gbo owun Abà
Ìràwé lèbèlèbè mba Ikin gbe'le
Won o gbo owun Ikin
Difa fun Omuro
Tíi se omo bibi inu Agbonmiregun
O nti orun bo wa si aye,
o de ile aye tan
O fi eyin ti, o nfi ekun sun irawun ire gbogbo
Owun e ri e wa ro fun Ikin
Òmùrò, owun e rí e wá rò fún ikin
Owun e ri e wa ro fun mi, Òmùrò owun e rí e wá rò fún mi, Òmùrò.
Ase

Eke (rafter) lives with house
Rafter does not hear the voice of house
Ekute lives with hut
It does not hear the voice of hut
Irawe live with Ikin Ifa
They did not hear the voice of Ikin Ifa
Ifa was consulted for Omuro
Orunmila's child
When he was coming from the spirit sphere to earth

And when he got to earth
He was distraught with life's disappointing strings
Take your problems to Ikin Ifa
Òmùrò, take your problems to Ikin Ifa
Bring your problems to me--Orunmila
Òmùrò, bring your problems to me, Orunmila
Ase

                    NOTES:

BOOK OF ODI

ODI IROSUN – Our continued rebirthing of consciousness leads to fulfillment of destiny. Possible ebo to Ori and Esu for protection. Speaks of need for ebo against negative forces (ajoogun).

idin osun
idin kowo
adifa fun eti to n lo re gba adalewa obinrin efon
won ni ebo ni kose
esu aisebo
esu aise etutu
e o ri ifa ojo ni bi ti n se
Riru ebo ni i gbe ni
Airu ki i gb'eeyan.
Ase

idin does not sleep
idin does not have peace of mind
cast divination for ear

who was going to snatch the Beautiful One (ada lewa)
the wife of mosquito
he was asked to offer sacrifice
he did not do the ebo
and till still to this date
mosquito disturbs the ear
It is doing ebo that brings blessings (ire)
Neglect of ebo pays no one
Ase

IROSUN ODI – This odu speaks of the need for using our ancestrally given talents to continue to grow. The person must work hard but watch their health carefully. This person should not involve themselves in other people's problems. Speaks of the need to be careful regarding intimate relationships. Do not succumb to temptation.

Páà okùn
N níí já mójúu réfe
A dífá fún Olósùn ti ón lóròọ ré já dijú
Wón ní nňkan burú fún un
Òrò òún leè dáa báyìí?
Wón lóròọ rè ó níí já dijú mó
Wón ni yóó móọ jayé
Ẹbọ ní kó rú
Wón ní èlà ilèkè okùn kan lẹbọ
Giripá òrúkọ lẹbọ è
Ó bá rúbọ
Ayé yẹ Olósùn
Ó lówó lówó
Bí ti ń láya ní ń bímọ
Ó kólé
Ọkàan rè balè
N ní wá ń jó ní wá ń yò

Ní ń yin àwọn Babaláwo
Àwọn Babaláwo ń yin Ifá
Ó ní béè làwọn Babaláwo tòún wí
Páà okùn
N níí já mójúu réfe
A dífá fún Olósùn ti ón lóròọ ré já dijú
Wón ní nňkan burú fún un
Ẹbọ n wón ni ó şe
Olósùn gbébọ ńbè
Ó rúbọ
Ayé làwá ń jẹ ò
Ayé làwá ń jẹ
Òrò àwà ò já dijú mó ò
Ayé làwá ń jẹ.
Ase

Abruptly for the string
It cuts off the line of beads
D'afa for Olosun whose things they claim are proving knotty
They say he is living in abject poverty
"Would my things get better at all?"
They told him he wouldn't experience difficult times again
"You will henceforth be enjoying life.
You should only offer ebo
A string-line of broken beads is part of the ebo
A mature goat is also part of the ebo" they said
He offered it
And life pleased him
He had plenty of money to spend
He started to have wives and children
He also built houses
Peace of mind crowned them all
He then started to dance and sing
He was praising his Babalawo

His Babalawo was praising Ifa
He said it was as his Babalawo had said
Abruptly for the string
It cuts off the line of beads
D'afa for Olosun whose things they claim are proving knotty
They said he was having a difficult time
He was asked to do ebo
Olosu Heard about the ebo
And did it
We are enjoying life
We are enjoying life indeed
We are not ever going to experience difficulties again
We really are enjoying life
Ase

ODI OWONRIN – in this odu, our creative abilities are finally recognized. This person must avoid falling into depression. Speaks of possible initiation into ifa. Speaks of relationship issues. Possible ebo to Esu and Ogun for protection from harm coming from the other person in the relationship.

Idin a rin rin ma rin
idin a rin rin marin
idin ridin ridin
lomo de n roko agbala
adifa fun orunmila
won ni ko bori iya re nitori ire gbogbo
Kee pe o
Kee jinna,
E waa wo'fa awo ki,
B'o ti nse
Ifa de, alase
Ope, abise wara

Ase

Idin a rin rin marin
idin a rin rin marin
it is in a sluggish way the children cultivate the bush of the backyard
cast divination for Orunmila
he was asked to make ebo to his mother's Ori
in order to receive all good fortune
he did the ebo and he was blessed
Very soon,
At no distant date,
Come and see the Babalawo's prediction
Coming to pass
Ifa has come, the great authority
Palm-tree, whose predictions come true speedily
ase

OWONRIN ODI – This odu speaks of unexpected changes that can, if handled properly, lead to continued rebirth, or confusion. Speaks of the need for generosity. We must give in order to receive. Must be close to Ifa. If female should be apetebi or receive Ifa. Calls for protection of one's children.

owonrin sidin
kokoro n sidi
idin woyi woyi lobe
adifa fun ori
ori n tikole orun bo waiye
won ni ebo ni kose nje oori mi gbemi o
ori mi lami o
ase

owonrin producing maggots
iwori producing maggots

lots of maggots in the soup
cast divination for Ori
when he was coming from heaven to earth
thus please my Ori save me
ase

ODI OBARA – A rebirth of consciousness brings spiritual elevation. This person needs to be more spiritual; prayers and meditation, etc. This person has a powerful enemy. Must atone for any misdeeds that this person can use against him/her. Possible need to receive Ogun.

idin bere
idin bere le kaja
adifa fun egungun nijo towun ti osanyin jo n jija kadi
won ni ebo ni kose
egungun nikan ni n be leyin ti toju ebo
ebo ti e lo da ju
Kee pe o
Kee jinna,
E waa wo'fa awo ki,
B'o ti nse
Ifa de, alase
Ope, abise wara
Ase

idin get in a crouch
idin get in a crouch to fight
cast divination for Egungun
when he was having a wrestling match with Osanyin
they were asked to offer ebo
it was Egungun that made the offering and he was the one that won
Very soon,
At no distant date,

Come and see the Babalawo's prediction
Coming to pass
Ifa has come, the great authority
Palm-tree, whose predictions come true speedily
ase

OBARA ODI – Continued spiritual growth creates continued rebirth of consciousness. This person needs to create protection for his/her family. Obara speaks of humility. In this odu, arrogance will lead to the confinement of Odi. This odu usually comes for someone experiencing difficulties. Might need to receive hand of Ifa. Possible ebo to Ogun to remove blockages. A lack of humility is causing losses.

obara o bodi idi ko mole
e je ki kanyin kanyin ile yin o ta yin die
adifa fun bembe
ti n lo si tapa lenpe
won ni o kara n le ebo ni ko ma se
nje obara ko dun
ikan yi kodun
Riru ebo ni i gbe ni
Airu ki i gb'eeyan
ase

obara o bodi
idi o mole e je ki kanyin kanyin ile yin ko ta yin die
cast divination for bembe
when he was going to tapa lenpe
he was asked to do ebo for a safe trip
thus obara does not sound
this does not sound
It is doing ebo that brings blessings (ire)
Neglect of ebo pays no one

Ase

ODI OKANRAN – A rebirth of consciousness brings the ability to think outside the box. Or hard headedness creates myopia. This hard headedness gets the attention of Esu. Ebo and prayers to Esu to allow you to be more open to advice and new thinking. Must have an Esu, and be close to Sango who brings humility. There might be a problem with one's ancestors.

idin ranyin ranyin awo oti
lo sefa fun oti
oti n raye a pemu won ni
ebo ni kose
esu aisebo
esu aise etutu e o ri ifa ojo ni bi tin se
Riru ebo ni i gbe ni
Airu ki i gb'eeyan
ase

idin ranyin ranyin the priest of alcohol
cast divination for alcohol
when he was coming down from heaven to earth
he was asked to offer ebo
so that people will not gather to drink him
he didn't offer the ebo
and since then people have been drinking him
It is doing ebo that brings blessings (ire)
Neglect of ebo pays no one
ase

OKANRAN ODI – Taking a new approach leads to growth. This odu speaks of the need for maturity and the need to control one's emotions. Emotional maturity. This person might be having problems at work. Ebo to Ogun and Esu. In this odu is a story of Sango and Ogun in competition. This person should not let their ego get them into useless competitions. This odu speaks of death. Might need to receive Ifa.

iwaju siwaju ipako tele
adifa fun olokanran ti n se omo iya idin
won ni korubo ko ma ba sinku idin
nje ewi folokanran ko sindi
gbogbo owo egbon di taburo
ewi folokanran ko sindin
Ero Ipo
Ero Ofa
E waa ba ni ni jebutu ire
Ase

the forehead takes the front and the back of the head takes the back
cast divination for olokanran the sibling of idin
he was asked to offer ebo
so that his sibling will not die
thus tell olokanran to bury idin
all the wealth of the senior brother became that of the junior brother
thus tell olokanran to bury idin
Travellers to Ipo
Travellers to Ofa,
Come and join us where there's plenty of good fortune
ase

ODI OGUNDA – Rebirth leads to a removal of obstacles to progress. This person might be suffering, but patience and ebo to Ogun will lead to peace of mind and improved circumstances. This person needs to be more sociable in order to expand their social network. This odu warns us to be careful who we choose as mates. And, as always with Odi, watch out for STD's.

dindi gunda

dindi gunda
adifa fun orunlojo ilu nijo ti won lo re se aremo fun oba leyo ajori
dundun nikan lo n be leyin to n rubo ebo ti
o da adaju
Riru ebo ni i gbe ni
Airu ki i gb'eeyan.
E waa ba ni ni ire gbogbo
Ase

dindi gunda
dindi gunda
cast divination for numerous number of drums
who were going to celebrate with the king of Ijori
they were asked to offer ebo before embarking on the journey
it was only dundun that offer sacrifice
and it was only dundun that could perform at the event
It is doing ebo that brings blessings (ire)
Neglect of ebo pays no one
Come and join us where there is plenty of ire
ase

OGUNDA ODI – clearing of obstacles leads to continued growth. Need to watch out for conflict. Ebo for victory. Ifa says this person will meet someone soon who would make a good spouse. Ebo for long life. Ebo to Ori and Ifa for wealth. Ifa says someone is attacking this person but no need for juju. Just be close to Ifa and walk straight and Ifa and Ogun will handle it.

Labugabuga awo or iota
A dafa fun akapo nijo ti nsunkun pe
Ohun monle ola t'ohun
Ifa wa'file aje mi nanmi o
Labugabuga iwo l'awo ori ota

Ela wa file aje mi nanmi
Labugabuga iwo l'awo ori ota
Ase

Labugabuga the diviner for Ori Ota
Cast divination for akapo Ifa (disciple of Ifa)
When he was weeping that he doesn't know
Where the house of wealth is located
Labuganbuga, you are the one who knows where ori ota's fortune lies
Ela, come and reveal my house of wealth to me
Labungabula you are the fortune teller of ori ota
Ase

ODI OSA – In this odu, the rebirth of consciousness leads to external changes that bring abundance. Or failure to let go of the past leads to loss as a result of the external changes. Must act in upright manner. If wanting to get pregnant, you will. If you don't, best use birth control. In this odu we have the story of the Osun staff as protection from witches. In the story the Osun staff turns into a man and is actually helping save the Iyami from a witch. This odu then, speaks of this person being victimized by witches and or sorcerers. Ebo to Osun staff can stop the attacks. Might need Ibori, Ifa and Esu. Avoid confrontation, and keep cool.

idin sa
idin so awo ata
lodifa fun ata
nijoti olowun n lore pa olo je
won ni ebo ni kose
nje ata tolowun o pa olo ko le pa olo mo
olo lo tun pa ata je
ase

idin sa

idin sa the priest of pepper
cast divination for pepper
when he planned to kill grinder
They were advised to do ebo
it was grinder that offered ebo
and it is the grinder that continues killing pepper

OSA ODI – The sudden changes wrought by Osa lead to a rebirth in consciousness. Warns us to stay on path spiritually and to listen to advice; at least consider it, even from strangers. Ifa forsees success at work. Ifa for protection from negative entities. This is powerful odu and if Ifa points to negative influences, ebo and akose, probably black soap med for wash will be needed. It is this person's destiny to triumph, with Ifa, Ogun and Ori's help.

Ona Osa koila
Ona Osa ma di o
Orunmila I ebo niki a se ki ona le la fun Osa
Kee pe o
Kee jinna,
E waa wo'fa awo ki,
B'o ti nse
Ifa de, alase
Ope, abise wara
Ase

Osa's way is not open
Osa's way is blocked
Orunmila advised ebo to open the way
A clay lamp, palm oil, money, Ifa medicine (make black soap with ewe okro)
Very soon,
At no distant date,
Come and see the Babalawo's prediction

Coming to pass
Ifa has come, the great authority
Palm-tree, whose predictions come true speedily
Ase

ODI IKA – Rebirth brings an increase in personal ashe. Ebo to Esu for business success. This odu, however, if comes in ibi, usually points to instability in the person's life. Ebo to bring stability. Avoid sticking your nose in other people's business. Be forgiving with people; hexing will backfire. Might be attracting attention of the mothers. Act right, so they have no reason to harm.

aka bori ko le bopin
adifa fun eye won bowokan fun ekun
won ni ebo ni ki won se
eye rubo lati ojo na ni ekun ko le rin kan se fun eye mo
Ero Ipo
Ero Ofa
E waa ba ni ni jebutu ire
ase

aka covers his head but is unable to cover his destiny
cast divination for bird and lion
they were told to do ebo
only bird offered ebo
and since then lion cannot harm bird
but can only watch him in the sky
Travellers to Ipo
Travellers to Ofa,
Come and join us where there's plenty of good fortune
ase

IKA ODI – Increased personal ashe brings a rebirth of consciousness. The client might be being treated badly and unfairly.

Of course, ebo can end this. If wanting children, this is a good time. Twins are a possibility. Ebo to Ogun and/or Iyami to remove the negative people and/or spirits around you.

Biri mi kadi
Esu bobo n y'odi
Adifa fun Jaguda (robber)
Tin t'orun bo a Saye
Jaguda, dankun mo jami
Mo sa di ikin
Ifa se ebo ni won ose
Won si gbebo gbe won rubo
Ko pe ko jinna
Ire gbogbo way a de turturu
Ase

Biri mi kadi
Esu bobo n y'odi
Cast Ifa for Jaguda
When he was coming from orun to aye
Jaguda, don't assault me
I ran to Orunmila for protection
I was told to do ebo
I did the ebo
Not long after
Come and see how I have received all blessings
Ase

ODI OTURUPON – Rebirth brings good health. Lack of planning can lead to illness. This odu warns of STD's and other reproductive system problems. If a woman, a trip to the gynecologist for check-up might be a good idea. If a man, also might want to be proactive. This odu provides the cure for impotence.

idin turu
ipon turu
adifa fun esu odara
to ti n kore ile loja loja
loba loba
o ni oku oke igeti ile orunmila
orunmila rubo
esu dele ile re o bere
si ni bi ire gbogbo fun orunmila
ase

idin turu
ipon turu
cast divination for Esu Odara
who was carrying everyone's good fortune
and cast Ifa for Orunmila
Orunmila offered the ebo
and when Esu got to his home
he found the offering of Orunmila on his porch
not knowing the sacrifice contained pieces of bone
Esu drank the sacrifice and started vomitting all the good things and fortune he was carrying
in the house of Orunmila
and Orunmila became rich
ase

OTURUPON ODI – Illness leads to a rebirth. Many times, when we recover from illness, we come back stronger. If we recover and become more fearful, we will bring bad luck. This odu brings lots of ire, but need to receive Ifa to make it flow. This person needs to lighten up a little; he/she is too uptight. Must change their attitude and find happiness. This odu also speaks of enemies. Ebo for victory. Might need to do full Iyami ritual, especially if pregnant. If a family member is sick, ebo is necessary.

Orisa to se didun
Lo se aidun
Difa fun Orunmila
Won ni k sebo Ayo
Ko si sebo Ibanuje
O gbebo, o rubo
Atawo, atisegun
E y'egba e y'atori
E ba wa le Ibanuje
E y'egba e y'atori
Ase

The Orisa which causes delight
Is also responsible for displeasure
This was the declaration of Ifa to Orunmila
Who was advised to do offering for happiness
And also do offering against sadness
Orunmila did the offering
Both awo and herbalist
Draw out your whips and switches
Help us chase out sadness
Draw out your whips and switches
Ase

ODI OTURA – Rebirth of consciousness brings connection to source. This odu speaks of the importance of family sticking together. This odu speaks of a test for this person. Must be open to doing things differently or counter-intuitively to pass the test. This person might have Aje power. Possible ebo to avoid pain in reproductive organs

idin atago keyin aparo
owun oju n wa loju n ri

adifa fun nini tin se eru orisa
adifa fun aini ti n se eru orisa
won ni ebo ni ki won se
orisa n la pele o
agba lowo nini gba fun aini
o so eni kan sos di igba eni
ase

idin atago keyin aparo
it is what the eyes want to see that they see
cast divination for riches, the servant of Orisa
and also for poverty, the servant of Orisa
it is the poor that offer ebo and obey Orisa
That is why orisa collect from the rich and give to the poor
Orisanla, the father, who turns a single person into many
ase

OTURA ODI – Connection to spirit leads to rebirth. Speaks on relationships. Speaks of people as the source of their own problems. Person might be spinning their wheels. Might be working against destiny or other problem. Ebo to Ori. Patience with spouse. If pregnant, ebo to Iyami to avoid a miscarriage. Warns men to be good to women.

Òtúá sì í
Òdògbò n ardí
A díá fín Àsàbí tí n fomi ojúú sògbérè omo
Ebo omo n wón ní ó se
Òún le bímo láyé báyìí?
Wón ní iwo Àsàbí rúbo
Iré ó rò ó lórùn
Iléè re ó kùún fówó
Yóó kùún fómo

Sùgbón rúbo
Àṣàbí bá rúbọ
Omó bá kúnlè
Àwon omọ òhún ò yàn kú
N ní wá n jó ní wa n yò
Ní n yin àwon Babaláwo
Àwon Babaláwo n' yin Ifá
Ó ní bẹ́è làwon Babaláwo tòún wí
Òtúá dì í
Òdògbò n radì í
A díá fún Àsàbí ti n fomi ojúú sògbérè omo
Wón ní ó sá káalè
Ebo omo n wón ní ó se
Àsàbí gbébo nbè ó rúbo
A mòmò rÀṣàbí o
A rÀsà
Iré gbogbó wolé Awo gerere
Ase

 Otura di i
Odogbo n radi i
Cast Ifa for Asabi who was crying because of children
She was asked to make an offering
"would I have babies?" she asked
"do the ebo," they said
"all the good fortune you have will be easy to manage
Your house will fill with money
It will fill with children
Just do the ebo"
She did the offering
The ground became littered with children
They did not die prematurely
She then began to dance and sing
She praised her awos

Her awos praised Ifa
She said it was exactly as predicted
Otura di i
Odogbo n radi i
Cast Ifa for Asabi who was crying because of children
She was asked to take care of the ground
And do ebo for children
She heard and did the ebo
We have seen Asabi
We have seen culture
All good things have entered the house of the awo in multitudes
Ase

ODI IRETE – Rebirth provides the renewed strength to persevere. This odu speaks of an unstable life. This person should have hand of Ifa and Esu to end difficulties and bring ire. This verse speaks a lot about marriage. If this person is planning to get married, this must be delved into by the diviner. Warns us to mind our own business to avoid problems.

ope kan dun lemu
ope kan dun lekuro
adifa fun alakole
omo enikan la ju igba eni lo won ni korubo nitori aje
o rubo o bere
si ni di alaje
Ero Ipo
Ero Ofa
E waa ba ni ni jebutu ire
ase

one palm tree is sweet to provide palmwine
one is sweet to provide ekuro
cast divination for alakole

when he was seeking for wealth from Olodumare
he was asked to offer ebo
he did the ebo
and became rich and wealthy
Travellers to Ipo
Travellers to Ofa,
Come and join us where there's plenty of good fortune
ase

IRETE ODI – Determination and perseverence lead to a rebirth. Or stubborness leads to confinement. This odu speaks of success in one's profession. Ebo to Obatala and Ogun to remove obstacles. Warns us not to ignore advice. Possibly affected by negative spirits.

Iretedi awo ologose
Lo d'ifa fun ologose
Ologose nsunkun pe ohun ko l'ola
Ebo ni won ni ko se
O si gbebo nbe o rubo
Nje ologose nlo la ope nlo ro
Eyin k'omo pe aro wo rubo kiku so si
Ase

Iretedi the awo for Ologose
Did divination for Ologose
When he was crying for lack of wealth
He was told to make an offering
He did it
Now come and see how Ologose has wealth and has orisa too
Don't you know that ebo accepted will not let you suffer?
ase

ODI OSE – Rebirth leads to a blessing of abundance. Speaks of the need for this person and his/her children to receive Ifa for protection and success. This person should be close to Esu and Olokun for blessings. Ebo to Ori to end difficulties. Follow the advice of the ancestors.

idin se irele se
igi ogba se ki n tu mi ro
adifa fun orunmila
baba n sawo lo sode ikirun won ni ebo ni kose
ko le lo re
ko le bo ire
Kee pe o
Kee jinna,
E waa wo'fa awo ki,
B'o ti nse
Ifa de, alase
Ope, abise wara
ase

idin se
irele se
when the tree in the garden bends
I will replace it
cast divination for Orunmila
when he was embarking on a journey to the town of ikirun
he was asked to offer sacrifice for a succcessful journey
Orunmila did the ebo
and his voyage was a success
Very soon,
At no distant date,
Come and see the Babalawo's prediction
Coming to pass
Ifa has come, the great authority

Palm-tree, whose predictions come true speedily
ase

OSE ODI – Abundance brings a rebirth of consciousness. Or greed leads to confinement. Speaks of having children and a good relationship that leads to happiness. Ebo to Iyami to avoid problems during pregnancy. Ibori to remove obstacles. This odu tells us to exhibit good character and kindness even if not acknowledged. If having bad luck, it is possible there is a person who is cursing you.

Ewe ori igi ni kofe ilele wa
Ti ilele naa ko lo ori igi
A d'Ifa fun Osanyin
Ti n raye lai nik'u
Ebo ni won ni ko se
O si gbebo nbe o rubo
Ko I pe, ki I jina
E w aba ni l'aiku kan n giri
Ase

The leaves from the head (ori) of the tree don't like to fall to the ground
The leaves on the ground refuse to go back up
These were the ones who did divination for Osanyin
Who desired to live a long life
He was told to do ebo
He did it
Not long after that
Come and see how long he lives
Ase

ODI OFUN – Rebirth brings a new beginning. Letting go of past behaviors leads to our prayers being answered. Victory is guaranteed, but must avoid getting in silly arguments. Speaks of illness. This person has been blessed since birth and must show gratitude. This odu speaks of protecting one's children.

idin funfun ko riran a fi eni ti yio fi tie gbo erupe ile awo oye
lodifa fun oye
oye n sunkun ki apa owun la kaye
won ni ebo ni kose
ki apa re le kaye
o rubo
apa re kaye
Ero Ipo
Ero Ofa
E waa ba ni ni jebutu ire
ase

idin funfun ko riran a fi eni ti yio fi ti gbo ile is the priest of harmattan
cast divination for harmattan season
he was asked to offer ebo
so that he can be felt through out the world
he did the ebo
and since then you can feel him everywhere in the world
Travellers to Ipo
Travellers to Ofa,
Come and join us where there's plenty of good fortune
ase

OFUN ODI – Receiving blessings brings a rebirth of consciousness. Or bad behavior leads to confinement. Speaks of a blessing of wealth. This person's ire is dependent on their development of good character; following Ifa's ethical principles. Ebo for long life. Might need to receive Egbe. This odu speaks on ebo being more efficient than charms or medicines. This person should be close to Obatala and Ifa to receive blessings and protection from enemies.

Orunmila l'Ofun
Ei naa l'Ofun bara mi agbonniregun
Ofun dele Alara
Ofun dele Ajero
Ofun dele Owarangun Aga
Awon o mon ebo o j'ade lo
Ofun dele Orunmila
Orunmila nikan l'omo n ebo
Nje kinni Ofun n di
Ofun n di owo
Ofun n di eyo
Eyin komo npe ohun rere l'Ofun n di
Ase

Orunmila says there is good fortune on the way
I say there is good fortune on the way
Good luck comes to the house of Alara
Good luck comes to the house of Ajero
Good luck arrives in the hose of Owanrangun-aga
They were told to make offering
Only Orunmila made the offering
Good luck has arrived
Ofun is providing money
Ofun is providing luck
Don't you know it is Ofun that brings the blessing of money?
Ase

NOTES:

THE HOLY ODU

BOOK OF IROSUN

IROSUN OWONRIN – Full use of one's talents leads to the ability to handle unexpected changes. This person must listen to the ancestors for warnings of impending unexpected changes. Speaks of this person having friends who wish them ill. Speaks of adhering to taboos. Warns us to not get involved with a person who is already in a relationship with someone else. This person should have their own Ifa and Osanyin.

sinmi titi lawo sinmi titi
sin mi jina lawo sin mi jina
bo le sin mi titi ko sa ti ba mi dele irosuun elerin
adifa awele onidi o ren bête ti yio ma fi obo daran kiri
won ni ebo ni kose
Riru ebo ni i gbe ni
Airu ki i gb'eeyan.
E waa ba ni ni ire gbogbo
ase

escorting me for a while is same as escorting for the long journey
if you can't escort me for long
just make sure you assist me to get to the house of irosun elerin
cast divination for awele
who liked orenbete's rear end
she was going to use sex to kill people
people were asked to offer ebo to be saved from her

It is doing ebo that brings blessings (ire)
Neglect of ebo pays no one
Come and join us where there is plenty of ire
ase

OWONRIN IROSUN – Unexpected change brings a blessing from the ancestors. Or the fear of change leads to stagnation. This person must not be impatient and easy to anger. Calm, cool and collected brings the ire. Warns not to rely on the advice of others so much and develop our intuition. This person might suffer from fear and anxiety. Faith in Ifa will bring those feelings to an end.

oja loja owonrin
gele ni gele irosu
adifa fun akoko o n sawo lo si ode iresa
won i ebo ni kose
akoko awo won lode iresa
lodifa fun won lode iresa ebo omo ni won se eropo
ero ofa e wa ba ni laru segun
arusegun la ba ni lese obarisa
ase

the back tie (wrap for baby) is that of owonrin
head wrap (women's) is that of irosun
cast divination for akoko that was going on journey to town of Iresa
akoko the priest of Iresa
was the one who cast divination for people of Iresa
they were asked to offer ebo
so as to receive a blessing of children
they offered the ebo
and they triumph over their enemies
they have children
ase

IROSUN OBARA – Fulfillment of potential brings inner transformation. Or arrogance and greed lead to disgrace. Might be suffering from negative attacks (witches). Avoid alcohol. Ebo to Ogun for protection.

sasu ni omo olo osun nwi
irosun ega ni omo olo osun npe
adifa fun oya
oya n sunkun omo re ile ira
won ni korubo nitori ire gbogbo
ase

sasu sound is what comes out of pestle
irosun ega is what come out of pestle of osun
cast divination for Oya
that was seeking of bearing a children
she was asked to do offering
she did and was giving birth
ase

OBARA IROSUN – Inner transformation leads to renewed motivation to fulfill one's destiny. This odu speaks of the need for Ifa initiation and spiritual discipline to receive one's blessings. If a woman, initiation into Iyami. Ebo to Ifa and Ori for prosperity. Speaks of conflict. Ebo to Ogun and Sango for victory.

aseseyo iroko ni se ewe gba koko
gba koko adifa fun obara ti yio kun osun si ese osi
ti yio da ese kan otun si
won ni o kara nle ebo ni ko ma se
eropo ero ofa e wa ba ni larusegun
arusegun la ba ni lese obarisa
ase

the growing of iroko tree

makes the leaves attractive
cast divination for obara
who painted his left leg red and spared the right leg
he was asked to offer ebo
the people of opo and ofa
come and meet us at the acceptance of offering
ase

IROSUN OKANRAN – In this odu, using our ancestrally gifted talents leads to new ideas. Says avoid getting into a war of insults. Speaks of conflict. This person should receive Ifa and work it.

irosun kanran won o kanran
adifa fun adekanbi omo won leyo igi
won ni ki won rubo
nitori oyun inu re
eropo ero ofa eniyan to gbe ebo nibe
ebo ire gbogbo ni se
Kee pe o
Kee jinna,
E waa wo'fa awo ki,
B'o ti nse
Ifa de, alase
Ope, abise wara
ase

irosun kanran won o kanran
cast divination for adekanbi the son of eyo igi
she was asked to offer sacrifice because of the pregnancy
she did the ebo
and delivered her child safely
Very soon,
At no distant date,
Come and see the Babalawo's prediction

Coming to pass
Ifa has come, the great authority
Palm-tree, whose predictions come true speedily
ase

OKANRAN IROSUN – Thinking outside the box brings the blessing of re-aligning with destiny. In this Odu, Sango speaks loudly. This person is an argumentative, angry person and this behavior is blocking his/her good fortune. Speaks of troubled relationship and the need for a renewal of vows. Speaks of the need for forgiveness. If planning a new endeavor, now is a good time, but keep the plans to yourself. This odu brings prosperity with proper ebo to Ogun and Olokun.

okanran roro
okanran o seje
adifa fun olan losin omo asa
won logbe gbowo
won ni ko kara nle ebo ni kose
nje olanlosin se o de o
omo asamo logbe gbowo
olanlosin loruko ta n pe okola
Ero Ipo
Ero Ofa
E waa ba ni ni jebutu ire
Ase

okanran roro
okanran o seje
cast divination for olan losin (olan losin is the name of a tattoo artist)
who was giving tribal marks in place of money
he was asked to offer ebo
thus the people accepted the marks in place of money
Travellers to Ipo

Travellers to Ofa,
Come and join us where there's plenty of good fortune
ase

IROSUN OGUNDA - Using the gifts our ancestors provided us leads to the removal of obstacles to our success. This person's arrogance is blocking his/her blessings. Must always comply with recommended ebo. This person should try to keep the family together; it is through the family that the blessings come. Try to work out problems in their marriage. Remove those influences from your life that are causing the breakup of the family, whether they be other people or behaviors. This person needs to propitiate Esu constantly and be generous with people. This person has created Elenini and must destroy them.

Bi o ba ma gun eda moyan
ki o gun eda moyan
bi o ba si gun eda mo yan
ki o ba irosun je oruko
adifa fun orunmila
baba n sunkun alainire gbogbo
won ni ebo ni kose
o rubo o
si ni di onire gbogbo
Kee pe o
Kee jinna
E tete waa ba wa ni jebutu aje suuru
Ase

if you wish to pound eda rat with yam
please do
and if you are not pounding rat with yam please do
cast divination for Orunmila
when Orunmila was seeking for good fortune

he was asked to offer yam pounded with rat to Ifa
he did the offering
and he was blessed with all forms of good fortune
Very soon,
At no distant date
Come and join us where there's plenty of money and peace of mind
Ase

OGUNDA IROSUN – The removal of obstacles leads to realignment with destiny. This person is having problems at work but must persevere. Must work on behavior and avoid arguments. Must always maintain optimism. Speaks of turning bad fortune into good fortune through ebo and behavior modification. Speaks of conquering enemies. Ebo of coconut, banana, sugar cane and honey to Ori, Ifa and Egbe to bring sweetness to this person's life.

Eguntan-moyo
Emi tikon owo ri d'lOlowo
Eguntan-moyo
Emi tikon aya ri d'alaya
Eguntan-moyo
emi ti kobimo ri olomo
Eguntan-moyo
Emi tikosan ri de ti san o
A dafa Agutan tiogba egun asese ti o gba egun aro
Won niki o wa sebo, egun ori re a tan
Ebo: eyele, obi, ataare, orogbo ati egberinla owo
ogbo o ru
ase

The curse is over, i am happy
I was poor, now I am rich
The curse is over, I am happy
I was single, now I'm married

The curse is over, now I'm happy
I never had a child, now i have children
The curse is over, now I'm happy
I was disabled, now I'm cured
Ifa was divined for Sheep
Who had curses from the maimed and the lame
She was asked to do ebo so that the curses on her Ori would be banished
The ebo: pigeons, kola nuts, alligator pepper, bitter kola and money
She listened and did the ebo
Ase

IROSUN OSA – Using our ancestral gifts brings abundance through changes. What we do today affects our tomorrow. In this case, something we did in the past is going to pay off soon. This odu speaks of negative spirits around this person. Ibori is called for accompanied by personal work on developing good character. Speaks of enemies, ebo to conquer.

irosun san ara gagagaga
adifa fun olukoso lalu bambi
omo arigba ota segun afiri wele wele se te
o n be laarin ota sangiliti o n fi ojojumo komi nu ogun
won ni ebo ni kose
eropo ero ofa e wa ba ni larusegun
arusegun la ba ni lese obarisa
ase

irosun san ara gagagaga
cast divination for olukoso lalu bambi (Sango)
the one that uses thunder stones to conquer his enemies
when he was amidst tribulation
he was asked to offer ebo
he did the ebo

and triumphed over his enemies
ase

OSA IROSUN – Our destiny is realigned by rapid change in circumstances (Oya). Calls for Ibori and ebo to Ifa. Warns of working too hard and not getting enough rest. Do not get involved with someone else's spouse. Ebo to come out clean of a scrape. Warns to follow Ifa's advice. Blessing of wealth through promotion. Be careful how you treat women. Possible ebo to Egbe.

Osa lee sun
O sa lee han-anrun fonfon
Difa fun Orí
Ti nlo ree gba igba iwa lowo Olódùmarè
Won ni ki won sakaale, ebo ni sile
O gbebo o rubo
Ko pe ko jinna
E wa ba ni ni wowo ire gbogbo
Nje mo yab're Aje
Mo yan t'aya
Mo yan t'aya tan
Mo yan t'omo
Emi yan t'aiku
Mo fi pelu e o
Ase

You can really sleep
You can snore loudly
That was Ifá cast for Orí
When going to take the calabash of destiny from Olódùmarè
Orí was advised to make offering
He complied
Before long not too far
Join us in the midst of all Ire (blessings)

I have chosen the Ire of wealth
I have chosen the Ire of spouse
After choosing the Ire of spouse
I chose the Ire of children
I next chose that of longevity
As addition to all my Ire
Ase

IROSUN IKA – Fulfillment of potential brings increased ase (personal spiritual power). Possible problems with in-laws. Warns not to divulge one's plans to others. Advises to have clean thoughts. Might need to do Tefa for protection from Iku (death). Possible ebo to Ogun and Ori to clear the way for blessings.

ero ma sunka
ero ma sun igede
o dile ijero koko ko
adifa fun ekuku
ti yio ni oyun sinu
won ni korubo ko le bi tibi tire
ogbebo orubo
keipe
kei jina e wa ba ni larusegun
arusegun la n ba ni lese obarisa
ase

ero ma sun ka
ero ma sun igede
odile ijero koko
cast divination for Ekuku
who was seeking for safe delivery
she was asked to offer ebo
not long after she delivered safely
come see us receive blessings from the king of Orisa

ase

IKA IROSUN – Focusing and consolidating our ase leads to our ability to better use our talents. This Odu speaks about Osun, and the need to do ebo to Osun. This person must be easier on themselves and pat themselves on the back once in a while. Must be less fearfull. Possible ebo to Iyami for protection from enemies. Warns to avoid fighting with anyone. Ebo to Esu and Aje for wealth.
Ajikawon mole ina
Aji ka won mol ojo owuro
D'Ifa fun Ika
Ti yoo ka Irosun mole
Nitori akokoro ori eran gbigbe
Kutukutu n'Ika ti ka Irosun mole
Titi ale fi le kokooko
Ase

To be encircled inside one's home by early morning fire
To be hemmed in inside one's home by early morning rain
Were the awos who cast ifa for Ika
When going to hem Irosun inside Irosun's house
Simply because of the dry animal skull (kept in his house)
He was told to offer a dry animal skull
He did not make the offering
Ika hemmed in Irosun since early in the morning (dawn)
Until very late at night
ase

IROSUN OTURUPON – Our health depends on our alignment with destiny. Warns of illness of unborn child. Ifa says we must comport ourselves well in public. Orunmila, Ogun and Obatala speak in this odu. Ebo to Ori, Ogun, Ifa and Esu to make life better.

enikan ki se ibi ko gba ore

THE HOLY ODU

enikan ki se ore ko gba ibi
adifa fun oba ijomu
to lowun yio pa oba akure
won ni ebo ni kose
nje ahun yo da o pa ara re
oba ijomu to lowun yio pa oba akure
ahun yo da para re
ase

nobody does bad and recieves good in return
nobody does good and recieves bad in return
cast divination for the king of Ijomu
that was planning to kill the king of Akure
he was asked to offer ebo
he did the ebo
thus the tortoise has killed himself
the king of Ijomu that planned to kill the king of Akure
the tortoise has killed himself with his sword
ase

OTURUPON IROSUN – Maintaining one's health is the road to fulfilling one's destiny. This person needs to stay healthy; exercise, eat well, etc. This odu brings wealth. This person probably should receive Aje. Ebo to Ifa for protection from enemies. Obatala for ire. If thinking of marriage, Ifa says the person is good for you. If thinking of a major purchase this will also be good. Possibly in wrong career or trade. Our popularity brings improved relationships. This person will suffer, but with patience and ebo, will receive blessing.

F'agada la'mi
Dia fun won n'Isokun
Won o ju ogun geerege
Ebo ni won ni ko waa se

O gb'ebo, o ru'bo
Ko pe, ko jinna
E wa ba 'ni ba wowo ire gbogbo
Ase

Oturupon sokun
F'agada lami
Ifa's message for the inhabitants of Isokun
When they were not more than 20 in number
They were advised to offer ebo
They complied
Before long, not too far
Come and join us in the midst of all Ire of life
Ase

IROSUN OTURA – Full use of our ancestral gifts brings connection to our higher self. This odu implores us to act with iwa pele. This person must show gratitude. If there is a project that was left undone, must finish it. Must give offerings to Ifa regularly to receive blessings. Should receive Ifa and possibly Olokun. This person will be successful, but that generates enemies. Ebo to Oya for protection. Speaks of impotency problems,

atere kan ri awo ode egba
na n gbaja awo ode ijesa
o wo susu se kan
adifa fun orunmila baba ti n se awo re lokunkun
won ni ebo ni kose
nje fitila tan ina ki n riran
emi o mka se awo okunkun
ase

atere kanrin the priest of egba land

na n gbaja the priest of Ijesa
owo sun su sekan
cast divination for Orunmila
when he had been doing things in the dark
he was asked to make offering
so that everything hiding in the darkness can really come out into the open
thus let the fire light up and let me see
I do not want to be a priest of darkness
ase

OTURA IROSUN – Connection to source leads to fulfillment of destiny. This odu calls for humility and honesty as the path to peace and harmony. Must avoid getting sucked into useless challenge of egos. Ebo to Ifa and Osun staff to ward off all ibi (illness, loss, etc.) and to Sango and Esu for victory, possibly related to promotion at work.

Òjò ògànjọ́ níí bórùn ebè baba
A díá fún Òtúá
Ti ó mÒsun lé ikú lo
Ebo n wón ní ó se
Òun le lé Ajogun gbogbo kúù Ilé òun báyìí?
Wón ní kó rúbo
Wón ní kó lòó bo Òsun
Ó bo Òsun
Ó bo òkè ìpòrí è
Ayé ye Òtúá
Ikú jáde lo
Àrùn lo
Òfò lo
Òràn lo
Òsé lo

Iré ló wolé tò ó
N ní wá n jó ní wá n yò
Ní n yin àwon Babaláwo
Àwon Babaláwo n yin Ifá
Ó ní bẹ̀ẹ̀ làwon Babaláwo tòún wí
Òjò òganjò níí bórùn ebè báábá
A díá fún Òtúá
Ti ó mÒsun lé ikú lo
Tètè lé ikú ló ò
Tètè lékú lo
Òtúáamósùn
Tètè lékú lo
ase

It is the midnight rainfall that levels with the ridge in fullness
Cast Ifa for Otura
That would use Osun to chase away death
"Would I be able to chase away death from my house?"
He was asked to do ebo
He was asked to offer ebo to Osun
He offered ebo to Osun
He also offered ebo to Ifa
Life so pleased him
Ifa and Osun scared death away
Sickness went away
So did loss
Offense
Sadness
It was ire gbogbo (all good fortune) that entered his house
He then started to dance and sing
He was praising his Babalawo
His Babalawo was praising Ifa
Ifa was praising Olorun
He said it was exactly as his Babalawo had said

It is the midnight rainfall that levels with the ridge in fullness
That would use Osun to chase away death
Please chase death away quickly
Chase death away fast
Oturaamosun
Chase death away fast
Ase

IROSUN IRETE – Using our talents to the fullest brings us renewed motivation and determination. This odu calls for spiritual discipline. Possible ebo to Orunmila to block ibi (sickness, loss, etc.). Possible ebo to Oshun and Ifa to release ire. This person must be compassionate and joyfull. Speaks of an important event in this person's life and the need for ebo to Esu so it will be succesfull.

jeje awo ile olosun
lodifa fun olosun
o ma kun le soro jeun titun lodun
won ni ebo ni kose
nje jeje wa lan bo osun
ase

jeje the priest of Olosun
cast divination for Olosun
who was going to celebrate Oshun
he was asked to offer ebo
he did ebo
and he was successful
thus it is gently and respectfully we are worshipping Oshun
ase

IRETE IROSUN – Patience and determination are the path to self actualization. This odu asks us to balance the masculine/feminine in ourselves. Speaks of many enemies. This person most likely has led a difficult life. Ebo to Esu, Orunmila and Iyami to end difficulties. The person needs an attitude adjustment.

Irete Rosu
A d'Ifa fun Olofin
Won niki Olofin wa rubo
Ki oran gedegbe na de
Eyele funfun, adiye funfun, ati egbejila owo li ebo
Kee pe o
Kee jinna
E tete waa ba wa ni jebutu aje suuru
Ase

Irete Rosu
Did divination for Olofin
Olofin was told to make an offering
In order to avoid unexpected trouble
He did the ebo
And avoided the unforeseen problem
Very soon
At no distant date
Come and join us where there's plenty of money
and peace of mind
Ase

IROSUN OSE – Alignment with destiny leads to ire. This odu says we need to use our ancestrally given talents and skills to accomplish our destiny. That act, by default, leads to abundance. Speaks of possible pregnancy and the need to protect it from witches. This odu does speak of Iloso – witches, Ebo to stop the problem. This person might be having a hard time, but with ebo, good times are assured. Must maintain a cool head. Improvement in business forecast.

eji bele ni pawo lori
iri wele ni ka etu laya
adifa fun ponse ajagun obele
won ni ko rubo
salaiku ara re
ero opo ero ofa e wa ba ni bayo
e wa wo ire
Riru ebo ni i gbe ni
Airu ki i gb'eeyan
E waa ba ni ni ire gbogbo
ase

it is heavy rain that weakens an awo
it is a snow that weakens etu
cast divination for ponse ajagun obele
he was asked to offer ebo
for long life
he did the ebo and he lived long
It is doing ebo that brings blessings
Neglect of ebo pays no one
Come and join us where there is plenty of ire
Ase

OSE IROSUN – The gift of abundance brings the ability to fulfill one's destiny. This person is guaranteed a long life and many blessings. They should receive orisa Aje for wealth and be initiated to Oshun for protection. Might need to be initiated Egungun. Of course, all this good fortune is accompanied by an equal amount of negativity so this person should wear a white head covering when she/he feels the need and do washing of Ori regularly. If going through a difficult period, ebo to end it. Many jealous enemies.

Gunnungun lowo bi ti a nrere loo ye si

Osifibi iyeere bange bange boo manle
A d'Ifa fun Ose
Ti nre le Olosun lo re e toro omo
Ebo ni won ni ko se
O si gbebo nbe o rubo
Nje Ose olosun lo l'aso
A daa le ko ma n lolaso
Ose olosun lo l'aso
Ase

The vulture goes to a hidden place to lay her eggs
And covers them with her long wings
Cast Ifa for Ose
When she was going to marry Olosun and have children
she was advised to make an offering
she did it
Ose Olosun is the owner of the cloth (egungun masquerade costume)
Let him crawl along the ground
Ose Olosun is the owner of the cloth
Ase

IROSUN OFUN – Staying on track with our destiny leads to the miraculous. This odu speaks of the need for patience and coolness. A hot head leads to loss. Arrogance will bring illness. Don't make promises you can't keep. Ori is prominent in this odu, must do ibori and pray for elevation regularly. Must worship Orisa funfun – the white dieties. Needs to receive Olokun. Should always wear light colored clothes.

okuta pa
adifa fun orunmila
o n sawo lo sile olofin

won ni ebo ni kose
orubo o segun esu
ti orunmila ba n lo sile olofin o ma n mu esu dani
ti orunmla ba kuro ni be
esu yio pada lo sile olofin leyin lati lo ba orunmila je,
orunmila rubo lasiri esu ba tu
Kee pe o
Kee jinna,
E waa wo'fa awo ki,
B'o ti nse
Ifa de, alase
Ope, abise wara
ase

okuta pa
cast divination for Orunmila
who was going to work Ifa at olofin's house
whenever he goes to do divination, he takes Esu along
this time Esu spoiled Orunmila's work
but Orunmila had made ebo
and Esu's secret was revealed
thus Orunmila overcame Esu's plans
Very soon,
At no distant date,
Come and see the Babalawo's prediction
Coming to pass
Ifa has come, the great authority
Palm-tree, whose predictions come true speedily
ase

OFUN IROSUN – Good fortune brings alignment with destiny. This person is connected to spirit. He/she must always listen. Spirit provides a clear vision of his/her destiny. This person might be suffering from sadness and depression. Ebo to Oshun of honey to help bring joy into the person's life. Speaks of new relationships. Possible Elegbe child. Must sleep under red blanket.

Ofun fun ire ka
Ofun ko pariwo
Eniyan bi iruwonyi sowon l'aye
Eni maa dasa kow'orunni'le ola
A d'ifa fun awon eniyan
A ni iku mi a maa won l'owo ise orun
A niki won rubo koma baa si okunkunati ibanujel'ona won
Won gbo sugbon won ko rubo
Ase

Ofun is giving out goodness
Ofun does not make any noise about it
People like Ofun are hard to find on earth
Anyone who wants to perform wonders should look up to Orun
Orun is the home of honor
Ifa was performed for human beings
Who were told that death would always bring them to see the wonders of Orun
They were asked to do ebo so that darkness and sorrow be banished from their paths
They heard but did not do the offering
Ase

BOOK OF OWONRIN

OWONRIN OBARA – Unexpected changes bring a transformation. Blessings are about to materialize. Be on the look out lest they pass you by. Speaks of receiving unexpected wealth. This person is confused and needs ibori for clarity. This person also needs to put their arrogance in check. Humble themselves enough to follow Ifa's advice and do required ebo. Receive Ifa for wealth. Generosity and kindness will lead to ire.

Owonrin Iparo (Owonrin Obara)
Owonrin Awo ale inu omi
Obara Awo ale odo
Ati Owonrin Awo ale inu omi
Ati Obara Awo ale odo
D'Ifa fun Olunkan
Omo nkan dun l'Eyo
To ju Oyin lo o

Ko ma si oun to dun l'Eyo
Bii ka ji
Ki ara o le o
Ara lile l'oogun oro eni
Ko ma ma si oun to dun l'Eyo
Bii ki ajinde o maa jeni o
Ara lile loogun oro eni o
Ase

Owonrin, the Awo of the river bed
Obara, the Awo of the stream bed
Both Owonrin, the awo of the river bed
And Obara, the awo of the stream bed
Were the ones who cast Ifa for Olunkan
The child of "that special thing that is so sweet in the city of Oyo"
That is sweeter than honey
There is nothing so sweet in Oyo
That is comparable with waking up
And feeling hail and hearty
Sound health is the therapy for all treasures that one possesses
There is nothing so sweet in the city of Oyo
That can be likened to one's well being
Sound health is the therapy for all the treasures that one possesses
ase

OBARA OWONRIN – The unexpected changes inherent in Owonrin are successfully managed due to the transformation experienced in Obara. The transformation has to do with how we react to stimuli. The reborn, transformed person will handle crisis differently than before (no more irrational behavior). Speaks of avoiding jealousy and similar negativity. Warns of money dispute. Ebo to Ifa to end suffering and bring joy and prosperity. It will take perseverance and patience. Ebo to Oba to avoid impending confrontation.

obara owonrin olofin awise
adifa fun esu bele ti n sawo lo si iserimole
won ni ebo ni kose
won ni korubo fun ire aje lati okere ko le ko ire naa bo wa sile
Kee pe o
Kee jinna
E tete waa ba wa ni jebutu aje suuru
Ase

obara owonri olofin awise
cast divination for Esu Bele
who was going to Iserimole town to do Ifa work
he was asked to offer ebo so he could return with good fortune
he did the ebo
he returned with all good fortune
Very soon
At no distant date
Come and join us where there's plenty of money and peace of mind
ase

OWONRIN OKANRAN – Unexpected changes bring a new start, a new chapter in this person's life. This person might be suffering depression. It is a downward spiral that brings bad fortune (ibi), so must be corrected. Offering of honey to Oshun at the river. Possible warning of serious ibi like death or loss of property. Possibly needs to receive Ifa and Esu, plus Osun staff or Osanyin for protection. Also ebo to Iyami.

owonrin pokan awo ako igi

lodifa fun ako igi won bo wokan fun abo igi
won ni won karale nle ebo ni ki won se
won gbe ebo won rubo
keipe ko i jina e wa ba ni ni jebutu ire
jebutu ire la ba ni lese obarisa
ase

owonrin pokan the priest of male tree
cast divination for male tree and female tree
they were asked to offer ebo for a good relationship
they offered the ebo and they were happy
thus come and meet us at blessing of Orisa
ase

OKANRAN OWONRIN – The willingness to try a new approach leads to the ability to handle unexpected change. This odu tells us of the value of gratitude, and not to take ourselves too seriously. Must stop being so argumentative. Weekly Obatala head wash. Possibility if impending legal problems. Ebo to Esu and Ogun for protection, to Ifa and Olokun for prosperity.

okanran wonyin wonyin
awo aja
lodifa fun aja
aja n tikole orun bo waye
won ni ebo ni ko ma muse
oni oun ti se ebo okanran wonyin wonyin
ase

okanran wonyin wonyin
the priest of dog
cast divination for dog
when he was coming from orun to earth
He asked, "will I have the love of humans?"

he was asked to offer ebo
he complied
since then he was shouting
"I have made an offering to okanran wonyin wonyin!"
this is the meaning of dog barking till today
ase

OWONRIN OGUNDA – unexpected changes help remove obstacles from our path. This person has possibly become uncentered. Speaks of conflict. Ebo to Ori for peace of mind, as well as a bath. Ogun and Esu speak a lot in this odu. this person might need to receive Ogun. if this person is ill, ebo is needed immediately. Possibly someone close to this person is working against them. This person must be truthful regardless of how hard that may be.

Peregun susu
A d'ifa f'Owon, a bu f'Eguntan
A niki won wa rubo
aye Owon ati ti Eguntan aya re a gun
Ogbo o ru
Riru ebo ni i gbe ni
Airu ki i gb'eeyan
E waa ba ni ni ire gbogbo
Ase

Peregun susu was divined for Owon and Eguntan
They were asked to do ebo
so that things would be well with Owon and his wife Eguntan
He heard and did the ebo
It is doing ebo that brings blessings
Neglect of ebo pays no one
Come and join us where there is plenty of ire
Ase

OGUNDA OWONRIN – Obstacles are removed through the successful handling of unexpected change. Ogun speaks a lot in this odu. This odu advises us to listen to our ancestors for guidance. Ebo to Ori to bring ire of long life and prosperity. Ebo to Ogun to conquer enemies and alleviate stress.

díá fún Ìṣẹ̀ṣe
tí íṣe oló rí Orò n'Ífẹ
njẹ́ kínni Ìṣẹ̀ṣe ẹni
Ọ̀lódùmarè ni Ìsẹ̀ṣe ẹni
Iṣẹ̀ṣe làbá bọ
kàí tèní b'Òrìṣà, Ìsẹ̀ṣe
Orí ẹni ni Ìṣẹ̀ṣe ẹni
Iṣẹ̀ṣe là bá bọ
kàí tèní b'Òrìṣà, Ìsẹ̀ṣe
Ikin Ifá ni Ìṣẹ̀ṣe ẹni
Iṣẹ̀ṣe là bá bọ
kàí tèní b'Òrìṣà,Ìsẹ̀ṣe
Ilẹ̀ Aiyé ni Ìsẹ̀ṣe ẹni
Iṣẹ̀ṣe là bá bọ
kàí tèní b'Òrìṣà, Ìsẹ̀ṣe
Ìyà ẹni ni Ìsẹ̀ṣe ẹni
Iṣẹ̀ṣe là bá bọ
kàítèní b'Òrìṣà, Ìsẹ̀ṣe
Bàbá ẹni ni Ìsẹ̀ṣe ẹni
Iṣẹ̀ṣe là bá bọ
kàí tèní b'Òrìṣà,Ìsẹ̀ṣe
Okó ni ni Ìsẹ̀ṣe ẹni
Iṣẹ̀ṣe làbá bọ
kàí tèní b'Òrìṣà, Ìsẹ̀ṣe
Òbò nini Ìsẹ̀ṣe ẹni
Iṣẹ̀ṣe là bá bọ

kàí tèní b'Òrìṣà, Ìsẹ̀ṣe
Olúwo ẹni ni Ìsẹ̀ṣe ẹni
Ìsẹ̀ṣe là bá bọ
kàí tèní b'Òrìṣà, Ìsẹ̀ṣe
Ẹ jẹ́ ká bọ Ìsẹ̀ṣe ò Olówó
Ìsẹ̀ṣe là bá bọ
kàí tèní b'Òrìṣà, Ìsẹ̀ṣe
Ìsẹ̀ṣe ni Bàbá ètùtù
ase

Divined for Ìsẹ̀ṣe (Progenitors)
The leader of the Òrò society of ancient Ífẹ
They asked, what is ones Ìsẹ̀ṣe?
Ọ̀lódùmarè is ones Ìsẹ̀ṣe
It is Ìsẹ̀ṣe we ought to appease Before appeasing any Òrìṣà, Ìsẹ̀ṣe (Primordials)
Ones Orí (Destiny) is ones Ìsẹ̀ṣe
It is Ìsẹ̀ṣe we ought to appease
Before appeasing any Òrìṣà, Ìsẹ̀ṣe
Ones Ikin Ifá (ones personal Odù) is ones Ìsẹ̀ṣe
It is Ìsẹ̀ṣe we ought to appease
Before appeasing any Òrìṣà, Ìsẹ̀ṣe
Ilẹ̀ Aiyé (Mother Earth/Nature) is ones Ìsẹ̀ṣe
It is Ìsẹ̀ṣe we ought to appease
Before appeasing any Òrìṣà, Ìsẹ̀ṣe (Primordials)
Ones own Mother is ones Ìsẹ̀ṣe
It is Ìsẹ̀ṣe we ought to appease
Before appeasing any Òrìṣà, Ìsẹ̀ṣe (Primordials)
Ones own Father is ones Ìsẹ̀ṣe
It is Ìsẹ̀ṣe we ought to appease
Before appeasing any Òrìṣà, Ìsẹ̀ṣe
Vagina (likely referring to one's marital relations within home or one's mother's genitals) is ones Ìsẹ̀ṣe

It is Ìṣẹ̀ṣe we ought to appease
Before appeasing any Òrìṣà, Ìṣẹ̀ṣe
Penis (likely referring to one's marital relations within home or one's father's genital) is one's Ìṣẹ̀ṣe
It is Ìṣẹ̀ṣe we ought to appease
Before appeasing any Òrìṣà, Ìṣẹ̀ṣe
Ones Olúwo ("Elder Priest") is ones Ìṣẹ̀ṣe
It is Ìṣẹ̀ṣe we ought to appease
Before appeasing any Òrìṣà, Ìṣẹ̀ṣe
Please let us appease Ìṣẹ̀ṣe
Before appeasing any Òrìṣà
Ìṣẹ̀ṣe is the Progenitor of all ètùtù (appeasements)
Ase

OWONRIN OSA – Proper handling of unexpected changes leads to blessings. Both Owonrin and Osa speak of change. If we embrace change, it will bring us ire; if we resist, we will have difficulties. To embrace change takes strength and courage. This odu says no blood ebo. Also, it is the odu with the story of when Esu provoked the two good friends to fight over differing perceptions of reality. Thus the odu comes with the message to be open to the possibility that your truth might not be someone elses and to avoid arguments. Ebo to Oshun for promotion.

owonrin wosa wayi wayi Ebo to
adifa fun won lode iseyin
omo abo igi idi ki won to mo oko
won ni won kara nle ebo ni ki won ma se
Kee pe o
Kee jinna
E tete waa ba wa ni jebutu aje suuru
ase

owonrin wosa wayi wayi
cast divination for people of iseyin
that offer ebo to idi tree before marriage
they were ask to offer ebo to prosper
they complied
their marriage was prosperous
Very soon
At no distant date
Come and join us where there's plenty of money and peace of mind
ase

OSA OWONRIN – External changes come unexpectedly. Possibility of chaos if not prepared. Must handle with courage. Must handle responsibilities and not run away from problems. Maintain positive attitude. Ebo to Aje for wealth. Speaks of enemies and the need for frequent offerings to Ifa for ire and to vanquish enemies.

Ola gaara Ola gaara
Teye agbe loni igbo
Teye aluko loni odan
Teye Olausasa loni
Ibamun Idi
Eepa ohun enu iwomu
Akara ohun enu iwomu
D'Ifa fun Kuegbe omo Irorere
Nife igba ti n raye ata niku
Ebo no won ni ose
O si gbebo nibe o rubo
Kuegbe eleku
Morere ki iku o ma pa
Kuegbe awo
Kuegbe eleya
Morere kiku ma pa

Kuegbe awo
Kuegbe Olobi alata
Morere kiku ma pa
Kuegbe awo
Ase

Ola gaara, Ola gaara
The mother of Agbe bird owns the forest
The mother of Aluko bird owns the grass field
It is Alansasa's mother that owns the the Ibamu Idi
Peanuts in the mouth chewed to pieces
Bean cakes in the mouth chewed to pieces
This was Ifa's message for Kuegbe, child of Morere of Ife
When he came to live a long life
He was asked to make an offering
He complied
Kuegbe, who offered a rat
Morere, death (iku) should not take Kuegbe the awo
Kuegbe who offered fish
Morere, death should not take Kuegbe the awo
Ase

OWONRIN IKA – An unexpected event will force you to focus your personal power (ase). This is one of the powerful and unstable odu that require special care by the diviner. Asks for patience and perseverance through tough times. Don't allow visitors to stay in the home for time being. This odu speaks of the importance of medicinal leaves in our tradition. Speaks of ebo against witchcraft. Happiness is essential to prosperity in this odu. Might need to receive Olokun or offer ebo to Olokun. Ebo to Ori for protection against a close enemy.

awonwo   awonwo

adifa fun awele
ti yi o ni oyun apesin sinu
won ni ebo ni kose
e a ba ni larusegun
arusegun la ba ni lese obarisa
ase

awonwo awonwo
cast divination for awele
who prayed for pregnancy of a blessed child
she was asked to offer ebo for a safe delivery
she did the ebo and gave birth to a blessed child
ase

IKA OWONRIN – Increased ase from your efforts provides the power to deal with unexpected change. This odu speaks of enemies. Speaks of blessing coming through Esu and Obatala. This person must forget the past and move forward with positivity. No regrets. Must be generous with visitors. Ebo to Ogun or might need initiation for protection against iku. Ebo to Ori for long life. Ebo to the ancestors and Iyami for good fortune.

Ika-wonrin-wonrin wonkankan
D'ifa fun won ni Iwonwo-Ija
Omo afigba s'ode
Omo afoori patako soja
Won ni ki won gbe Somurege omo re f'oko awo
O lohun o f'Alawo o fun
Iba f'omo f'Alawo
Ki ba ma ku o
Oniwonwo-Ija, ire de!
Ase

Ika Owonrin

Cast Ifa for Oniwonwo-Ija
The king of Iwonwo-Ija
Child of the one who planted the Igba tree (garden egg tree) outside his home
And who planted Oori tree (black plum tree) at the market place
He was advised to give his beautiful daughter to an awo for marriage
He refused to give his daughter's hand in marriage to an awo
Had he followed Ifa's instruction
His daughter would not have died
Oniwonwo-Ija, all good fortune has arrived!
Ase

OWONRIN OTURUPON – Protection from illness is assured by successfully handling the stress of unexpected change. Speaks of blockage and being off our path. Speaks of loss. This person has to pay special attention to his/her valuable things at this time. This odu brings peace and prosperity with ebo to Ifa. Speaks of the need for generosity.

towonrin logun
toturupon logbon
a papo o di adota
adifa fun orunmila
to n lo re ya esu lowo
won ni ebo ni kose
jebutu ire la ba ni lese obarisa
ase

that of owonrin is twenty
that of oturupon is thirty
we combine it together making fifty
they are the awo that cast divination for Orunmila
when he was going to lend some money to Esu Odara

he was asked to offer ebo
so that he can collect his money back
come and see the blessing of the king of Orisa
ase

OTURUPON OWONRIN – Maintaining our health will allow us to handle unexpected changes. Joy and happiness are within reach. Warns of STD's. Also warns of possible legal problems, so must be very careful not to engage in any illegal activities. This person is having much difficulty and should receive Ifa and his children and always go to Ifa for any important decisions.

Owo ri mi o tele mi
Oturupon Owonrin
Aya ri me o tele mi
Oturupon Owonrin
Omo ri mi o tele mi
Oturupon Owonrin
A d'Ifa fun Olasimbo Atepamose Kolamalelo
A niki Olasimbo wa rubo
Ki ola ma le lo
O gbo o ru
Ase

Money sees me and follows me
Oturupon Owonrin
A wife sees me and follows me
Oturupon Owonrin
A child sees me and follows me
Oturupon Owonrin
Divined for Olasimbo Atepamose Kolamalelo
Who was told to make an offering so that he would not lose his honor

He heard and did the offering
ase

OWONRIN OTURA – Changes bring a connection to spirit. Offering of eko to ikin for ire. Ebo to Oya and Ori for peace. Iwa pele is the road to prosperity; must be virtuous. This person's life is a mess. Ebo for stability and prosperity.

orere awo elejigbo
lo kifa fun elejigbo
ti won ni ko joko ko ma wo ikin re loju
ko ma lo si oko tifa ni ko ma gbo
won ni korubo
nitori ire gbogbo
ase

orere the priest of elejigbo
was the one that cast Ifa for elejigbo
when ifa asked him to take care of him (ikin)
that he should not be a farmer
he was ask to make ebo
he complied
he became a babalawo and received all good fortune
ase

OTURA OWONRIN – Connection to spirit allows us to handle sudden change. Speaks of the need for courage and take action without fear. Ebo to Ifa and Egbe for protection from enemies. This person is much criticized for laziness; ebo to Ogun for strength and stamina, but mustn't do hard work for a living. Ebo to Esu for all ire (ire gbogbo). Ebo to Ifa (amala, gin and kola) for good health and prosperity.

Eefin gori aja

O ru gobugobu
Eefin I paakun nii rin koroyi-koroyi
D'ifa f'Okanmbi
Ri won fi ledo Oye
Ti won o pin logun
Eyi ti yoowaa fi gbogbo aye sogun je
Ebo ni won ni ko wa se
O gbebo, O rubo
E ya wa o, e wa o, e wa sin
Gbogbo omo eni
E ya wa o, e wa o, e wa sin
Ase

The smoke rose to the ceiling
But rose ineffectively
The smoke made from burning twisted vines
Walks in twists and turns
These were the declarations of Ifa to Okanmbi
Who had been appointed the next king
However he was denied his inheritance
But who would inherit the world in the end
He was told to do ebo
He complied
Branch here and pay homage
All our children
Branch here and pay homage
Ase

OWONRIN IRETE – Unexpected changes lead us to renewed determination to succeed. Must remain positive and avoid despair; all problems have a solution. Must keep moving forward; don't look back. This odu assures victory over enemies, including someone close to this person. Must avoid fighting or antagonizing other people.

Should have a spiritual bath and give kola, coconut and ori butter to her/his Ori. A close friend is an enemy. Ebo to Esu for victory. Might need to receive Ifa for long life.

owonrin rere
irete rere
awo omi difa fun omi
o n tikole orun bo waye
won ni ebo ni kose
bi omi ba bale alapa orojo omi bale ni laluja
bi omi ba bale alapa
ase

Owonrin rere
irete rere
the babalawos of water
that cast divination for water
when she was coming from heaven to earth
she was asked to offer ebo so she could always face forward
she did the ebo
and since then she has always moved in forward direction
ase

IRETE OWONRIN – Our determination helps us manage sudden change. This odu contains the story of when Orunmila went to the town of the Iyami (Olota) and did not die. It speaks of the need for balance between feminine/masculine and protection. This odu assures victory over competition and or conspirators. Ebo to Ifa for all ire including a good job. Speaks of the need to show gratitude.

Ki wo sap o duro simi kemi wo sap o duro si o
A d'ifa fun Orunmila
Lojo ti n s'awo rode Ota
Ebo ni won ni ko se

O si gbebo nbe o rubo
Nje iwo leye emi
Naa leye Iyala Olota
Ase

Collaborate with me and I will collaborate with you
Divined for Orunmila
The day he was venturing into the town of Ota (sacred city of Iyami) to do Ifa work
He was advised to make an offering
He complied
Now, you continue to do evil works
But I belong to the Iyami cult of Ota
Ase

OWONRIN OSE – Unexpected change brings unexpected ire. Or, failure to prepare for and adapt to change leads to continued poverty. This odu speaks of the hard luck case. In order to turn things around, ebo is needed. This person must not skimp on the ebo. Also must do river wash to remove poverty. Must also make better choices as to who he/she associates with. Must only associate with positive, successful people. Must observe taboos. It is probably the breaking of taboos that has led to this person's bad fortune. Ebo to Oshun of sorghum wine and ewusi to bring order to this person's life.

owonrin wese wese
adifa fun seke seke
ti yio ma se owo eniyan ni didi
won ni ebo ni kose
ko ma ba mu amubo
Riru ebo ni i gbe ni
Airu ki i gb'eeyan
E waa ba ni ni ire gbogbo

ase

owonrin wese wese
cast divination for handcuffs
who was doing the job of catching people
they asked him to offer ebo
so that he will not fail in catching people
he offered ebo
since then he has been catching people successfully
It is doing ebo that brings blessings
Neglect of ebo pays no one
Come and join us where there is plenty of ire
ase

OSE OWONRIN – Abundance protects us from unexpected changes. Or we experience chaos as a result of greed. Speaks of the need to handle one's responsibilities, including paying one's debts. Might need to receive Osanyin. This person has talents as a healer. Ebo to Ogun for victory. Ebo to Oshun at river for protection. Might need Ifa initiation. This person needs to be courageous and fight if pushed into a corner. Has to be close to Orisa. Needs heavy Ori work.

Wonrin wonrin ti won
A d'Ifa fun Onile kaa
Abu fun Onile koto
Ebo ni won ni ko se
O si gbebo nbe o rubo
Ose owonrin
Wonrin wonrin ti won
Eyin o mo po Onile kaa ni Sango?
Ose owonrin
Wonrin wonrin ti won

Ase

Ose owonrin
Wonrin wonrin ti won
Cast Ifa for Onile kaa
And also for Onile koto
He was told to make offering
He did it
Ose wonrin
Wonrin wonrin ti won
Don't you know that Onile kaa is Sango?
Ose wonrin
Wonrin wonrin ti won
Ase

OWONRIN OFUN – Unexpected change brings the miraculous. Speaks of the need to bring out family Egungun masquerade. Ifa says keep business and family separate. Our actions will pay off. Continue to do good even if not appreciated as it will come back to you. Possible ebo to Odu (feminine diety). Possibility that someone close to this person is in danger of death.

gidi gidi gbon bi os e
adifa fun eleyin a po n si
omo ato sadi nijoogun
won ni korubo
ko ma ba ku lodun
orubo ko ku mo
ase

gidi gidi gbon bi ose
cast divination for he who can survive war
they asked him to offer ebo so that he will not die in this year

he complied
and his life was spared
thus Orunmila is the one who can protect us during war
ase

OFUN OWONRIN – The realization of our prayers protects us from chaotic change. Must maintain positive attitude and be greatful for what we have. This person is destined to be wealthy but must maintain spiritual discipline and propitiate there Orisas. Ebo to Iyami to receive a promotion at work or business success. Might need to receive orisa Aje for wealth. Needs to do ibori – head wash and offering – for prosperity. Good time for new relationship.

ofun fun won ke
ofun fun won rin
a difa fun olakaami
won ni:
edumare nmuree bowa
ki a rubo ki apa ota ma ' le ka ni
ki ota ma le fi ohun ini-eni s' ofo
obe meta akuko meta ati egbaata owo
o gbo o ru
Ero Ipo
Ero Ofa
E waa ba ni ni jebutu ire
ase

Ofun gave to them so they would have joy
Ofun gave so they would have laughter
Divined for Olakawi
Who said Olodumare gives good things
He was told to do ebo
So his enemies would not have any power over him
And cause him to lose his property

THE HOLY ODU

He complied
His enemies failed
Travellers to Ipo
Travellers to Ofa,
Come and join us where there's plenty of good fortune
ase

NOTES:

BOOK OF OBARA

OBARA OKANRAN – Inner transformation brings new opportunities. Sometimes, our thinking becomes predictable and we miss opportunities right in front of us. Speaks of conflict at work or at home. Ebo to Esu for resolution. But also, in order to resolve the disagreement, the person has to try to look at things differently. A cool head prevails. Head wash for coolness. Must not harbor evil thoughts or seek vengeance. This person is possibly off path with their destiny. Ebo to Esu and Ogun to correct the path and avoid loss. This person's good fortune is closely tied to Ogun. Ebo to protect one's children.

Bi awo gbofa
bi awo o gbofa e je ki afi obara okanran
lo won wo obara okanran ko se ki lenu omo awo
adifa fun orunmila baba n gbogun
lo re ja atewo won ni ebo ni kose
o ru lo ba segun
nje orunmila pele o
ogun were were ti n ja atewo

ase

whether a babalawo is good at reciting Ifa verses or not
Let's ask him to recite obara okanran
obara okanran is not always recited by a young awo
cast divination for Orunmila
when baba was embarking on a war with palm tree
he was asked to offer ebo
he complied
and conquered palm tree
come and meet us at the triumph of ebo
ase

OKANRAN OBARA – Taking a new direction brings inner transformation. This person needs to follow his/her ancestor's traditions. This odu has much ire. Might need to do Egungun ritual. Ebo to Esu to protect one from unfair accusations. Speaks of an enemy at work, Ebo to Esu and Iyami for protection of family.

okanrran bambam
lodifa fun oloba bedu
o feyinti o n moju ekun sunrawun tomo
won ni ebo ni kose
ire omo je dajule wa
Kee pe o
Kee jinna
E tete waa ba wa ni jebutu aje suuru
Ase

okanran bam bam
cast divination for oloba bedu
when she was seeking children
she was asked to offer ebo
she complied

and bore many children
Very soon
At no distant date
Come and join us where there's plenty of money and peace of mind
ase

OBARA OGUNDA – Transformation helps remove obstacles from our path. Ori is prominent in this odu. Ebo to Ori and head cleaning to open the way for blessings. This person needs to connect with their higher self (iponri) so his/her Ori can communicate with Iponri. Must stay out of trouble; and stay away from troublemakers. Must avoid gossip. Ebo to Esu for money.

okika abeso poro poro
adifa fun olobara ti n se egbon ogunda
won ni korubo nitori aburo re ogunda
eropo ero ofa e wa ba ni ni jebutu ire
jebutu ire la n ba ni lese obarisa
ase

okika with mysterious seed
cast divination for Olobara, the brother of Ogunda
he was ask to offer ebo
so that his junior brother Ogunda would not die
he did the offering
thus come and meet us at the acceptance of ebo
with all good fortune in the path of orisa
ase

OGUNDA OBARA – This odu says we need to clear the obstacles to our inner transformation. Usually the main obstacle is fear. Ogunda Obara: Ogun and Sango. Speaks of conflict and the need to have a battle plan. Head wash and ebo to Ori for wealth. Speaks of a troubled relationship. This odu brings the blessing of success with the proper ebo.

Àkò garùn
Àkò gasè
A díá fún Òsìn gàgààà
Èyí tí n lo rèé werí olà lódò
Wón ní kí Òsìn ó rúbo
Wón níre ó tó o lówó
Wón ní sùgbón wón n só'o lódò
Òsìn bá rúbo
Ayé bá ye é
Ní wá n jó n ní n yò
Ni n yin àwon Babaláwo
Àwon Babaláwo n yin Ifá
Ó ní béè làwon Babaláwo tòún wí
Àkò garùn
Àkò gasè
A díá fún Òsìn gàgààà
Èyí tí n lo rèé werí olà lódò
Àwá werí olà a ríre
A werí olà a ò kú mó
A werí olà a ríre
ase

Ako bird extends it neck
Ako bird extends it legs
Casts divination for the big Osin bird
The one going to wash the Ori of wealth in the river
They asked him to offer sacrifice
'Good fortunes would get to you' they predicted
But he was warned about his enemies who were on the lookout for him in the river
Osin performed the sacrifice

Life pleased him
He then started to dance and rejoice
He was praising his Babaláwo
His Babaláwo was praising Ifá
He said it was exactly as his Babaláwo had said
Ako bird extends it neck
Ako bird extends it legs
Casts divination for the big Osin bird
The one going to wash the head of wealth in the river
We have washed the head of wealth
and we have seen fortunes
We have washed the head of wealth, we will not die again
We have washed the head of wealth, we have seen fortunes
ase

OBARA OSA – Inner transformation leads to positive changes in one's environment. Usually a consequence of us going through spiritual growth is we start to shed our old friends, etc. as they can't relate to the new you. Might need to have Egungun ceremony performed or make offering to male ancestors. Warns this person to be careful of being the victim of fraud. Speaks of the need to focus. Ebo to Ogun and Ori for protection. If a man, should not exhibit anger towards women.

omo oniyenyen tuye
lodifa fun ajija gogo go
ajija gogo go
lodifa fun won lotu ife
nijoti ti iku n ko won bi eni ko omo eran
won ni o kara nle ebo aiku ni ki won mase
won gbe ebo won rubo
keipe keijina e wa ba ni larusegun
arusegun la ba ni lese obarisa

ase

omo oniyenyen tuye
cast divination for ajija gogo go
ajija gogo go
cast divination for people of Ife
on the day death (iku) was killing them as if they were animals
they were asked to offer ebo to stop sudden death
they offered the ebo
and since then they live long
come and see the blessing of the king of Orisa
ase

OSA OBARA – The successful handling of external changes brings an inner transformation. Speaks of the need for humility. Osa births Oya and Obara births Sango. Speaks of relationships as symbiotic. The marks for Osa and Obara are perfect opposites. Speaks on the need for compromise. Speaks of being in the right profession; in alignment with our destiny. Ebo to Aje and Yemoja for wealth. Ebo to Oya and Sango for victory.

Ojo niibaraje
A d'ifa fun Akeregbe
Nigbi Akeregbe gbekele obirin ati awon omode
a niki Akeregbe wa ru'bo
Ki awon tin se elegbe lehin re
ma le yeesile lojiji lojo tiowa ninu ola re
O gbo ko ru
Riru ebo ni i gbe ni
Airu ki i gb'eeyan
E waa ba ni ni ire gbogbo
ase

Cowards give way to grief
Was divined for Akeregbe (gourd)
Who depended on the women and young children
He was advised to make ebo
So that he would not be let down suddenly by his supporters
While he was in his glory
he heard but did not do the ebo
It is doing ebo that brings blessings
Neglect of ebo pays no one
Come and join us where there is plenty of ire
ase

OBARA IKA – Inner transformation brings an increase in or focusing of our personal power (ashe). This is one of the four powerful but unstable odu. Special care must be taken by the diviner. Must do all things in moderation. Moderation is the path to ire. This odu speaks of impending good fortune in the form of material wealth. Ebo to the Ori of the person's spouse. Warns against a loss of influence, but ebo will turn that around.

Bi mo ti feri mo fe kore mi ori
adifa fun olobara
ti yio tinu ika la wa
ebo ni won ni ki won se
nje olobara o n tinu ika la waye more
Kee pe o
Kee jinna
E waa wo'fa awo ki
B'o ti nse
Ifa de, alase
Ope, abise wara
ase

the way I want to be is what I want my friend to be
cast divination for Olobara
who would become successful at the side of Ika
he was asked to make offering
so that they both would be successful
thus it is Olobara that became successful
through his friendship with Ika
Very soon,
At no distant date,
Come and see the Babalawo's prediction
Coming to pass
Ifa has come, the great authority
Palm-tree, whose predictions come true speedily

ase

IKA OBARA – An increase in our ase brings an inner transformation. This odu warns us to avoid extramarital affairs. Instead, focus on creating truly loving relationships and healthy families. Ebo to the ancestors for long life. Possibly needs initiation into Egungun and or Egbe. Blessing of children. Should initiate them into Ifa. Might need to receive Olokun and Aje for blessings.

Iwonran awo f'Olokun
Lo d"Ifa fun Olokun
Ijo ti Olokun n f'omi oju sungbere Aje
Ebo won ni ose
Osi gbebo nbe o rubo
Iwanran man mande o awo Olokun
Iwo loso Olokun deni Aji ki
Iwo loso Olokun d'eni Aji Ajige
Ase

Iwonran the diviner for Olokun
Divined for Olokun
Regarding her luck in acquiring wealth
She was told to make ebo
She complied
Iwonran has arrived, Olokun's diviner
It was you that made the ocean surge
You were the one that uplifted Olokun
Ase

OBARA OTURUPON – Transformation leads to an increase in our health. Much of our health issues are caused by emotional issues like stress. The inner transformation through spiritual growth brings a wider outlook on things which reduces stress and uncertainty. Must work on one's short temper. Warns of impending trouble. Ebo to Esu. Speaks of abiku child.

agutan afenu bolo bolo
adifa fun won ni itoku agbe
won feyinti won moju ekun sunrawun ire gbogbo
ebo ni won ni ki won se
won rubo won di alaje
Riru ebo ni i gbe ni
Airu ki i gb'eeyan
E waa ba ni ni ire gbogbo
ase

the sheep with mysterious mouth
cast divination for the people of Itoku Agbe
when they were requesting for all good fortune (ire gbogbo)
they were asked to offer ebo
they complied
and they received all good fortune

It is doing ebo that brings blessings
Neglect of ebo pays no one
Come and join us where there is plenty of ire
ase

OTURUPON OBARA – Protecting one's self and family from illness brings transformation. Esu is prominent in this odu. Possible initiation to Esu. This odu comes with the promise of many blessings. Ebo to Esu and Ori to bring the blessings. Ebo to Esu from protection from ajoogun and enemies. Speaks of the need for spiritual elevation. Possible domestic problems. Should try to work them out.

Oturupon pon-on deere
Apaa re ni oka a o
Obara a faa deere
Apaa re ni oka o
D'Ifa fun Atepo
O nlo sode Iweme
D'ifa fun won lode Iweme
Won maa gba Atepo sile
Won ni ki awon ara Iweme rubo
Ki won ma gba alejo oran
Won koti ogbonyin s'ebo
Ipin aisebo, egba aiteru
Atepo lo se ile Iweme d'ahoro
Ase

Oturu strapped it awkwardly on her back
Because her strength was not sufficient to support it
Obara dragged it lazily on the ground
Because her strength was not sufficient to support it
These were the declarations of Ifa to Atepo (light skinned woman)
When she was venturing to Iweme town

The same was also declared to the inhabitants of Iweme town
When they wanted to accept Atepo as a guest
They were advised to do ebo
Lest they accept a problematic guest
They did not do the ebo or heed Ifa's warning (against receiving guests in town)
The outcome of the failure to do the ebo
And the consequences of rejecting rituals
Atepo was responsible for the sacking of Iweme town
Ase

OBARA OTURA – Successful inner transformation brings a connection to Spirit, or Ori to Iponri. This is a great odu for it represents the whole point of what we want to accomplish. Warns us to watch out for an enemy close to us. This person is having a difficult time; the person's good fortune is being blocked. but ebo to Obatala and Ori will end the bad times. Ebo to Esu for victory. Might be involved in a competition of some sort. Might need to receive Ifa for protection from enemies.

obara tu yala yala
adifa fun won ni ikowusi omo aleku gori odi lo
won ni ki won rubo ki won le segun ota
won rubo won segun
ase

obara tu yala yala
cast divination for people of Ikowusi
when they were amidst trouble
they were asked to offer ebo
they offered the ebo
the troubles were ended
thus we have sent away death at Ikowusi

we have sent away disease at Ikowusi
we have sent a way tribulation at Ikowusi
ase

OTURA OBARA – Connection to higher self brings a transformation of consciousness. This odu speaks a lot about success in business or career. This person has been struggling, but this odu brings an end to that. Pereverence is the road to blessings in this odu. Maintain one's faith in their Orisa and provide ebo. Speaks of business partnership. All partners should do head wash and ebo to their Ori's for success. Ebo to this person's Orisa for victory. Possible ebo to Ifa and Obatala for prosperity.

Etura bayi, Obara bayi
a da fun omuye meji
nwon ni ki awon mejiji rubo ki gran won le ni ori
apa kan rubo, apa-kan ko ru
Awon ti o rubo
Nigba ni awon omo iya meji ti a ma nso pe
E ko
ri bi ohun-kan won ti gun?
Awon ti ko rubo nigba ni awon ti a ma nso pe Nwon ba
Etura ba
Obara ba
Ase

"Etura like this, Obara like this"
was the one who cast Ifa for two children of the same mother
They said that both should make a sacrifice
so that their affairs might be successfully concluded
One side sacrificed; the other side did not
Those that sacrificed at that time are the two children of the same mother of whom we say,
"Don't you see how their things are in order?"

Those that did not sacrifice at that time are the ones of whom we say,
"They are worthless; Etura is worthless and Obara is worthless."
Four pigeons and two shillings is the sacrifice.
Ifa says that two children of the same mother
should make a sacrifice so
that they will be able to join forces
and so that people will not be saying,
"They are worthless."
Ase

OBARA IRETE – A transformation of consciousness brings renewed determination. This odu portends many blessings. Ebo to Oshun of a mirror for peace of mind. Must avoid self deception. This person needs to be generous with people and get out more often. Possible ebo to Ifa for long life, Sango for good relationship and Esu to forestall a problem with one's siblings. This odu speaks on the relationship of Sango and Oshun.

amoran oloran ma mo tarare
adifa fun olobara ti yio dete ni gongo imu
won ni ebo ni ko se
won ni ki o sora re ki o ma ma da
si oro oloro
nitori ki o ma ba karun
ebo ni won ni kose
Ero Ipo
Ero Ofa
E waa ba ni ni jebutu ire
ase

he who mettles into someone else's business and ignores his own was the one who cast divination for Olobara

who would suffer from an infection in his nose
he was asked to stop interfering into other people's business
so that he will not be affected by nose infection
Travellers to Ipo
Travellers to Ofa,
Come and join us where there's plenty of good fortune
ase

IRETE OBARA – Determination and perseverance lead to transformation. This person might be having problems of too many enemies. Must stick to his/her guns and not cave. Must maintain a cool head and have faith in Ifa. Ifa is with this person and will bless them if they follow his ethical principles and listen to advice of their parents. Possible initiation to Ifa.

Oni je nje laa ja oni mu n mu laa mu
Oni gba n gba laa gba
Bomo e so ba n gba igba laye
Omo babalawo a mo n gbeku gbe ja
Bomo a gbe ba n gbagba yun pa ko
Omo babalawo a mo n gbagba oti fere-fere
A d'Ifa fun Orunmila
Lojo ti n lo lee bu ju are ni je bu
Ebo ni won ni ko se
O si gbebo nbe o rubo
Ela loko niju ni Esu naa wo
Si eyele mi ju o ru kun gbudu gba da ni ise
Gbogbo o mo n ju wa bami
Kee pe o
Kee jinna
E waa wo'fa awo ki
B'o ti nse
Ifa de, alase
Ope, abise wara

Ase

We eat and drink in abundance
We collect plenty of gifts
When the son of the servant suffers in bitterness
The son of the babalawo is enjoying his prestigious position
When the son of the farmer is sweating hard in the bush
The son of the babalawo is drinking and having a good time
Cast Ifa for Orunmila
On the day he was looking for all his good fortune (ire gbogbo)
He was told to do ebo
He complied
He received all good fortune
He gave thanks to Ela and Esu for all the blessings
The pigeon offered brought all the favors granted
and brought me all good fortune
Very soon,
At no distant date,
Come and see the Babalawo's prediction
Coming to pass
Ifa has come, the great authority
Palm-tree, whose predictions come true speedily
Ase

OBARA OSE – Transformation leads to blessings. Speaks of victory over enemies. Speaks of the need to heal a family dispute for a blessing from the ancestors. Ebo to Ogun to protect one's children from getting into trouble. Speaks of the need for positive thinking and to stop self critiscism. Patience and humility and ebo to Aje for business success.

obara sele se pepe
adifa fun ayan o n lo re ra adie leru
won ni ebo ni kose

o ko korubo lo ba lo ra adie leru
nigbati o dele
ni adie ba bere si ni le ka
lo ba paje
Riru ebo ni i gbe ni
Airu ki i gb'eeyan
E waa ba ni ni ire gbogbo
ase

Obara sele se pepe
cast divination for Ayan
who was going to buy hen as a slave
they asked him to offer ebo
but he refused
when he brought hen to his house
hen started going after him
until hen killed him
It is doing ebo that brings blessings
Neglect of ebo pays no one
Come and join us where there is plenty of ire
ase

OSE OBARA – Abundance provides the opportunity for inner transformation. Must follow Ifa's directions to end indecision. This odu brings many blessings. Must be good to women or the Iyami will block the blessings. Ebo to Esu for the blessings to manifest. This odu says we are the architects of our own misfortune. Head wash, ebo to Ori and a change in behavior to end troubles.

Ose lo ba bi emon
Gbedo gbedo kan o gbe koto
Dia fun Ose
Tii somo won lode Ilogbo

Aroleke kan o ro baba
Dia fun Obara
Tii somo won lode Ilogbo
Esinsin nii ji nii fowo rawo ibeje-ibeje
Dia fun Alabahun Ajapa
Tii sore Obara
Ebo ni won o waa se
Ose p'erin si Ilogbo
Olobara p'agbo ni Ilogbo
Nje ona s'alabahun deji
Ewo ni n ba lo
ase

No mortar carver can carve a calabash pot
Ifa's message for Ose
Their offspring in Ilogbo Land
No bead maker can fashion a guinea corn
Ifa's message for Obara
Their offspring in Ilogbo land
The housefly is it that wakes up and rubs its hands gingerly together
Ifa's message for Alabahun Ajapa, the tortoise
Who was the friend of Obara
He was advised to offer ebo
Ose killed an elephant in the forest in Ilogbo
And Olobara killed a big ram in Ilogbo
Indecision turned the road into two for Alabahun
Which way would I take out of the two
ase

OBARA OFUN – Transformation leads to manifestation of prayers. Following Ifa's words and doing ebo bring abundance and end hard times. Speaks of the need for humility and less talk more listening. Ebo to Esu and Ogun for protection from enemies. Must be careful around women.

obara funfun nigin nigin
adifa fun onile ka merindilogun
won ni korubo salaiku ara re eropo
ero ofa e wa ba ni ni jebutu ire
jebutu ire la ba ni lese obarisa
ase

obara funfun nigin nigin
cast divination for the owner of sixteen houses
when coming from orun to earth
he was asked to offer ebo
he complied
come and meet the king of Orisa
as the acceptance of ebo leads to good fortune
ase

OFUN OBARA – Manifestation of prayers brings a transformation of consciousness. Ebo for increase in business. Calls for a change in attitude. Be more gratefull and less negative. Ebo to Esu and Ori for success. Ebo to Ifa for protection from enemies. Ebo to Sango for long life.

Ofun Bara
A d'ifa fun Olu-Ota
A niki Olu-Ota wa rubo
Nitori awon abinu-eni
Nitoripe olu-Ota a maa r'eni war a l'owo oun
Olu-Ota a maa ta
A maa ri owo gba wara
O gbo o ru
Riru ebo ni i gbe ni

Airu ki i gb'eeyan
E waa ba ni ni ire gbogbo
Ase

Ofun Bara
Was cast Ifa for for Olu-Ota
Who was told that many people would bring him their business
And consequently he would become rich
He was told to do ebo against enemies
He did the ebo
It is doing ebo that brings blessings
Neglect of ebo pays no one
Come and join us where there is plenty of ire
Ase

NOTES

BOOK OF OKANRAN

OKANRAN OGUNDA – A change in perception brings a removal of obstacles. This person probably will need to receive his/her own Ifa and or Ogun. This person might have ability to see spirits. Must learn how to deal with that and receive Egungun. Accept help when offered. Stand and fight; don't run away from the issue.

okanran kangu kange kangere
adifa fun oniwowo ado
omo arumo logun danu
on ti ikole orun bo waye won ni okara nle ebo ni kose
orubo nje lapalapa logun lo ogun owun ko de ja
Kee pe o
Kee jinna
E tete waa ba wa ni jebutu aje suuru
Ase

okanran kangun kange kangere
cast divination for Oniwowo Ado (praise name of sonponna)
when he was coming from orun to earth
he was asked to make ebo
he complied
thus he was able to defeat his enemies
Very soon
At no distant date
Come and join us where there's plenty of money and peace of mind

ase

OGUNDA OKANRAN – Removal of obstacles provides an opening for a new direction in one's life. This person has to keep it moving. Ebo to Ogun to avoid loss. Ebo to Egun to remove obstructions to the ire. Speaks of keeping feet on the ground and balancing prayer with action. Must propitiate Ifa regularly for ire and Ogun for protection from enemies. Ifa will end this person's struggles with ebo and good character (iwa pele).

Ògúndá fò ó dÒkànràn
Olòkànrán fò ó dÒgúndá
Erinmi nlá subú lAgbagba
Agbagba nlá subú lErinmi
A díá fún èìnlójo igi
Wón n tòrun bò wálé aye
Erinmi nlá subú lAgbagbaÀwon èìnlojo igi ní n bèèrè lówó Ifá
Ilé ayé tí àwón n lo yìí dáa báyìí?
Wón ní kí wón ó rúbo'
Wón ní mee bí báwón bá dé ilé ayé tán
Sebí ebo náà làwón ó móo rú
Ògún fò ó dÒkànràn
Olòkànrán fò ó dÒgúndá
Agbagba nlá subú lErinmi
A díá fún Àkó
N tòrun bò wálé ayé
Wón vá fi Àkó se àgbà
Wón dé Àkó ládé
Wón níwo Àkó rúbo o
Ìwo ni ón dé ládé yìí o
Wón lébo ni kóo mò o'
Kí wón ó mó baà sí adé orù re o
Àkó ò gbó ebo yàn

THE HOLY ODU

Gbogbo igi bá dé ilé ayé
Wón bá pète pèrò'
Bó bá sì di ojó ketàdínlógún
Wón ó bàá sí adé tí ón fi dé Àkó lórí
Wón ní sebí àwón wí fún o
Sùgbón nígbà Àkó bá dádé
Enìkan ò gbodò sá a lóbe
Bééyán bá dán irú è wò
Olúwa è rí òràn
Tée dòní
Àwon èìnlójo igi ni wón ghé èníní tì 'I
Ó ni Ògúndá fò ó dÒkànràn
Olòkànrán fò ó dÒgúndá
Erinmi nlá subú lAgbagba
Agbagba nlá subú lErinmi
A díá fún èìnlójo igi
Wón n tòrun bò wálé aye
Wón ní wón ó rúbo
Wón kò won ò rúbo
Àkó nìkàn ní n be léyìn tó dádé
Gbogbo igi
E sì pète pèrò
E wáá badé Àkó jé
Gbogbo igi
ase

Ogunda flies off; it becomes Okanran
Olokanran flies off; it becomes Ogunda
A big hippopotamus falls off Agbagba
Agbagba falls on a hippo
Cast Dafa for uncountable number of trees
They were coming from orun to aye
The troop of trees were asking Ifa
"The Earth that we are going to, is it going to be good?"

They were told to do ebo
"Once we get to earth
Is it not the same ebo that we would be performing?" They asked
Ogunda flies off; it becomes Okanran
Olokanran flies off; it becomes Ogunda
A big hippopotamus falls off Agbagba
Agbagba falls on a hippo
Cast dafa for Àkó tree
He was coming form orun to aye
The other tress then voted in Àkó tree as their leader
They crowned him
"You, Àkó, do ebo," they warned
"You are the one who has been crowned
You should observe all prescriptions for ebo
So that the crown on your head (ori) would not be removed"
Àkó tree refused to listen attentively to the prescribed ebo
The troop of trees arrived on earth
They all connived and conspired against Àkó tree
Once it is the seventh day
They would remove the crown from Àkó tree's head
It was then that they reminded him of their previous warning
Within the period that Àkó tree is crowned
No one should remove the bark or strike the trunk with a knife
If anyone does that
That person would be in trouble
Until today
The troop of trees conspired against him
He said, "Ogunda flies off; it becomes Okanran
Olokanran flies off; it becomes Ogunda
A big hippopotamus falls off Agbagba
Agbagba falls on a hippo
Cast Dafa for uncountable number of trees
They were coming from orun to aye
They were asked to do ebo

They refused: they didn't do the ebo
It is Àkó tree coming from behind and wearing a crown
All trees
Y'all connived
You destroyed Àkó's crown
All trees
ase

OKANRAN OSA – Considering new directions leads to positive external changes. This odu brings much good fortune. Speaks of the peaceful resolution of conflict and knowing when to hold em or fold em. Ebo to Sango for successful strategy. Ebo to Oya to end hard times and bring prosperity.

kamu gege lu gege awo ile alakoko
igbin ko ni ara ina ni yiya
awodi o bale ko gbe adiye aba
oluwo marun ojubona mefa awon ni
won sefa fun orunmila baba n lo re fi irukere tumo re
ogun ti won fi esi si
eyi ti won fi oko ja
irukere ledu fi tumo re
ifa ko tumo iku
ko tumo arun
ko tumo gbogbo irunbi
Kee pe o
Kee jinna
E waa wo'fa awo ki
B'o ti nse
Ifa de, alase
Ope, abise wara

ase

kamu gege lu gege the priest of akoko
a snail is not fit for absorbing heat
awodi (hawk) does not come down and prey on the egg that is about to hatch
five head of awo
and six ojubona
they are the people that cast divination for Orunmila
when he was going to use irukere to dismiss evil
all the war they face with amunitions
it was an irukere Orunmila used to conquer it
Ifa conquers death, conquers disease and conquers all evil
Very soon
At no distant date
Come and see the Babalawo's prediction
Coming to pass
Ifa has come, the great authority
Palm-tree, whose predictions come true speedily
ase

OSA OKANRAN – Positive changes open the door to new opportunities. Calls for positive attitude and courage. Speaks of victory over enemies and to not harbor malice in one's heart. This person needs to focus and stay the course. Ebo to Oya for abundance.

Osa Kanran
O rin Kanran
Irin kanran kanran
Ni irin ekun
A d'Ifa fun agba ti o l'owo
Ti o ma wo awo Olowo
Kanran kanran

Ebo ni won ni o se
Osi gbebo nibe o rubo
Koipe bee ni ojun
Ewa bani ni jebutu ise
Ase

He runs ill tempered
He walks ill tempered
Ill tempered walking is the walk of the leopard
This was Ifa's message for Agba
Who does not have money and looks longingly at another person's money
He was told to do ebo
He complied
Not soon thereafter
Come and join us in the blessing of all good fortune (ire gbogbo)
Ase

OKANRAN IKA – Taking advantage of opportunities leads to an increase in one's ase. Speaks of one having the courage to take a stand. Says don't start what you can't finish. Accept the good with the bad and maintain focus. This person needs to change some ingrained behaviors such as lack of confidence. Must act like a successful person in order to be one.

okanran kawo bope bi kope
adifa fun kanna kanna
eyi ti gbogbo eye o fi jolori
won ni ebo ni ko ma muse
ogbebo orubo
keipe keijina
e wa ba ni larusegun
arusegun la ba ni lese obarisa

ase

okanran count if it is complete or not
cast divination for kannakanna
who was going to make the head of all birds
he was asked to offer ebo for long life
he complied
not long or sooner he became successful
come and meet the king of Orisa as the acceptance of ebo
leads to good fortune
ase

IKA OKANRAN – Increase in personal power (ase) leads to new opportunities. Speaks of the need to change one's behavior. Patience and a cool head for success. Snails for Ifa and Ori. Use your intelligence to improve material life. Warns of loss. Do not curse anyone. Don't be careless. Don't jump to conclusions. Good time to start a new venture.

Erin niko dududu jako
Aroni oro ese ija dina egan
Adifa fun Oluwere magbo ojo ti Obalufon
Eyin ibadire han ferefe
Ebo won ni ose
Osi gbebo nbe orubo
Nje Obibo sarewa owa bomi pitipiti
Igbinde ma ni ero ako ko omi
Ifa pe ro simi l'ona
Igbinde ma ni ero akoko omi
Ifa pe ro simi n'ile
 Ki o pe ro simi l'ona
Igbinde ma ni ero akoko omi
Ifa pe ro simi l'ori
Ki ope ro simi nikun

Igbinde na ni ero akoko omi
Ase

The elephant takes of plants when moving
The flying bird never blocks the road
Cast Ifa for the big river at Obalufon
Whose depths were going to be seen secretly by the people
He was told to do ebo
He complied
May Ifa protect me quickly
Snail has come to bring me tranquility and peace
Ifa pacifies my home
Ifa pacifies my road
Ifa pacifies my stomach
Ifa pacifies my Ori
Snail brings me tranquility and peace
Ase

OKANRAN OTURUPON – New directions regarding one's health protects us from illness. This person needs to stop being grumpy and sad all the time. Must maintain one's faith in Ifa. Ebo to one's Orisa for gratefulness. Don't try to do things outside your talent level. Calls for faithfulness and honesty with one's spouse. Ebo to Olokun for prosperity. Might need to receive Olokun.

ka guniyan isuko ninu opan ore
ka gun iyan esinmirin ninu opan iroko
kagun iyan aga owun ni kan soso ninu opan ide
adifa fun olokanran ti n sunkun otutu lae lae
won ni ebo ni kose
ase

we should pound yam inside ore tray

we should pound esinmirin yam inside iroko tray
we should pound aga yam alone inside golden tray
these were the awos who cast Ifa for Olokanran
when he was complaining of being cold forever
he was asked to offer ebo
so as to be free from illness
he did the ebo
and was healthy
ase

OTURUPON OKANRAN – Staying healthy brings new opportunities. Ifa says we need to be patient and all will be well. "Little by little we eat the head of the rat." Must be gentle. Speaks of great blessings. Ebo to Ori, Obatala and Oshun. Must be fearless and childlike to have a long, prosperous life. Must receive protection from curses.

Omotolamoyo Iyowukode maat'enis'ehin demi
A d'Ifa f'Efunbunmi
Won ni
Efunbunmi a bimo pupo sugbon ki o wa rubo
Ki omo re tiopon si ehin yi
Nigbati o gba dagba ma baaje odaran omo
O gbo ko ru
Riru ebo ni i gbe ni
Airu ki i gb'eeyan
E waa ba ni ni ire gbogbo
Ase

Omotolamoyo Iyowukode maat'enis'ehin demi
Divined for Efunbunmi
Who was told that she would have many children
But that she should first make an offering
So that the child she carried on her back might not

become a criminal later in life
She heard but did not make the offering
It is doing ebo that brings blessings
Neglect of ebo pays no one
Come and join us where there is plenty of ire
Ase

OKANRAN OTURA – A fresh new direction brings connection to spirit. Speaks of the need for coolness. Snail water to be drunk by this person and water with shea butter to Esu. Head wash with snail water, efun, shea butter. Should avoid alcohol. Respect and be grateful for one's elders. Family disputes must be resolved.

akara bo sinu epo
o gbayi ododo
adifa fun ota ti n se omo iya osun
won ni korubo
ki won ma ba fi ara won sile
Ero Ipo
Ero Ofa
E waa ba ni ni jebutu ire
ase

when bean cake enters into palm oil
it takes on a red color
cast Ifa for stone, the sibling of Oshun
they were asked to make an offering
so they wouldn't leave each other
Travellers to Ipo
Travellers to Ofa
Come and join us where there's plenty of good fortune
ase

OTURA OKANRAN – Connection to spirit brings new opportunities. Perseverance and courage are the road to ire. Ebo to open the gates to plenty of ire. Must change bad behavior and bad talk. Speaks of one causing legal problems for themselves. Enemies bring losses. Ebo to Ogun, Ifa and Iyami to protect from loss due to enemies. Ebo to Obatala for long life. Might need Ifa initiation for protection from negative spirits.

Orunmila ni eku
Moni Awise
Oni awise eku ni eku yi o ko omo re sapamo si niton iku
Oni Awise omo eja ni eja yi o ko omo re sapamo si ni tori awon dedo dedo
Oni awase omo eran ni eran yi o ko omo re sakpamo si ni tori iku
Oni awase omo eni ni omo eni yi o ko omo re pamo si Orunmila
Iwo n se n fo bi ede
Iwo n se n fo bi eye
Oni ki a so fun eni ti o da oun ki o ti He kun re mo ori ni ojo kan
Ki o ma si se jade
Ti o ba ti le se be ko
ni bo si owo iku
Be ni
ko si ni bo si owo ejo
Kee pe o
Kee jinna
E tete waa ba wa ni jebutu aje suuru
Ase

Orunmila pointed to the door
They told him it was significant that the door was locked with a key
He replied that by locking doors
Rat protects her children from death
Fish protects her children from the fisherman

Animal protects her children form the hunter's traps
Humans protect themselves from their enemies
Orunmila says when this odu is revealed
The person must stay inside their home
behind locked doors for a couple of days
To avoid getting into trouble
Very soon
At no distant date
Come and join us where there's plenty of money
and peace of mind
ase

OKANRAN IRETE – Taking a new direction gives us renewed determination. Speaks of victory over enemies. Calls for initiation to Ifa. Ebo to Esu and Olokun for prosperity. Ebo to Ogun for protection from enemies. This person might be going through difficulties, but ebo will usher in the good times. Ebo to one's ancestors. Humility is needed.

okanran rete rete
adifa fun ate to n lo re bawon noja ejigboromekun
won ni korubo ko le jere bo oja ejigboro mekun
o rubo ate jere bo oja
ejigboromekun
Ero Ipo
Ero Ofa
E waa ba ni ni jebutu ire
ase

okanran rete rete
cast divination for ate (a mat used in displaying goods at the market)
when he was embarking on a journey to ejigboromekun market
he was asked to offer ebo

so that he could gain a healthy profit
he heard and offered the ebo
and returned with much profit
Travellers to Ipo
Travellers to Ofa
Come and join us where there's plenty of good fortune
ase

IRETE OKANRAN- Perseverance and determination lead to new opportunities. Speaks of the need for harmony in our personal relationships. Our spouse or future spouse will bring success. In this odu, one must follow Isese, all that encompasses the tradition, especially one's ancestors, for blessings. Ebo to one's Egungun masquerade for prosperity. This odu speaks a lot of receiving honor, like a title, job promotion, etc. Ebo to Ori for honor. Speaks of avoiding gossip and small talk.

Ogan bidi bii ri bi
Babalawo a d'Ifa fun Aje
Nigba ti o n ti orun bow a s'aye
Ebo ni won ni ko se
O si gbebo nbe o rubo
Won ni Aje lo ni so
Fi so side awo Aje lo ni so
Kee pe o
Kee jinna
E tete waa ba wa ni jebutu aje suuru
Ase

Ogan bidi biiri bi
Was the awo who cast Ifa for Aje (diety of riches)
When she was coming from orun to earth
She was told to do ebo

She did it
Now look what Aje has to say
That she is owner of all wealth on earth!
Very soon
At no distant date
Come and join us where there's plenty of money and peace of mind
Ase

OKANRAN OSE – Opening up to other possibilities brings abundance. This odu brings plenty of good fortune. Initiation into Oshun to end poverty and bring ire. Must not be malicious. Ebo to Ori for business success. This person might be going through hard times or on the verge. Ebo to Oshun and Ori to stop it.

ise n se erin erin gbinu igbo
ise n se efon efon n sun eluju odan,
ise ko se oba bayi loju mi ri
adifa fun adetula
e yi to n lo re ponmi ola fun oba
won ni o kara
n le ebo ni ko ma se
ase

it is poverty that makes elephant to reside in the forest
it is poverty that makes efon to reside in the forest
poverty has never affected a king like this before
cast divination for Adetula
he who went going to fetch the water of wealth for the king
he was asked to offer ebo
he offered ebo
and when he fetched the water (symbol for Oshun) for the king
and poured the water for the king in his back yard
wealth in abundance poured out

and he became a rich man
ase

OSE OKANRAN – Abundance opens the way to the possibility of considering a new direction. This odu is very close to orisa Aje, the diety of wealth. This person should receive Aje. Ebo to Aje, Oya and Ori for wealth. This odu asks us to be patient and kind; that good times are near. Must always speak the truth as one sees it. Asks us to be closer to Ifa and one's Orisa. Ebo to Sango to conquer enemies at work.

Ose dede
olOkanrannaa dede
ojo ogbogbo kii ro manjumo
ti alayo nyo ni sekelewe
a d'Ifa fun Orunmila
baba orinrin yoo ba enire pa'de
ebo ni won ni ko se
o si gbebo nbe o rubo
peki tin orin mokan onire gbogbo
eni rere l'ope ngbe n'ire
eni rere
Riru ebo ni i gbe ni
Airu ki i gb'eeyan
E waa ba ni ni ire gbogbo
ase

Ose dede
OlOkanran naa dede
The rain of melancholy does not stop until dawn
The rain of happiness falls bit by bit
Cast Ifa for Orunmila
When he was going for a long walk
Looking for a person of gentle character

He was advised to do ebo
He complied
I have walked a short distance and have found wealth
Ifa will lead me to good people
I have walked a short distance and have encountered all ire (good fortune)
It is doing ebo that brings blessings
Neglect of ebo pays no one
Come and join us where there is plenty of ire
Ase

OKANRAN OFUN – New direction brings manifestation of prayers. The new direction most likely involves an attitude adjustment from pessimism to optimism. Head wash, and ebo to Obatala. Ebo to Esu and Ogun to avoid embarrassment or ridicule leading to loss. Might meet someone new who brings good luck.

okanran fun okanran o fun
adifa fun orisa n la osere magbo
won ni korubo nitori aseyori
oru bo
lo ba bere sini se aseyori
Kee pe o
Kee jinna
E waa wo'fa awo ki
B'o ti nse
Ifa de, alase
Ope, abise wara
ase

okanran fun okanran o fun
cast divination for Orisa nla osere magbo (Obatala)
he was asked to offer ebo for success

he complied
and became a successful person
Very soon
At no distant date
Come and see the Babalawo's prediction
Coming to pass
Ifa has come, the great authority
Palm-tree, whose predictions come true speedily
ase

OFUN OKANRAN – The manifestation of our prayers opens the way to new possibilities. This odu says we must be more disciplined spiritually. This person needs a thorough cleansing of head, body and home. Must honor taboos and watch what one eats. Possible disagreement; must find compromise. Ebo to Obatala and Sango to avoid being the victim of an injustice. Must not abuse one's position of power. This odu speaks a lot about enemy attacks, especially verbal. Must avoid engaging them; trust in Ifa. Ebo to Ogun for victory.

Agogo ní n ró e pé péré
Àràn gèjè ní n ró mò kómo jo mò kómo jo
A díá fún Kóórì
Èyí ti n fomi ojúu sògbérè omo
Òun le rómo bí báyìi?
Wón ní ó rúbo
Wón ní àgbédò adie lebo
Ló bá pa adìe fúnra è
Nbè náà ló ti sè e
Nbè náà ló ti je é
Kò rómo kankan bí
Ó tún dèèkejì
Ó tún pa adìe

Ó tún dá a je
Kò rómo pûn
Nígbà ó dèèketa
Ó bá loòdò Òrúnmìlà
Hówù!
Wón ní kóun ó fi àgbébo adìe rúbo léèkíní
Òún fi rúbo léèkejì
Wón sì ní àwon omo n tèlé òun kíri
Òrúnmìlà níwo Kóórì loò seun
Ò n pa adìe
O sì n dá a je
Òrúnmìlà ní kí Kóórì ó lóò fi ìdodo kan ògiri
Lénu ibi ti ìdodo è bá ga mo lára ògiri
Kó sàmì síbè
Kó wáá pa adìe mìún
Kó mú eje adìe òhún
Kó fi yí ojú àmí ohun
Kí èjè adìe ó wáá sàn wálè
Kó sì ta epo díè sí ojú ibè náà
Òrúnmìlà ni kó mó je nbi adìe
Òrúnmìlà ní tí ò bá ti je nbè
Àwon omo ó tèle
Kóórì bá se bêè
Ó bá kó gbogbo àwon èèyàn jo
Kò jè nnú è
Omó bá dé
Kóórì bímo yè
Ní bá n jó ní n yò
Ní n yin àwon Babaláwo
Àwon Babaláwo n yin Ifá
Ó ní bêè làwon Babaláwo tòún wí
Agogo ní n ró e pé pére
Àràn gèjè ní n ró mò kómo jo mò kómo jo
A díá fún Kòòrì

Èyí ti n fomi ojúú sògbérè omo
Tí sì n rodò ti ò rómo kó wálé
Ó lo nígbà èèkínní
Béè ni ò romo mú wálé
Ó lo nígbà èèkejì
Kò rómo mú wálé
Ni ón bá n korin fún Kóórì
Wón n pé bí ó lo
Kó móo lo
E jé Kóórì ó rodò
Bí ó lo kó móo lo
Ó japá
Ó jetan
Ó jèdí
Ó jèdò
Bí ó lo kó móo lo
Wón ní bí ti n padìe ní n dá je é
Ìgbà èèketa l'Òrúnmìlà se Ifá fún Kóórì
Ó ní Kóórì o
Ó mò dé aréwe yò
Fún mi lómo kan n gbé jó
Ase

Assemble yourselves is the sound of the gong
Àràn gèjè sounds I will gather children
Cast divination for Kóórì
The one crying because of children
Would I have children is the question she asked Ifá
They told her to perform sacrifice
A matured hen is the sacrifice
She killed the hen herself
On the spot where she cooked it
It was on the same spot that she ate it
She got no child

She came calling the second time
She killed another matured hen
She ate the hen by herself
She found no baby
Thereafter on the third occasion
She went to consult Òrúnmìlà
'Why has these misfortunes beclouded me'? She asked
'They told me to sacrifice a matured hen each on two previous occasions'
'I offered it'
'And they told me that children are following me around', Kóórì said'
"You are the one that did not follow the instructions given to you," Òrúnmìlà replied
'You killed all the animals mandated for you'
'You ate it alone'
Òrúnmìlà then told Kóórì to use her navel to touch an upright wall
The height to which the navel reaches on the wall
'You should mark that spot'
'You should then kill another hen'
'Collect its blood this time around'
'And use it to smear the spot of the navel mark
'Such that the blood would drip down through the trace from the mark'
You should also smear some red palm oil on the same spot
You must never eat out of the chicken, Òrúnmìlà said
Once you do not eat out of the chicken
The children would come to you
Kóórì did as instructed
She assembled people
She did not taste out of the chicken
The babies then started to come
She had successful childbirth
She then started to dance and rejoice
She was praising her Babaláwos

Her Babaláwos were praising Ifá
She said it was as her Babaláwos had said
Assemble yourselves in totality is the sound of the gong
Àràn gèjè sounds I will gather children
Cast divination for Kóórì
The one crying because of children
The one going to the stream without fetching water with them
She tried the first time
Yet could not find a baby to bring home
She went the second time
She could not bring home a child
They then started to sing mocking her
If she wants to go
Let her go
Let her go to the stream
If she wants to go, let her go
She ate the wings alone
She ate the laps
She ate the buttocks
She ate the liver
Let her go if she wants to go
They said it was on the same spot where she killed the hen that she devoured it
It was on the third occasion that Òrúnmìlà prepared an Ifá portion for Kóórì
Kóórì, they hailed her
The one that rejoices at the sight of children is back
Please give me one to cuddle
Ase

NOTES:

BOOK OF OGUNDA

OGUNDA OSA – The removal of obstacles brings positive changes in our surroundings. This odu speaks of the need to focus and center one's self to gain peace of mind. This person is going through a lot, but this odu brings an end to suffering and arrival of ire. He/she is surrounded by enemies. Must do ebo for victory. Ebo to Esu and Oya for prosperity. Ebo to Ogun to remove obstacles. Ebo to Ifa, Obatala and Ori for wealth.

Mon rari ni mon ra pongba
Afai Sosa kosun lese Iwin Oko
Aje ke laaro
Titi n gbebi ka
Baba latari
Kinni yoo gbebi kuro l'Ori Awo?
Agbe
Kinni yoo gbebi kuro l'Ori Awo?
Akuko
Iko ni yoo kobi kuro l'Ori Awo
Iye ni
Yoo yebi Ori Awo danu
Ase

Mon rari ni mon ra pongba
Afai Sosa kosun lese Iwin Oko
Aje ke laaro
Titi ale ome won ni ku
Cast divination for Orunmila
When he was surrounded by bad things (ibi)
What will drive the evil away from the Awo's Ori?
Agbe
What will drive the evil away from the Awo's Ori?
Akuko
Iye will help the Awo evade the bad things
Ase

OSA OGUNDA – External changes lead to removal of obstacles. When we approach change with courage and faith, the obstacles to progress are removed. Speaks of avoiding conflict and victory over enemies. Ebo to Ogun for victory. Ebo to Ifa and Obatala to receive blessings. Be careful who you trust.

Oyigiyigi ora awo Isode
A difa fun Orunmila
Nijo elegbe Ifa
Lawon yoo dimo pafa
Ebo won ni ko se
O gbebo o rubo
O gberu o teru
Elegbefa emo dimo pami
Afefelegelege oko kii dimo pagi oko.

Oyigiyigi ora priest of Isode
Cast Ifa for Orunmila
When his astral mates (Egbe) said we will collectively kill him
Orunmila was advise to do Ebo

He complied
My astral mates, do not collectively kill me
afefelegelege can never collectively kill forest tree..
  ase

OGUNDA IKA – This odu speaks of clearing obstacles to our building of spiritual power (ase). Time must be made for spiritual growth. We need to communicate with our Orisa, etc., to increase and focus our ase. This odu has the story of the origins of wood carvings and other spiritual icons used to focus our prayers, etc. Speaks on the need for honesty. Ebo to Ori for peace of mind and money. Watch one's words; they have power. Ebo to Ogun to remove obstacles; Sango for ire.

Nijo o buru
Ole n gbabe odu folun
Adifa fun O nigbaye ti n
Rook aleno l"odu
Nuro ebo
Ero at kesy
Ewa bani l'aiku kangidi
Ase

When things are bad
You will find a thief living with Odu
Cast Ifa for the farmer
When he was going to harvest his crops on the farm
He was told to do ebo
He did it
Come and see the place where the people do not die
ase

IKA OGUNDA – Focusing of ase leads to the removal of obstacles. This odu speaks of using one's ase to clear away blockages. This odu portends long life and prosperity for this person. Speaks of controlling one's anger; must stop being argumentative. Speaks of a blessed relationship. A blessing is coming. This person should maintain an even keel; not get too upset or too happy. Ebo to Ori for long life. Ebo to Ogun for courage. Receive hand of Ifa and ebo to Iyami for protection.

Jiji ni mo0 ji
Ni mo ri ire o
Ni kutukutu ni mo he iwa
Feere kile o mo
Ni mo ri iko Aje lode
D'ifa fun Olonko Egi
Omo ayinbo l'ori Aje suurus
Ko pe, ko jinna
E w aba mi ni wowo ire o
Ase

As I woke up
I saw Ire
Very early in the morning
I was presented with the gift of a pleasant destiny
At dawn, before the day broke
I saw the delegates of wealth in the street
These were the declarations of Ifa to Olonko Egi
The child of "He who sits marvelously on a pile of wealth"
Before long
Not to far
Come and join us in the midst of all ire
Ase

THE HOLY ODU

OGUNDA OTURUPON – Alignment with Ogun protects us from illness. Must develop good character and make ebo in order to receive blessings from Ogun. Calls for a change in behavior; less negativity and stubbornness. This odu has the story of when Ogun Married Obba. This person might be about to meet a very powerful woman. Ebo to Ori and Ifa for success.

Ogun dari ire sile Oturupon
A d'Ifa fun won n'Ife Ooye
Won ni
Odun oro de
odun owo
odun omo
Won niki won rubo
ki ija ma si
Won gbo won rubo
Kee pe o
Kee jinna
E waa wo'fa awo ki
B'o ti nse
Ifa de, alase
Ope, abise wara

Ase

Ogun directed good fortune (ire) to Oturupon's house
Was divined for the people of Ife Ooye
They said that the year of riches had come
the year of wealth had come
the year of children had come
They were told to do ebo so they might not have any quarrels
They did the ebo
Very soon
At no distant date

Come and see the Babalawo's prediction
Coming to pass
Ifa has come, the great authority
Palm-tree, whose predictions come true speedily
Ase

OTURUPON OGUNDA – Taking care of our health gives us the strength to remove obstacles. Speaks of ancestors and the need to keep family united. Speaks of the birth of a child and the need for ebo so the child may be healthy. Probably needs to receive Ogun. Ebo to Obatala and river wash with Awede for wealth. Warns of illness, ebo to protect and cure. Ebo to male ancestors for protection. Ebo to Ayan Agalu, the Orisa of drums for ire.

Jógede
Gbàgede
A díá fún Òòsàálà Òsèèrèmògbò
Níjóó tí n tòrun bò wálé ayé
Ebo n wón ní ó se
Jógede
Gbàgede
A díá fún Òkànlénú Irúnmolè
Níjóó wón n tòrun bò wálé ayé
Wón ní kí gbogboo wón ó rú eran méjì méjì lo
Òòsà lórí òun ò gbó
Òòsà bá rúbo
Wón ho awo eran òhún
Wón e kànlù
Ngbàa wón dé ilé ayé
Àwon Òòsà ró kù ò rílù jó
Wón bá dé àjo nbi wón ó ti jó
Enii wón n sápéé fún
Eni rí n korin lásán

THE HOLY ODU

Òòsà bá yo lóòókán
Ó ní Jógede
Gbàgede
A díá fún Òòsààlà, Òsèèrèmògbò
Níjọ́ọ́ wón n tòrun bò wálé ayé
Jógede
Gbàgede
Ifá jé n gbayì ntèmi
Bí Sàngó ti tó un
Kò rílù jó
Jógede
Gbàgede
Bí Ògún ti tó un
Kò rílù jó
Jógede
Gbàgede
Òòsà ní n be léyìn
Tí n jíjóo re
Wón bá fìlù bé e
Ògún ní háà
Òun náà bí nbi ìlú
Ògún bá lòó kan Àgèrè
Sàngó lòó kan bàtá
Gbogbo wón bá kànlù
Gbogbo ihun tí ò bá nílú nnú
Kò leè sehun rere kan tó dáa
Ase

Jogede and Gbagede
Cast divination for Orisaala Oseeremagbo (Obatala)
On the day he was coming from Orun to earth
He was asked to perform sacrifice
Jogede and Gbagede
Cast divination for uncountable Irunmole

On the day they were coming from orun to earth
They asked all of them to sacrifice two goats
Òòsà said he can not dare the consequences
Òòsà performed the sacrifice
They skinned the goat
And used the skin to make a drum
When they arrived on the earth
The other Orisa could not find a drum to dance to
They got to where they would congregate to dance
Some were being clapped for
Some were forming the rhythms only with their mouths
Òòsà, seen from afar, chanted
Jogede and Gbagede
Cast divination for Orisaala Oseeremogbo
On the day he was coming from orun to earth
Jogede and Gbagede
Ifá let me be renown on my own
As big as Sàngó is
He has no unique drumbeat to dance to
Jogede and Gbagede
As powerful as Ògún is
He has no unique drumbeat to dance to
Jogede and Gbagede
It is Òòsà coming from the back
That is dancing his deserved drumbeats
They drummed loudly
In desperation, Ògún exclaimed
'I also have an idea of a type of drum'
Ògún went to make Agere drum
Sàngó made Bata
All of them started making different kinds of drums
All celebrations devoid of drumbeats
Would not connote a good function
Ase

OGUNDA OTURA – Removal of obstacles allows a connection to spirit. Speaks of the need for focus and not running around senselessly. This person needs to stop worrying so much; it is affecting their health. Ebo to Saponna, Ogun and Iyami to end troubles and open the way for blessings. Head wash and Ibori for a cool head. This person needs to pay more attention to their children.

Isu u ku
Isu u fara jo oro
Abata sunwon, sunwon se gbedegun
D'Ifa fun Okankanleku Irunmole
Won lo reef e Ajere (ikin container)
Tii somo Ajalorun
D'Ifa fun Orunmila
Ifa nlo reef e Ajere
Tii somo Ajalorun
Orunmila lo wa fe Ajere
Tii somo Ajalorun nje Imonmo da ki n raye
Ki n ri Ajere o
Ase

The yam dies
The yam resembles cactus
The marsh is wet and serene
They were the ones who cast Ifa for the 401 Irunmole
When they were all going to ask for the hand of Ajere
The daughter of Ajalorun (the dog of heaven)
They also cast Ifa for Orunmila
Who was also going to ask for the hand of Ajere (aje ire, the blessing of wealth)
The daughter of Ajalorun (God's messenger)
Orunmila was the one who succeeded in marrying Ajere
Please let there be lightning for me to see
Let me be able to see Ajere let ther be lightning for me to see
The daughter of Ajalorun

Ajere
Ase

OTURA OGUNDA – Connection to spirit gives us the ase to remove obstacles. Must change behavior and align with the ethics of Ifa and receive Ifa for protection from Ajoogun and enemies. Needs to perform good deeds. Head wash to remove negative energies. Ebo to Obatala for wealth. Speaks of travel; ebo for a fruitful trip.

Eke o kun'ni
Ika o kun'mo eniyan
Bi eke ba nyole e da
Oun werewere abenu a maa yo won ni sise
D'afa fun Sagbagiriyan
Tii se Baale Asotito
Nje sotito, sododo
Eni to sotito
Ni Imole ngbe

Dishonesty doesn't pay
Wickedness isn't beneficial either
When a dishonest person plots his treachery
His conscience pricks him persistently
Those were Ifa's declarations for Sagbagiriyan
Who is the leader of the honest people
Pray; be honest; be truthfull
He or she who is honest
Is whom the Immortals support
Ase

OGUNDA IRETE – Removal of obstacles provides renewed determination and focus. Ebo to Oya for children. Speaks of ancestors and to honor one's father. Be truthfull and keep your thoughts to yourself. If have been less than truthfull with or abusive to your woman, ebo to Iyami for forgiveness. Ebo to Oya for children and Aje for wealth.

Kukunduku a b'ewe geru geru
Opo oogun a gun mo galegale
Bi o ba l'opo oogun, bi o bal'ekee
Eke o ni je o je
Inu-ire je ju ewe lo
Difa fun Ooni Alanak esuu
Eyi ti ko gbudo ko ohun Ifa si'le
Ma da mi
A g'bori ile, a j'eku
A g'bori ile, a j'eja
A g'bori ile, a 'j'ata
A g'bori ile, a mu mi
A g'bori ile, bo da mi
O d'owo ile ta ju mu
Kukundunku a b'ewe gerugeru
Opo oogun a gun mo galegale
Bi o ba l'opo oogun, bi o bal'ekee
Eke o ni je o je
Inu ire je ju ewe lo
Difa fun Ooni Alanak esuu
Eyi ti ko gbudo ko ohun Ifa sile
Ase

Sweet potato with fresh leaves
Possession of too many charms and spells intoxicates
If you have potent charms and spells and you are dishonest
Your dishonesty will render the charms and spells impotent
Honesty and good will work better than charms and spells
Divined for Ooni Alanak Esuu

Who must follow Ifa's advice and injunctions
Do not betray me
We stood on the ground and ate eku
We stood on the ground and ate fish
We stood on the ground and ate ataare
We stood on the ground and drank water
If you stand on the ground and betray me
I leave justice to Mother Earth (Onile)
Sweet potato with fresh leaves
Possession of too many charms and spells intoxicates
If you have potent charms and spells and you are dishonest
Your dishonesty will render the charms and spells impotent
Honesty and good will work better than charms and spells
Divined for Ooni Alanak Esuu
Who must follow Ifa's advice and injunctions
ase

IRETE OGUNDA – Determination and perseverance will lead to the removal of obstacles. This odu tells us that one's spirituality is the road to ire. This odu has the story regarding the two faced Esu. Exposes life's contradictions. Speaks of the importance of ebo. Ebo to Esu and Iyami. Calls for initiation into Ifa (Itefa). Ebo to Ifa and Ori for ire. Ebo to Egungun for long life. Head wash for coolness and calm. Speaks of death. Ebo to Orunmila, Egungun and Iyami.

Orunmila ni iyawo fere
Moni iyawo fere
Oni, Iyawo asin ni o fi npa eku
Iyawo osa ni o fi npa eye
Iyawo ekun ni o fi npa eran
Iyawo aje ni o fi nkpa eni
ase

Orunmila praised readiness

And also praised agility
Orunmila then explained the benefits of agility and readiness
Cannibal rat's sense of smell pointed him to the other rats;
Falcon with quickness is successfull killing other birds;
Tiger with agility kills other animals;
the student of Aje is always ready to bring good fortune (ire) to people
Ase

OGUNDA OSE – In this odu, the removal of obstacles brings abundance. Speaks of the need for honorable behavior. Speaks of many blessings with proper ebo and behavior. Must respect people and not make insults. Ebo to Ogun to defeat enemies and for long life.

E baa re ree re bi Ere
Ibi ti e ti lo naa
Le o pada si
D'afa fun Ojola
Omo Ere l'Apa
Ifa ni Isese lo maa leke
Isese lo maa gbeniyan
Ase

No matter how far you wander like the grindstone
No matter how far you wind and wend like the boa conscriptor
It is to your starting point
That you will return
These were Ifa's declarations to royal python
The child of boa conscriptor of Apa town
Pray, do not kill it
Do not kill royal python
The child of boa conscriptor of Apa town

Ifa says Isese (tradition) shall prevail
Isese will allow humanity to prosper
Ase

OSE OGUNDA – In this odu, abundance leads to removing obstacles. Abundance allows us to breath a little easier so we can pay more attention to clearing out obstacles. Calls for initiation. Might need to receive Ile Ori. This odu speaks of this person receiving plenty of blessings. Ebo to Olokun so that the ire may flow. Calls for ebo to Orunmila, Esu and Ori to drive away ajoogun and align with destiny. Possible abiku child.

Ise-Eguntan, aso ire li aiba lara Agbe
Ise-Eguntan, aso ire li aiba lara Aluko
Ise-Eguntan, aso ire li aiba lara Odidere
Gbogbo ire niit'owo Olokun
Olokun olori omi
Bgogbo ire niit'owo Oloosa, Osa ibikeji odo
Ise-Eguntan
Toto niki gbogbo ire maa to mi l'owo
Ase

Ise-Eguntan
we meet the clothes of good fortune on Agbe (blue turaco)
Ise-Eguntan
we meet the clothes of good fortune on Aluko (indigo woodcock)
Ise-Eguntan
we meet the clothes of good fortune on Odidere (African grey parrot)
All good fortunes (ire) are in Olokun's possession
Olokun, the head of all waters
All good fortunes (ire) are in Oloosa's possession
Osa the the second head of all waters

Ise-Eguntan
Toto commands all good fortune (ire gbogbo) come to me
ase

OGUNDA OFUN – Removal of obstacles clears the way for the manifestation of prayers. Speaks of blessings. Ebo to Obatala for ire. Might need to receive Obatala. Speaks of the need to resolve a family dispute or other conflict openly. Ebo to Ogun and Esu to conquer enemies and protection from thieves.

Seke-seke se eke
Eke kee Sika-sika se ika
Ika kaa
Ara kii ro eke
Okan osika o bale boro
Aseni nse araa re lose
D'afa fun Orunmila
Nijo ti seke-seke
Sika-sika ati Aseni maa je omo ikofaa re
Ti Baba maa gba iwa buburu yii lowoo won
Ase

A liar lies
His lies destroy him
The wicked person displays his wickedness
His wickedness damages him
There is no peace for a liar
No security for the wicked
The treacherous person is doing untold harm to him or herself
These were the declarations of Ifa to Orunmila
When the liar, the wicked and the treacherous were to become his students
Ifa would purge them of their lack of character

Ase

OFUN OGUNDA – the manifestation of prayers removes obstacles. This odu portends a lot of ire. But must do ebo to Ifa and Aje to end money problems. This odu is strong on Ori. This person should do ebo to Ori (ibori). might need to receive Ile Ori. should make water with ire leaves to wash his/her head every morning. must stay away from bad influences, bad friends and behave ethically.

Abata a ba'ya gbedegbede a da fun Orunmila ti o ti
nse ofun egbelegbe lai-lai
nwon ni ki o rubo
pe ni dun ni ni Olorun san gbogbo ohun kan re ti o ti nse ofun fun.
O ru eku, ija, igbin, ayebo adie, ati egbejila.
Ni igba ti Orunmila rubo yi tan
o ko ori eku, ori eja, ori adie ati ase igbin na sinu ohun kan o gbe sile
n'igba ti ile fi ma mo
awon erun ijalo ti su mo
bi o ti ni ki o gba won kuro ni o jin s'ile Olokun
bayi ni Orunmila bere si gbon akun
N'igba ti awon ti o ba je'hun ni ana
wa ki pe o ku ina owo
ati pe Olorun yio so ofun re di oro
Orunmila da'hun o ni ofun ti o se l'ana ko to'la
lati igba na ni a ti npe odu yi Ofun-ti-ola
ase.

"Mud has a mushy chest"
was the one who cast Ifa for Orunmila
when he had been suffering losses on all sides
from the beginning of time
They said that he should do ebo
so that during that year Olodumare might repay him for all his losses

He offered a rat, a fish, a snail, a hen, and money
When Orunmila had completed this offering
he put the head of the rat, the head of the fish,
the head of the hen, and the feelers of the snail
in something and left it on the ground
When dawn was breaking
ants (driver ants) gathered and covered the ebo
and when Orunmila began to sweep them away
he broke through the ground into a pit of Olokun
So Orunmila began to scoop up beads (wealth) from the pit
When those who had eaten with him the day before
came to greet him saying
"Greetings on spending money"
and "Olodumare will change your losses into riches,"
Orunmila answered that the losses he had suffered in the past
did not equal the wealth he had gained
From that time on, we have called this Odu Ifa "Loss then Wealth"
Ase

NOTES:

NOTES:

BOOK OF OSA

OSA IKA – Handling external changes with coolness and courage lead to an increase in personal ase. This is a powerful odu with lots of feminine ase (Aje power). Speaks of the need for cooling. Head wash and ebo to Ori, Ifa and Esu of cooling elements – water, snail, ori (shea) butter, efun, palm oil, pigeon, etc. must keep things to oneself. No divulging of plans to anyone. Speaks of enemies. Ebo to Sango and Ogun for victory and protection. Ebo to Ifa for ire.

Osa kadi
O rin kadi
O fo fere fere
O modi Ika gun
A dia fun Onile Oroke
Eyi tii somo Abewolegi
Won ni ko sa kaale ebo ni o se
O si gbebo nbe
O rubo
E wa n gbagogo
A be o gbagogo?

Awa momo n gbagogo
Nile Onile Oroke
Ibe la gbe n gbagogo
Ifa wa n gbo tiwa
Abi o gbo tiwa?
Onile Oroke
Ifa n gbo tiwa
Ase

He runs into hiding
He walks into hiding
He jumps up high
And climbs the boundaries of Ika
Cast Ifa for Onile Oroke
The child of Abewolegi
He was asked to take care of the ground and do ebo
He heard and did the ebo
Can you hear the gong sounding?
Or can't you hear it?
We are really hearing the gong sounding
In the house of Onile Oroke
There, we hear the gongs sound
Ifa, now listen to our plea
Doesn't he?
Onile Oroke
Ifa listens to our plea.
Ase

IKA OSA – An increase in our spiritual power brings positive changes to our environment. This odu speaks of the need for this person to change their behavior and become a person of integrity in order to receive their blessings of ire. Speaks of a husband and wife working together in harmony. Speaks of illness. Ebo to Iyami for health. If a man, might be result of behavior with women, so also ebo to Iyami. Sango and Ogun to conquer enemies. Speaks of maybe needing Itefa, Ile Ori or Obatala for ire.

Ika sara awo eti oya
D'afa fun won l'Egun tatala
Nijo ti won n gbogun lo ilu l'Aje
Ebo ni won ose
Won si gbebo nbe won rubo
A bo lowo Ogun nigbayi o
Abo lowo Ogun bokan
Soso opolo se
Bo lowo Okundun
Riru ebo ni i gbe ni
Airu ki i gb'eeyan
E waa ba ni ni ire gbogbo
Ase

Ika saran the priest of the Niger river's edge (Oya)
Cast Ifa for Egun tatala
On the day he was fighting at the town of the Aje (powerful women)
He was asked to do ebo
He complied
We do not have war now
We do not have war
Like the toad that is free from Okundun
It is doing ebo that brings blessings
Neglect of ebo pays no one
Come and join us where there is plenty of ire
ase

OSA OTURUPON – succesfull handling of changes in our circumstances brings protection from illness. This odu speaks of loss. Speaks of enemies. Ebo to ifa for protection. Ebo for long life. Must avoid gossip and hexing.

Oni logo omo eku b'afi ori kan
Igba edu lojo naa ni iwa re baje
Orunmila ni o di kiji
Ni Esu n hi bara Agonniregun
Ifa ni ilu ti Esu nlu tani njo
Won lomo eja bafi ori kan
Igba Edu lojo naa ni iwa re baje
Nmila ni o di kiji
Ni Esu nn hi bara Agonniregun
Ifani ilu ti Esu nlu tani njo
Won lomo eye, omo eran ni oni logo ti won bafi ori kan
Igba Edo logo naa ni iwa won baje
Orunmila ni o di kiji
 Ni Esu n hi bara Agbonniregun
Ifa ni ilu ti Esu nlu tani njo
Won lota eyundie, bafi ori kan
Igba Edu lojo naa ni iwa re baje
Ase

Orunmila ni o di kiji (sounding the drum)
Esu is beating the drum
Who is dancing to the drum?
The awo said, "it's Emu's child"
Orunmila replied that anyone that is Eku's child
and touches Edu pumpkin will die
Orunmila says "Orunmila ni o di kiji"
Esu is beating the drum and who is dancing to to its beat?
The awo said, "it is on the day the fishes, birds and animal's children
Touch Edu pumkin that they will die"
Orunmila says "Orunmila ni o di kiji"
Esu is beating the drum and who is dancing to to its beat?

The awo said it is the enemy of the Babalawo
Orunmila replied that it's on the day the egg touches the Edu pumpkin that it will break
Ase

OTURUPON OSA – Taking care of one's health leads to positive changes in circumstances. Ebo to Obatala and Yemoja for children and ire. This person needs to be calm and not be fearful. Must watch words; no gossip or bragging, etc. Might need initiation into Ifa (Itefa) for protection and all ire. Ebo to Ifa and Oya to end difficulties. Aje for wealth. Sango for victory over enemies.

Oturupon Osa a difa fun won ni Ilara
won ni iye omotitun ti a bi ninu odun ti a pon won sare ogun
won ni: kinni Ebo?
Won ko ru u
Riru ebo ni i gbe ni
Airu ki i gb'eeyan
E waa ba ni ni ire gbogbo
ase

Oturupon Osa was divined for the people of Ilara
They said all the babies born that year
would be carried on their mothers' backs
when running away from battle
The people asked what is the ebo
They did not offer the ebo
It is doing ebo that brings blessings
Neglect of ebo pays no one
Come and join us where there is plenty of ire
Ase

OSA OTURA

OSA OTURA – Successful handling of external changes bring a renewed connection to spirit. Speaks of loss leading to ire. This odu speaks of maintaining a cool head and being honest at all times. This odu is the one that contains the song, "speak the truth, tell the facts." Which means to be objective and tell the truth the way you see it based on facts. Speaks of protecting our children. Ebo to Obatala and head wash for coolness.

Osa Otura I Kinni Otito?
Emi I kinni Otito?
Orunmila I Otito ni Oluwa orun ti nto aye
Osa Otura I kinni Otito?
Emi I kinni Otito?
Orunmila I Otito li Eni-airi ti nto aye
Ogbon ti Olodumare nlo
Ogbon-nla
Opolopo ogbon
Osa Otura I kinni Otito?
Emi I kinni Otito?
Orunmila I-Otito ni iwa Olodumare
Otito ni Oro ti ko le subu Ifa li Otito
Otito ni Oro ti ko le baje
Agbara-nla, Ajulo, ire-ailopin
Orin Ifa na:
"S'otito: S'ododo, S'otito o si tun S'ododo;
enis'otito ni imale yoo gbe o"

Osa Otura says, What is truth?
I say, What is truth?
Orunmila says: Truth is Olodumare guiding the earth
Osa-Otura says, what is truth?
Orunmila says: Truth is the unseen one guiding the earth, the wisdom Olodumare is using--great wisdom, many wisdom's.
Osa Otura says, What is truth?

I say, what is truth?

Orunmila says: Truth is the character of Olodumare, truth is the word that cannot fall. Ifa is the truth. Truth is the word that cannot spoil. Mighty power, surpassing all. Everlasting blessing.

Ifa's song: Speak the truth, tell the facts. Speak the truth, tell the facts. Those who speak the truth are those whom they deity will help ase

OTURA OSA – Connection with spirit provides the ability to handle change in a positive way. This odu contains the ase of Oya; the ability to remain calm in the hurricane; to find the eye of the hurricane. This person is spiritually gifted. Might need initiation into Oya or Ifa. Must do ebo as prescribed. This person needs to be brave and calm. Head wash and ebo to Obatala for coolness. Ebo to Oya for bravery. Ebo to ancestors and Egbe for protection. Might need to receive Egbe. Ebo to Olokun and Aje for wealth.

Bi winiwini ba pe ka ma lagi lojude baba toun mo
A gbe lo ojude baba winniwinni loo la
Dia fun Otura
To ti ngasa
Ebo ni won ni ko waa se
O gb'ebo, o ru'bo
Igba Otura ti ngasa
Oun la ri baba lori esin
Ero Ipo
Ero Ofa
E waa ba ni ni jebutu ire
Ase

If someone insists that we must not cut the wood

in front of his father's house again
We will take it to another person's father's front yard to cut
Ifa's message for Otura
Who had been practicing exclusive goodness and benevolence
He was advised to offer ebo
He complied
When Otura had been practicing
exclusive goodness and benevolence
That was when we saw him on top of a horse (with honor)
Travellers to Ipo
Travellers to Ofa
Come and join us where there's plenty of good fortune
Ase

OSA IRETE – Handling change positively brings renewed determination for success. This odu portends good fortune. This person needs to be generous as one's generosity is returned with interest. Ebo to Ifa and Oya to open the way to blessings. Asks us to have faith in our gods. Speaks a lot about peace of mind. Ebo to Ori and Oya for peace.

Ó sá réte
Ó rìn réte
Àgbàrá gorí òkè
A sáré réte
A rìn réte
A díá fún Òrúnmìlà
Níjó ire gbogbo kò tí ò yalée rè mó
Àwon ire tí ón yaá lo yìí?
Wón yà wá báyìí?
Wón ní gbogbo iré ní o móo ya ilé è
Wón ní kó tójúu eran oyà
Wón ní kó fi rúbo

Òrúnmìlà se bẹ́ẹ̀
Ó fi eran òyà bo òkè ìpòrí è
Ire gbogbo bá n yale e
Ó sá réte
Ó rìn réte

Runoff water climbs a hill
It runs bumpily
And walks bumpily
Cast divination for Òrúnmìlà
On the day all good things refused to come into his house
"All these good fortunes that are turning away
Would they return?" He asked
They said all good things would come into his house
But he should prepare the meat of Oya
He was asked to use it as offering
He complied
He used the meat of Oya as an offering to his Ifá
All good fortunes then started turning into his house
Ase

IRETE OSA – Determination and perseverance bring blessings through change of circumstances. This odu brings much ire, but usually the person is going through hard times. Might need initiation to Oya for protection and to end hard times. Ebo to Ifa for ire. Must worship Orunmila. Ebo to Sango to conquer enemies who are working against you. Watch who you hang out with and what you get into. Speaks of death.

Irete Osa
A d'Ifa fun Aduroja-Abayako
Won ni kiowa rubo kiobaa le se te awon ota re
O gbo o ru

Won ni Aduroja-Abayako a se te awon ota re
Kee pe o
Kee jinna
E tete waa ba wa ni jebutu aje suuru
Ase

Irete-Osa
was cast for Aduroja-Abayako
on the day that he was about to meet his enemies
They told him to come and do ebo
in order to be able to conquer his enemies
He complied
They said that Aduroja-Abayako would conquer his enemies
Very soon
At no distant date
Come and join us where there's plenty of money and peace of mind
Ase

OSA OSE – Successful handling of changes in environment bring the blessing of abundance. This odu brings much ire. This person is successful but that brings jealousy. Head wash and ebo to Ori for protection from negativity. Ebo to Oya for long life and victory over enemies. This person has ofo ase, word power, so must be careful what he/she speaks. Don't jump to conclusions about who the enemy is.

Waa sere omo Olohun
Erin o ma gba iwase Awo Okodeere-Moba
Poo ni mo gba otaa mi loju
Awo Atokeere-ihin-wa
Awo Atokeere-ohun-wa
D'Ifa fun Talo-n-ru-Okanmbi
Ti nba Esu Odara sere akodi
Nitori aso o

THE HOLY ODU

Won ni ki won sakaale, ebo ni sise
O koti ogbonyin sebo o
Ipin aiteru
Egba aiteru
E ro rina kan n won o
Nje e je ka mu aso f'Esu
K'Esu o maa maso lo o
Tani o mo wipe Osa-Ase la nsa
E je ka mas f'Esu
K'Esu o maa maso lo o
Ase

Come and play
The child of the landowner
Laughter does not recognize the origin of any matter
The awo of Okodeere-Moba
With all my strength
I slapped my enemy in the face
The awo who came from a long distance over here
The awo who came from a long distance over there
They were the ones who cast Ifa for Talo-n-ru-Okambi
Who was struggling with Esu Odara
Because of his cloth
He was advised to make ebo
He did not comply
The consequences of refusal to do the ebo
The aftermath of ignoring the performance of ritual
Imagine how fire kept burning them
Please let us leave the cloth for Esu
For Esu to take
Who knows that we are all running from penury?
Please let us leave the cloth for Esu
Let Esu take the cloth
Ase

OSE OSA – Abundance allows for the successful handling of change. This odu speaks of knowing when to fight and when to run. Speaks of much ire, but enemies might be blocking it. Ebo to Esu, Ifa and Iyami to bring harmony. Ebo to Ifa for all ire. Speaks of confusion. Ebo to Ori and Egbe for focus and protection. Ebo to eguns for long life. Ebo to Ogun to end hard times.

Bi ogun bi ogun niko tan lowo oba
Bi apala ebu bi a pa la ebu kotan lowo awo onyagbe
A D'Ifa fun ti a nrere
Ti won ti ndare olaare deyin lailai
Ebo ni won ni ko se
O si gbebo nbe o rubo
Ifa ni aro niyo maaro ibi won lewon l'Ori
Apada niyo maa pari ibi won da pada si won sawerepepe Ifa a pe
Le pe
E wo ti ni igba egbo nke
Ifa jeki ire kowo timi
Ase

A king never gets bored of going to war
A broken yam is always found in the hand of a farmer
The farmer never gets tired of cultivating
Cast Ifa for ti a nrere
Whose road was blocked
He was told to do ebo
He did it
Ifa says the leaves of aro will turn evil (ibi)back to where it came from
Ifa says the leaves of apada will turn evil back to where it came from
Ifa says the leaves of sawerepepe will kill my enemies
It is the sound of the leaves of iba egbo
That will bring good fortune (ire) to me

Ase

OSA OFUN – Successful handling of external changes brings a manifestation of our prayers. This odu speaks of this person having a tendency to run from problems. Must change this behavior and stand and fight. Ebo to Oya for courage and stability. Might need initiation to Oya. Speaks of the need to honor taboos. This person's life might be chaotic. Ebo to end the chaos.

Safunmi
No funo
Ekan niko ti bi boroboro bole
A d'ifa fun Ojuninboju leru
Tinse oko Iyalode
Ebo won ni ose
Osi gbebo nbe o reubo
Keepe
Kee jina
Ebani ni jebutu ire
Ase

You give it to me
I don't give it to you
The nail does not stick itself by the back
But by its sharp point
Cast Ifa for the eye
Who was getting scared of the other eye
The husband of Iyalode
He was told to do ebo
He did it
Come and find us in the middle of lots of blessings (ire)
Ase

OFUN OSA – The manifestation of prayers brings ire. The development of good character brings sudden good fortune. This odu brings plenty of ire, but the person might be experiencing hard times. Ebo to Obatala, Oya and Ifa for abundance and an end to chaos. Must maintain positive attitude. Ebo to Ori to overcome problems and for long life. Ebo to one's father's eguns. Might need initiation to Ifa. This person's children should be initiated (Orisa).

Òfún sà á, sà á
Ó sà á bẹ́ẹ̀ ni ò tán mó
A díá fún Òrúnmìlà
Babá n sunkún òun ò lajé
Wón lébo ajé ni kí Babá ó se
Òrúnmìlà bá rúbo
Ajé bá ṣẹ
Òfún bá bèrè sí sà á
Ó sà á bẹ́ẹ̀ ni ò tán
Kee pe o
Kee jinna
E tete waa ba wa ni jebutu aje suuru
Ase
Ase

Òfún picked and picked
He picked it continuously yet it was not exhausted
Cast Ifa for Òrúnmìlà
Baba was crying that he had no wealth
They asked Baba to perform sacrifice
Òrúnmìlà then offered the sacrifice
Money then came out of the ground
Òfún started picking it
He picked and picked yet it was not exhausted
Yet it was not exhausted

THE HOLY ODU

It is Ifá that owns massive wealth
Very soon
At no distant date
Come and join us where there's plenty of money and peace of mind
Ase

NOTES:

NOTES:

BOOK OF IKA

IKA OTURUPON – Increased ase brings a blessing of good health. This odu brings ire in the form of relationships, children and creativity. This odu speaks of the relationship of Orunmila and Oshun. Speaks of a misunderstanding leading to an unnecessary conflict in one's relationship. Ebo to Ori and Ifa for suuru (peace of mind, patience, wisdom and coolness). Ebo to Oshun for ire. Ebo to Egungun and Ogun for success, Sango for protection.

Osi o tami
Kin je Obi baba tire
A d'Ifa fun Lanlehun ti somo Ogun
Ebo ni won se
Won si gbebo nbe won rubo
Eropo ero ofa
Erifa awo ki, Ifa nse
ase

No matter now much poverty I face
I will eat my father's kola nuts
Cast Ifa for Lanlehun, the child of Ogun

He was told to do ebo
He heard and did it
Pilgrims of Opo; pilgrims of Ofa
Come and see how Ifa's words come to pass
Ase

OTURUPON IKA - Maintaining a healthy lifestyle increases our ase. Speaks of pregnancy. Speaks of truthfulness as the road to ire. Speaks of healing one's child of possible illness. The child might need initiation. Must stay away from trouble. The main ebo in this odu is a change in behavior, which leads to prosperity.

O ji tuu omo onihun
O rinrin gbere-gbere-gbere bi omo onihun
O ji kutu faso igosu bose
D'Ifa fun Asiyanbi tii somo Oloro kan atijo
Ebo ni won ni ko waa se
O gbebo, o rubo
Bi igba ba ji
A fowo o re m'oko
Ifa oni ko to ifa ola to nbo
Bi gboro ba ji
A fowo o re m'oko
Ifa ono ko to Ifa ola to nbo
Eluluu ko maa ke tuturu
Ifa nka nu yoo to mi wa
Ase

He woke up gingerly like a child of a property owner
He walked majestically like the child of a property owner
He woke up at dawn and used expensive cloth to cover his legs
These were the awos of Asiyanbi
The child of a succesfull man of time past

He was told to do ebo
He did it
When the calabash grows
It rests its stem against the farm
Today's gain is not as much as the one coming tomorrow
When the pumpkin grows
It rests its stem against the farm
Today's gain is not as much as the one coming tomorrow
Let the Senegal lark heeled cuckoo bird herald the news
Great profits are sure to come looking for me
Ase

IKA OTURA – Increased ase through spiritual discipline and iwa pele, lead to a connection with spirit. Speaks of turning things around; the end of hard times and the blessing of peace and prosperity through meditation, etc. speaks of enemies. Ebo to Esu and Orunmila for protection. Needs to receive Esu and hand of Ifa. Might need initiation to Ifa as it is Ifa this person must be close to. Might be in a bad relationship.

Ika Otura, Akowonjo, Lapawonpo
Bami k'owo jo
Bami ko aya jo
Bami ko omo jo
Kiowa ko gbogbo ire jo sile mi
Kee pe o
Kee jinna
E waa wo'fa awo ki
B'o ti nse
Ifa de, alase
Ope, abise wara

Ase

Ika Otura, The gatherer, the joiner
Help me to gather money
Help me to gather wives
Help me to gather children
Come and gather all good things (ire gbogbo) in my house
Very soon
At no distant date
Come and see the Babalawo's prediction
Coming to pass
Ifa has come, the great authority
Palm-tree, whose predictions come true speedily
Ase

OTURA IKA – Connection to spirit increases our personal ase. This odu speaks of lots of ire. However, the person might be blocked. Must have head wash and Ori work to remove negative energy. Ebo to Iyami and Ogun for protection from enemies. Ebo to Aje and Orunmila for wealth. Ebo to Sango for success. Might need to receive Egbe.

Biebi ba n pa inu
Akasu banba laa fi bee
D'Ifa fun Teyingbiwa
Tii yo san wo ipin l'orun
Mo san wo ipin mo ni isinmi
Teyingbiwa
Mo san wo ipin l'orun
Teyingbinwa
Ero Ipo
Ero Ofa
E waa ba ni ni jebutu ire
Ase

If the stomach is feeling hungry
A large leaf of eba is used to appease it
This was Ifa's declaration to Teyingbinwa
Who would pay his dues of his destiny in orun
I pay my dues of destiny and I have peace of mind
Teyingbinwa
I have paid the dues of destiny in orun
Teyingbinwa
Travellers to Ipo
Travellers to Ofa
Come and join us where there's plenty of good fortune
Ase

IKA IRETE - Increased ase provides renewed determination. Speaks of avoiding loss through ebo. Speaks of ancestral support. Ebo to one's ancestors. If considering a new venture or expanding current business, it is a good time. Speaks of one's hard work being the road to ire. Might need Tefa, also a child who is getting into trouble needs Tefa or at least hand of Ifa; but definitely ebo to Orunmila for ire. Must avoid fights and arguments. Must adhere to taboo of self hexing. Ebo to Ori for ire and bath.

Asa n wewe
awo Omode
A difa fun Esu Panada
Eyi ti o ri eeru je
Esu Panada to sawo ti o reru je
Lo difa fun Okoko niyele
omoo won ni Isalu okun
Nijo ti n fomi ojuu sogbere omo
Ero Ipo
Ero Ofa
E waa ba ni ni jebutu ire

Ase

Asa n wewe
The Babalawo of Omode
Cast Ifa for Esu Panada
The one that had been practicing his preisthood
without having any free gifts
The Esu Panada that had been a priest for a long time
without having free gifts
He was the one that cast divination for Okoko niyele
Their child at the other side of the ocean
On the day she was crying because of children
Travellers to Ipo
Travellers to Ofa
Come and join us where there's plenty of good fortune
Ase

IRETE IKA – Determination and perseverance bring increased personal ase. Times are tough, but with ebo and doing the best job possible at work, the hard times come to an end. This odu brings the ire of success. Ebo to Ori and Ifa for success and protection. Also warns of protecting against loss. Ebo to Ogun to prevent loss.

Ateka ode Ibadan
A D'ifa fun won lode Ibadan
Lojo ti won se ohun gbogbo ti okan ko ni laa
Ebo ni won ni ko se
O si gbebo nbe o rubo
Nje Ateka ma da awo Ibadan
Bawo o be se aroye awo kii la
Kee pe o
Kee jinna
E tete waa ba wa ni jebutu aje suuru

Ase
Ase

Ateka, the awo for Ibadan
Cast Ifa for the people of Ibadan
When everything they did met with failure
He was asked to do ebo
He did the ebo
Aleka has become the babalawo of Ibadan
Many people are coming to him with gifts
Very soon
At no distant date
Come and join us where there's plenty of money and peace of mind
Ase

IKA OSE – An increase in one's ase brings the blessing of abundance. This person has had a tough time of it. Spiritual discipline is needed so that one's prayers may manifest. Must change one's attitude. Be grateful, hopefull and kind. Being the best at work leads to better times. Speaks of many detractors. Ebo to Ori, Ifa and Iyami for protection. Don't fear these people; ignore them and be confident in the protection provided by the ebo, akose and your good character and hard work.

Apendelero nii f'oju gb'omi
D'Ifa fun Owo
Tii se Iya Orisa
Omo Owo
Won kii ku koju Owo
Orunmila ma jee ki n ku
Loju eni yii n feran mi o
Omo Ese
Won kii ku koju Ese
Orunmila maa je ki n ku

Loju eni yii n feran mi o
Ase

Potsherd is the one who uses its face to collect water
Divined for owo (hand)
Who is the mother of Orisa
The child of Owo
Orunmila, please do not let me die (before my time)
In the presence of my loved ones
The child of ese (feet)
Will never die in the presence of Ese
Orunmila, please don't let me die
In the presence of my loved ones
Ase

OSE IKA – The blessing of abundance brings an increase in ase. Speaks of honoring the ancestors. Speaks of the need for iwa pele to protect oneself from enemies' accusations. Many enemies; Ebo to Sango and/or Ogun for victory. Speaks of this person experiencing loss and general bad luck. Ebo to Ifa and Esu to turn bad luck into good luck and prevent any further losses. The Orisa are waiting to help, but must be asked with sincerity which means you are ready to do your part. What we do today affects our tomorrow. Follow tradition.

Ose pakaja
Orin pakaja
A d'Ifa fun Onimoka Ona Ofa
Eyi ti baba ree okun la lojo lailai
Won ni se e baba re ni o mo o se
Awa o kokun kokun
Ao kokun l'aje
Ao kakun kokun

Ao kakun kokun
Ao kakun n'ire gbogbo
Ayamo bi Onimoka Ona Ofa kokun kokun l'aye
Ase

Ose pakaja
Orin pakaja
Cast Ifa for Onimoka Oni Ofa
Whose ancestors had never made any money producing ropes
He was compelled to carry on his ancestor's traditions
We make ropes
We make ropes to be rich
We make ropes
We make ropes to have wives
We make ropes
We make ropes to have children
We make ropes
We make ropes to have all good fortune (Ire gbogbo)
It is definetly not true that Onimoka Ona Ofa did not get rich making ropes
Ase

IKA OFUN – Increasing our ase through communication with spirit leads to the manifestation of our prayers. This odu contains the 16 laws of Ifa. This person must act ethically. In this odu, one's good fortune comes from one's Ori. Ebo to Ori and head wash. Self discipline is needed.

Aje b'ori ogbon
Otosi so opo oro
A bu ni lole omo oun ti nse ni
A kunle, a yan eda
A dele aye tan

Oju n kan gbogbo wa
Eda ose e pada loo yan omiran
Ayafi bi a taye wa
Ase

Wealth surpasses wisdom
A poor person utters ineffective words
Those who castigate us for being lazy
Do not understand our predicaments
We knelt down and chose our destiny in orun
While on earth
We are all in a hurry
We cannot go back and change our destiny
Unless we reincarnate
Ase

OFUN IKA - prayers answered brings an increase in personal ase. Ebo to obatala for ire. Ebo to Iyami for end of troubles. Must take personal responsibility to bring ire. Speaks of betrayal and having enemies close. Not a good time for a new venture. Must watch your temper and be kind, especially to children. Bad behavior leads to loss. Ori is prominent in this odu and is the one who will guide you, protect you and bring blessings. Ebo to ori and head wash. Ebo to egungun for prosperity.

Pelepele lojumo n mo
Pelepele allele n le
Pelepele la n pmukuuru u pele
Ba o ba fi pelepele pamukuuru u pele
A ro'ni titi lo de ponpolo itan
D'Ifa fun Oniwayo
Ti nlo soko Ororo-Ewa
Won ni ko sakaale, ebo ni sise

O f'ebo salo
Ki nlo so Oniwayo dahun?
Ororo-ewa
Ki nlo wa pa Oniwayo gbangba?
Ahun Ororo-Ewa
Lo pa Oniwayo gbangba
Ahun Ororo-Ewa
Riru ebo ni i gbe ni
Airu ki i gb'eeyan
E waa ba ni ni ire gbogbo
Ase

The day dawns gently and easily
The night falls gently and easily
The insect biting one's scrotum needs to be killed gently
If not killed gently
The pain goes into the marrow of one's thigh bone
These were the declarations of Ifa to Oniwayo (a deceitful man)
When planning to marry Ororo-Ewa (a beautiful woman)
He was advised to offer ebo
He delayed making the offering
Who turned oniyawo into a tight fisted man?
It is Ororo-Ewa, his wife
What then killed Oniyawo eventually?
It was the stinginess of Ororo-Ewa, his wife
It is doing ebo that brings blessings
Neglect of ebo pays no one
Come and join us where there is plenty of ire
Ase

NOTES:

BOOK OF OTURUPON

OTURUPON OTURA – Maintaining a healthy lifestyle brings a stronger connection to spirit. This odu speaks of the need for patience and planning. Speaks of the need for spiritual discipline. This odu establishes the 5 day week. The Egun speak a lot in this odu. This person might be under spiritual attack and needs to do ebo to Egungun and Egbe for protection. Ebo to Ifa for ire. Might need to receive Ifa. Must be hospitable. Ebo to Sango and or Ogun for victory over enemies.

Oturupon Otura
Ita jare Irele jare
Dia fun Orunmila Baba nsoore lotu Ife
Won ni ibi lo nse Nje ita jare
Irele jare K'otu-ife
roju K'otu Ife raaye Kaboyun
Ile-Ife o bi ibi tibi tire Kagan
Ile Ife o towo ala bosun Ita jare
Irele jare
Ase

Pray to Ita and Irele (Oro cult deities) for assistance
So declared the oracle to Orunmila

When he was doing good in Ile-Ife
And it was misconstrued to be wickedness
Say it loud and clear that Ita and Irele we pray
Let there be peace in Ile Ife
Let there be prosperity in Ile Ife
Let the pregnant women deliver of their babies with ease
Let the barren one conceive and give birth
Ita and Irele we beseech thee!
Ase

OTURA OTURUPON – Connection to spirit brings stronger health. Warns of the need to do ebo promptly. Be nice to people. Eguns speak in this odu. Ebo to Eguns for protection. Needs to receive Ifa for long life and peace of mind. Needs to stop arguing and fighting with people. Ebo to Ogun to help with this. Ebo to Esu for ire. This person needs to receive Ile Ori, have head rogation, etc. so that their Ori may guide them and bring them ire.

Otura baa lie
Eti mejeeji nii kangun igbe
D'Ifa fun Orunmila
Ifa n sawo lo sode Aimowaa-hu
Won o ba ti iwu-lowo I ba ti pe o
Esu aimowaa-huu won ni o
Won a ba ti bimo-bimo iba ti pe o
Esu aimowaa-huu won ni o
Won o ba ti n'ire gbogbo iba ti pe o
Esu aimowa-huu won ni o
Ase

Otura Oturupon
The two ears are closest to the forest
Divined for Orunmila
When going to the land of those who lack proper manners

They would have been blessed with wealth for a long time
But for their lack of good manners
They would have been blessed with a spouse
But for their lack of manners
They would have been blessed with children for long
But for their lack of manners
They would have been blessed with all ire for long
But for their lack of manners
Ase

OTURUPON IRETE – Maintaining good health allows us to overcome adversity. Portends the ire for success in current project with ebo. Must be honest and not be vengefull. This odu brings lots of ire in the form of success. Ebo to Ifa, Olokun and/or Aje for wealth and success. Ebo to Egungun for protection.

Oturupon Rete
A d'Ifa fun iya Adepon
Won niki iya Adepon wa rubo
Ki awon omoomo re ma baa ri'ibi arun Ete
O gbo ko rubo
Iya Adepon oruko ti aipe Ibepe
Riru ebo ni i gbe ni
Airu ki i gb'eeyan
E waa ba ni ni ire gbogbo
Ase

Oturupon Rete
Was divined for the mother of Adepon
She was advised to do ebo
So that her children might not suffer from leprosy (illness)
She didn't do the ebo
Adepon's mother is what we call the pawpaw (papaya)
It is doing ebo that brings blessings

Neglect of ebo pays no one
Come and join us where there is plenty of ire
Ase

IRETE OTURUPON – Determination and perseverance make us stronger. Speaks of the need to treat all people fairly. Speaks of the need to appease the Iyami. Speaks of the need for coolness. Head wash for coolness. Calls for initiation into Ifa to remove blockages and difficulties, bring healing and bring ire. Ebo to Olokun for prosperity, OrisaOko for progress.

Ajopante Ogede
Lo D'Ifa fun Onire
Opeji igba ti nfi
Omi oju s'ogbere ire
Ebo ni won ni ko se
O si gbebo nbe o rubo
Onire mo wadi
Onire mow a yara
Ope agunka ti nbe leyin re ju odi lo
Ase

Ajopante Ogede
The awo of onire
Cast Ifa for Onire Opeji
When they were crying because of not being blessed
He was told to do ebo
He did it
Onire(owner of ire) is not worried
Onire is not looking disturbed
The Orisas will always be with him
Ase

OTURUPON OSE –

Maintenance of health brings the blessing of abundance. Speaks of the need to be a responsible person. Speaks of the need to honor tradition. Speaks of the need for patience and kindness. This odu calls for coolness. Ori is prominent in this odu. Should receive Ile Ori and have river bath ritual to end poverty. Don't tell your secrets or plans. Ebo to Iyami for protection from enemies. Watch out for infections.

Òrúa jégédé
Awo ebá ònà
A díá fún Ato
Níjó tí n sòwò rojà Èjìgbòmekùn
N lo rèé pónko
Wón ní kó rúbo
Ato n pón èko lója Èjìgbòmekùn
Ó wo aso àdìre sára
Òkìkí kàn
Gbogbo èèyàn ní n ra èko lówó Ato
Èkejì Ato lórun bá ní òún ó loòdo Ato
Òún ó lòó ra èko lówó è
Wón sì ti so fún èèkejì rè pé aso àdìre ni Ató ró
Ató bá sùn
Oorun rè ò já geere
Wón ní kí Ató ó fi aso araa rè rúbo
Ató fi rúbo
Enìkejìi è bá n bò
Nbgà ó dé kò bá àdìre lára Ato mó
Èsù tí pààrò àdìre ara è
Enìkejì òrun ò bá rajà lówó è mó
Ó nó Òrúpa jégédé
Awo ebá òna
A díá fún Ato
Níjó tí sòwò rojà Èjìgbòmekùn

Tí n lo rèé pón èko
Wón ní ó sá káalè ebo ní ó se
Ato gbébo nbè
Ó rúbo
Rírú ebo
Èèrù àtùkèsù
A wá bÁto láìkú kanngiri
Àìkú kanngiri là ó wà
Ase

Orupa jegede
The awo of the roadside
Cast divination for Ato
On the day she was trading at the Ejigbomekun market
She was going to sell hard pap (eko)
She was asked to do ebo
Ato was making hard pap in Ejigbomekun's market
She was wearing an Adire cloth
She became very popular
People from all walks of life always came to buy pap from her
Her iponri (higher self) then decided to go and visit Ato
She wanted to go and buy pap from her on earth (take her life)
They told her before she left heaven that Ato would
be dressed in Adire
Ato then slept
Her sleep was full of nightmares
They asked her to make an offering of the clothes she was wearing
Ato complied
Her iponri entered the earth looking for
Ato that was dressed in Adire
She searched and could not find anyone selling pap
dressed in Adire
Esu had changed the Adire cloth on Ato
Her iponri as a result could not locate Ato

We now meet with Ato solid and undying
We would be found without death
Ase

OSE OTURUPON – The blessing of abundance brings improved health. This odu speaks of illness and provides the cure. Ogun is prominent in this odu. Ebo to Ogun to remove blockages and bring ire. If going on a trip, ebo to Ogun for ire. Must watch how we talk to people, especially women. Ebo to Iyami for forgiveness. Ebo to Egbe for their support. Ebo to Sango for success. Red cloth for ancestors for protection.

Atodunmodun l'Erin ti n rin
Erin o fara k'asa
Atosumosu, l'Efon ti nrin
Bee ni o tese bo poolo
Eeyan ti o mo'ni leni
Ti o mo eeyan leeyan
Eeyan ti o ba ko ede d'ele
Nii pe t'obinrin o si laye
D'Ifa fun Ewuji
Ti yoo gba seke Ide lalade Orun
Ebo ni won ma f'oju di oun o
O ni Seke Ide ti oun gba yi
Ki won ma f'oju di oun o
O ni eni to ba fori bale
Yoo maa laje
Yoo maa laya
Yoo maa bimo
Yoo maa bimo
Yoo maa de'bi aiku wa
Kenikan ma wipe eni ateyinto lobinrin o
Ase

For the many years that Elephant had been roving
Elephant had never been hit with a javelin
For the long months that Buffalo had been wandering
Buffalo had not slipped into a ditch
A person who does not appreciate the value of a fellow human being
Who does not recognize the importance of a fellow human being
A person who is ignorant
Is the person who devalues women
These were the declarations of Ifa to Ewuji (praise name of Oshun)
When going to pick up a brass rafter in orun
She was advised to do ebo
She did it
She said that the brass rafter that she got from orun
Let nobody underestimate her or be insolent with her
Those who show respect
They will be blessed with wealth
They will be blessed with a spouse
They will be blessed with children
They will be blessed with long life
Let no one use negative language regarding women
Ase

OTURUPON OFUN- Good health brings a manifestation of prayers. This odu says we should not worry so much or it will make us sick. Have faith in Ifa that our needs will always be met. This odu portends success. Speaks of honoring one's Orisa to open the way to ire. Be grateful and generous with one's blessings. You are a very lucky person and should give Ifa kola nuts constantly to keep being lucky. Ebo to Obatala and Esu for long life.

Eku-Iru Awo Ode Egba
Eku eru titu Awo Ode Ijesa
Ara owu ni won n buu seni owu

Oturu gbonwu lebelebe ma ran
D'Ifa fun Agbaagba mefa
Won n lo Ile Ife
Won n loo tooro Ogbo
Ebo ni won ni ki won waa se o
Won gbebo, won rubo
Ase ogbo o loogun
Ase jeejee ogbo o loogun
Bi a ba ri koto
Ma se ja lu
Ase ogbo o loogun
Ase jeejee ogbo o loogun
Bi o ba rile to njo
Ma kori bo
Ase ogbo o loogun
Ase jeejee ogbo o loogun
Bi o ba ri were to y'ada
 Ma duro dee
Ase ogbo o loogun
Ase jeejee ogbo o loogun
Bi o bay o tan
Ma lo wa bekun-bekun kiri
Ase ogbo o loogun
Ase jeejee ogbo o loogun
Ase jeejee loogun Ogbo
Bi idaamu be de
Ase ogbo o loogun
Ase jeejee loogun Ogbo
Ase

"good of you to do ebo," the Awo of Egba
"well done performing ritual," the Awo of Ijesa
Part of cotton wool is usually added to cotton wool
As extra measure to what was brought

Oturu combed cotton without spinning
These were the Awos who divined for the six elders
When going to Ile Ife
To plead for long life
They were told to do ebo
They did it
Longevity has no charm
Humility is the charm of longevity
If you see a ditch
Don't plan to jump in it
Longevity has no charm
If you see a burning house
Don't enter it
Longevity has no charm
Humility is the charm of longevity
If you see a mad man with a cutlass
Don't try to be a hero
Longevity has no charm
Humility is the charm of longevity
If you eat to your satisfaction
Do not go in search of a stomach ripper
Longevity has no charm
Humility is the charm of longevity
In times of tribulation
Do not commit suicide
Longevity has no charm
Humility is the charm of longevity
Ase

OFUN OTURUPON – Manifestation of prayers brings improved health. Calls for attention to one's spiritual path. Speaks of a troubled relationship. Ebo to Obatala for peace in one's marriage and happy children. Ogun is prominent in this odu. This odu speaks about one's job being in jeopardy but it is the right job for this person so they must fight to keep it. Ebo to Ogun and Ifa to keep job and conquer enemies. Must be courageous. Ebo to Ori for wealth. Ebo to Egungun for protection, Obatala and OrisaOko for progress and success.

Ofun-Oturupon a difa fun yewa
Iyawo Obatala oseere-igbo
won ni omo a po lowo re gbogbo aye ni yoo maa wa toro
won niki o rubo
ki won le maayin in nitori awon omo naa
obatala y orumila a maakowon
won niki o rubo
ki inu orumila le dun si
o gbo o ru
Kee pe o
Kee jinna
E waa wo'fa awo ki
B'o ti nse
Ifa de, alase
Ope, abise wara
ase

Ofun Oturupon divined for Yewa
The wife of Obatala oseere-igbo
She was told to do ebo
So that she would be blessed with many children
And the whole world would come to pay homage to her children
And that the children in turn would always praise her
Obatala said Orunmila would train them
She was told to make an offering
so that Orunmila would be happy to do so
She did the offering
Very soon

THE HOLY ODU

At no distant date
Come and see the Babalawo's prediction
Coming to pass
Ifa has come, the great authority
Palm-tree, whose predictions come true speedily
ase

NOTES:

Awo Fategbe Fatunmbi Fasola

BOOK OF OTURA

OTURA IRETE – A strong connection to spirit provides the determination and perseverance to continue on the path to illumination. Home is where the heart is. A healthy and strong home leads to blessings. Speaks of the need for moderation, gratitude and honesty. This odu brings many blessings. Speaks of the need to be close to Ifa. Speaks of ebo to Ifa, Esu and Aje for wealth. Speaks of success in business. Ebo to Ori to conquer enemies. Speaks of imminent misfortune; ebo to Ifa and Esu. Ebo to one's paternal eguns for success.

Adupe-mpoe lawo adupe-mope
Adore-moore lawo adore-moore
Eni ti ko dupe ana ko le gbore oni bo
A d'Ifa fun Okankanlenirun Irunmole
Won lo reef e Ope
Tii somo Orisa-Gbowuji
A d'Ifa fun Orunmila
Baba nlo ree fe Ope
Tii somo Orisa-Gbowujimo dupe, mo gbore
Mo dupe, ana
Mo gbore toni bo
Otura Irete, mo dupe
Ase

To show gratitude upon gratitude
is the Awo of all gratitude

To display benevolence upon benevolence
is the Awo of all benevolence
Whoever does not show gratitude for yesterday's benevolence
Such a person will not receive today's blessing
These were the awo who divined for the 401 Irunmole
When going to marry Ope (gratitude)
The daughter of Orisa-Gbowuji (Obatala)
They also declared the same for Orunmila
When he was in turn going to marry Ope
The daughter of Orisa-Gbowuji
I am grateful; I receive my blessings
I am grateful for yesterday's favors
I shall receive today's
Otura-Irete, I am grateful
Ase

IRETE OTURA - Determination and perseverance bring a reconnection with spirit. This person needs to adopt some form of spirituality to find peace and contentment. This odu speaks of protection from illness and death. Speaks of enemies and the need for caution. This person might be cheating on their spouse and needs to ask for forgiveness. It is a good time for change or start a business. Ebo to Esu to open the way to success. Ebo to Aje for wealth. Ebo to Ifa to end hard times.

Ese kan so lo lomi iyoku ipasa loke odo
D'Ifa fun Orunmila
Ifa o fi ese be si'le Aje
Ebo ni won ni ko se
O si gbebo nbe o rubo
Nje Aje wa mi wa nija yin ni mo wa
Aje wa mi wa!
Riru ebo ni i gbe ni
Airu ki i gb'eeyan

E waa ba ni ni ire gbogbo
Ase

One foot in the water and one foot out
Cast Ifa for Orunmila
He jumped on one leg into the house of Aje (the Goddess of Wealth)
He was told to do ebo
He complied
Now may Aje come to me
I am here! Aje come to me!
It is doing ebo that brings blessings
Neglect of ebo pays no one
Come and join us where there is plenty of ire
ase

OTURA OSE – Connection to spirit brings a blessing of abundance. This odu speaks of the end of hard times. River wash and ebo to Ori to remove negativity. Speaks of the need for protection. Be careful outside. Might need to receive Ifa or Ile Ori. Ebo for protection, Ifa, Ori, Esu, Oshun. Calls for honesty in one's relationship and the need for discreetness. Ebo to Ifa and Esu so one's hard work will pay off. Brings many blessings.

Oyere ori imo li o d'Ifa fun Otu
Otu nlo jagun ilu Ajase
Won niki o wa rubo, a segun
O gbo o ru
O segun
Riru ebo ni i gbe ni
Airu ki i gb'eeyan
E waa ba ni ni ire gbogbo
Ase

Oyere of the top palm frond was divined for Otu
Otu was going to fight a battle at the town of Alaje
He was told to do ebo
So that he would win the battle
He did the ebo
He overcame the enemy
It is doing ebo that brings blessings
Neglect of ebo pays no one
Come and join us where there is plenty of ire
Ase

OSE OTURA – *Òsétùrá* is the odu that gave birth to Esu Odara and is accordingly said to be the odu that causes the sixteen principal odus to interact and produce the remaining 239 omo-òdú, emphasizing the importance of his function in Ifá.
This odu portends many blessings. Ebo to Orunmila, Iyami, Ori and Esu for protection, wealth and abundance. These four are prominent in this odu. Must pray to Ori every morning. This odu is the one that delivers our offerings and is the source of ashe. Speaks of spiritual discipline to build our ase. Must act with iwa pele and respect elders especially women. Must be positive and watch one's words.

Penpe lesee tubu
Ela agemo ni o to gele
Iba to gele
Nba mu rele loo we
D'Ifa fun Awurela
Ti n sawo rode Ijebu
Apejin laa pe Oniru
Ajejin laa pe Oniyo
Apela, apela laa pe Awurela
Ni ijebu
Ose Awurela, Awo ire ni o

ase

tiny are the feet of Tubu
the stripe of a chameleon is not big enough to be used as head gear
had it been enough
I would have taken it home and adorned my head with it
These were the Awos who divined for Awurela
When going on a spiritual mission to Ijebu land
We call on the locust bean seller and pay her money
We visit the salt seller and make her rich
We call on Awurela with respect to Ijebu land
Ose Awurela is a good awo
Ase

OTURA OFUN - connection to spirit brings the manifestation of prayers. This person must be spiritual and close to Ifa, Obatala and Ori. This person's good fortune depends on their behavior (iwa pele). Orunmila is the source of the many blessings in this odu. Calls for initiation or receive hand of Ifa (ikofa) and give offerings to Ifa on the regular. Also, calls for ibori and Egbe for support. Ebo to eguns for protection and Oshun for childbirth.

Otura funfunfun
Awo Oyin lo dia f'Oyin (honey)
Otura funfunfun
Awo Ado lo dia f'Ado
Otura funfunfun
Awo Ifunfun lo dia fun Ifunnfun
Aye awon le dun ni won ndafa si
Ebo ni won ni ki won waa se
Won gb'ebo, won ru'bo
Ile Oyin ma n ho o

Ti Ado n yo
Ifunnfun naa o tile gbele
Riru ebo ni i gbe ni
Airu ki i gb'eeyan
E waa ba ni ni ire gbogbo
ase

Otura funfunfun, the white Otura
He cast Ifá for Oyin, (honey)
Otura funfunfun
He cast Ifá for Ado, Sugar-honey
Otura funfunfun
He cast Ifá for Ifunnfun, (another type of honey)
When wanting to know if their lives will be sweet or not
They were advised to offer ebo
They complied
The home of honey is filled with sweetness
That of Ado is also sweet
There is no bitterness in the home of Ifunnfun
It is doing ebo that brings blessings
Neglect of ebo pays no one
Come and join us where there is plenty of ire
ase

OFUN OTURA – Manifestation of prayers improves our connection to spirit. This odu asks for patience and perseverance to overcome hard times. We must let go of regrets and be forward looking with optimism. Speaks of maintaining love in one's relationship. This odu brings much ire, but the person might be going through tough times due to a lack of patience, a greedy nature, or mistreating people. Gratefulness, generosity and kindness bring the blessings. Ebo to Ori to end difficulties. Ebo to Ogun for progress.

Ebo to Ifa and Aje for wealth and prosperity. One's children might need Ifa's protection.

Ofun-to pola
Ofun fun olelebo-iyo
Ofun nwa ohun-to-dun-todun je
D'Ifa fun Esu Odara
Nlo gbe Epo ni iyawo
A ni, won koniiya ara won titi laelae
O gbo o ru
Eropo ero ofa
Erifa awo ki, Ifa nse
Ase

Ofun tasted palm oil
Ofun dropped olele in salt
Ofun was looking for all good things to eat
These were the awos for Esu Odara
Who was going to marry Epo (palm oil)
He was told to do ebo so they would never be separated
He complied
Pilgrims of Opo, pilgrims of Opa
Come and see how Ifa's words come to pass
Ase

NOTES:

BOOK OF IRETE

IRETE OSE - determination and perseverance lead to a blessing of abundance. This is a very powerful odu that requires special care by the diviner. Speaks of negative forces, but also speaks of wealth. This person needs a bath to remove negativity best done at the sea, ebo and medicine to protect from loss brought by negative entities (ajogun, etc.). However, in ire, this odu brings big blessing of abundance. Ebo to Ogun to stop the evil machinations of one's enemies. Must avoid anger and walk with iwa pele (the best protection). With ebo and change in behavior, the hard times end and the ire of wealth and abundance flows.

Okunkun gbe adie mi t'ori t'ori
D'Ifa fun Olode
Nwon ni oko ni no o nlo yi
Nwon ni rio yi aya kanfe n'ibe
Won ni ki o rubo
Ki o maba ti ara obinrin na ri ibi
O rubo
Riru ebo ni i gbe ni
Airu ki i gb'eeyan
E waa ba ni ni ire gbogbo
Ase

Darkness swallows the chicken's Ori completely
Was the awo who divined for hunter (ode)
They said he would be going to the farm
And he would find a wife there
He was told to do ebo
So that the woman would not bring him evil
He complied
It is doing ebo that brings blessings
Neglect of ebo pays no one
Come and join us where there is plenty of ire
ase

OSE IRETE – Abundance provides renewed determination to reach our goals. This person is going to receive the blessing of abundance, but must reciprocate with generosity in order to keep it. It's a good time for this person to start anything. Offering of kola and pounded yams to Ifa and Ori for blessings. Speaks of business success due to one's business partner. Oshun for health and abundance. Ifa initiation for ire.

Eni to jin si koto
Lo ko ara yooku logbon
D'Ifa fun Ose
Ti yoo bi Irete sile Aje
Ebo ni won no ko waa se
O gbebo, o rubo
Ibi owo yin e ti mi si
Ibi ire n'Ifa ngbe mii lo o
Ifa ngbe mi relu Ilaje
Ibi ire
L'Erigi-Alo n gbe mi ire
Ibi ire
Ifa ngbe mi ilaya
Ibi ire

THE HOLY ODU

L'Erigi-Alo n gbe mi ire
Ibi ire
Ifa n gbe mi I ilomo
L'Erigi-Alo n gbe mi ire
Ibi ire
Ifa n gbe mi relu inire gbogbo
Ibi ire
L'Erigi-Alo n gbe mi ire
Ibi ire
Ase

He who falls into a ditch
Will serve as a lesson for others
These were Ifa's words to Ose
Who would throw Irete into the house of wealth (Ile Aje)
He was told to do ebo
He complied
Push me to wherever you wish
Ifa carries me to a good place only
Erigi-Alo, Ifa is carrying me to the town of wealth
The location of Ire
Ifa is carrying me to the town of good spouse
The location of Ire
Erigi-Alo, Ifa is carrying me to the town of wealth
The location of Ire
Ifa is carrying me to the town of good children
The location of Ire
Erigi-Alo, Ifa is carrying me to the town of wealth
The location of Ire
Ifa is carrying me to the town of all Ire
The location of Ire
Erigi-Alo, Ifa is carrying me to the town of wealth
The location of Ire
Ase

IRETE OFUN - determination and perseverance result in our prayers being answered. This odu speaks alot of and to women. If a woman, should marry a babalawo. This person must treat their mother very well and do ebo to her Ori. Must treat people well; it is through this person's social network that they will have success. Watch who you have around you and treat them well. Ebo to Ifa and Oshun for long life. Ebo to Ori for success.

Atefun-tefun
Difa fun Okanlenirino Irunmole
Won nlo sode Apere
Atefun-tefun eyin oni
Awo Ori lo difa fun Ori
Ori nlo sode Apere
Won ni ki won sakaale, ebo ni sise
Ori nikan-nikan ni nbe, leyin ti nsebo
Ebo Ori waa da ladaju
Nje Ori gbona j'Orisa
Ori ma gbona j'Orisa
Ori nikan-nikan lo ko won l'Apeere
Ase

He who prints with efun on the back of Crocodile (Oshun)
Was the one who cast Ifa for the 401 Irunmole
When going to Apere (a place of perfection)
He who prints with efun on the back of Crocodile
Was the Awo who cast Ifa for Ori
When Ori was going to Apere
They were told to do ebo
Only Ori complied
Ori's ebo has been abundantly rewarded
Ori is the greatest of all dieties

It is only Ori who reaches Apere, the state of perfection
No other diety can support this voyage
Outside of Ori
Ori is higher than all the other dieties
Ase

OFUN IRETE - manifestation of prayers brings renewed determination. This odu calls for continual spiritual growth as the path to ire. The client needs to bring balance to his/her Ori. It is alignment and balance of Ori that brings peace of mind and prosperity allowing for the person to grow spiritually. This person needs to be willing to ask for help. Must not be greedy. be humble enough to consider all advice, and do not show off. Ebo to Ifa and Ori for success and Esu for long life. Ebo to Aje for money. Ebo to Iyami to protect one's children from illness.

Aje nii mu nii kole
Aya ni mu ntun le se
Oosa nii je ni l'eburu
Oosa to je ni l'eburu
Lo fun'ni laremo pe rannse
Osumare-Ego onile legbee Orun
Bo ba le
Won a l-Osumare lo jaare Ego
Ifa o to gege
Koo dara fun mi o
Ara to wu Oosanla nii fi sese-efun da
Ifa o to gege koo dara fun mi o
Ara to wu Ifa nii fii Otutu-Opon da
Ifa o to gege koo dara fun mi o
Ara to wu Esu niifi Eree da
Ifa o to gege koo dara fun mi o
Ara to wu Sango nii fe kele da

Ifa o to gege koo dara fun mi o
Ko nii degbo o ailu
Iro omo Olu-igbo
Ko nii degbo ailu
Bojumo ba mo
Inaki a da'lu, a da fon
Bojumo ba mo
Ifa je ki ndalu ki ndafun
Itun lo ni ki won fenu won tun mi se
Ifa lo ni ki won fenu won fa mi mora
Ifa je ko ye mi bii tii ye'yele
Ifa je ki ngbiwa gboo bi Oti
Ifa je ki aye mi o dun rinrin biaye oyin
Apa otun
Apa osi
L'eyele fi nko rere wole
B'Osumare ba gb'owo o la soke
Teru-tomo nii rii
Ifa je kin la ki gbogbo aye o mo mi
Ase

It is wealth which allows one to build a house
It is a spouse that helps one organize the home
It is Orisa Oke (Obatala) who provides opportunities for success
The Orisa who provides opportunities is also the one
who makes it possible for one to have a child to send on errands
Osumare (the rainbow serpent)
who resides closest to Orun
When she appears
People say that she is victorious over rainfall
Ifa, it is high time
You performed wonders in my life
It is wonders that Oosanla (Obatala) performs with sese-efun beads
Ifa, it is hight time

You performed wonders in my life
It is also wondrous that Ifa performs with Otutu-Opon beads
Ifa, it is high time
You performed wonders in my life
It is a befitting wonder that Sango performs with Kele beads
Ifa, it is high time
You performed wonders in my life
It will never be in the forest without beating its drum
Iro (baboon) the child of the Ori of the forest
Will never be in the forest without making a sound
When daylight appears
Iro will regale in splendor
When daylight appears
Ifa, please let me regale in splendor
It is Itun beads which authorize people to help in laundering my image for me
It is Ifa beads that permits people to use their mouths to call to me
Ifa, let my life befit me as it befits the pigeon
Ifa, let me be as popular as Gin
Ifa let my life be as sweet as honey
The right arm
The left arm
Are what the pigeon uses to bring prosperity home
When Osumare shows us prosperity in her appearance
She is seen by both the captive and the free
Ifa, please let me be prosperous for the whole world to know and recognize me
Ase

NOTES:

BOOK OF OSE

OSE OFUN – Abundance brings a manifestation of our prayers. This odu implores us to have faith in Ifa and that all problems have a solution. Speaks of ebo for protection from enemies. Should wear light colored clothes. Ebo to Obatala (might need initiation) for wealth and success. Must be calm and deliberative, humble and kind. Head rogation with white elements for peace of mind. Ebo to Egungun and Esu to end hard times and open the way for ire.

Ose funfun bi Aje
Ofun gbeje gbeje bi ate ileke
D'Ifa fun Isawuru
Ti nse omo Onibu
Igba ti n f'Omi oju s'ogbere ire gbogbo
Ebo ni won ni ko se
O si gbebo nibe o rubo
Ifa ma njeki n rahun aje ki n to l'aje
Ifa ma njeki n rahun ire gbogbo ki n to n'ire gbogbo
Arira oko ope monmon jeki n rahun
Isawuru kii rahun omi
Aira oko ope monmon jeki n rahun
Ase

Ose funfun bi Aje
Ofun gbeje gbeje bi ate ileke

Cast Ifa for Isawuru, the child of water's surface
Also for the water's surface
On the day they were crying for not having wealth
They were told to do ebo
Isawuru did not do the ebo
Water's surface did
Ifa will never let me suffer the lack of money
Arira will not allow me to suffer
Isawuru will be the one crying
Arira will not allow me to suffer
ase

OFUN OSE – Manifestation of prayers brings abundance. This person is probably going through hard times financially, causing much stress. Must do generous ebo to Ifa and their Orisas to end troubles and bring ire. Give more attention to your children. Must change attitude and behavior. Speaks of enemies but warns not to retaliate, but do ebo for protection. Do not be rude to people especially at work. Says to have big dreams. Speaks of illness. Should do blood cleansing.

"Ofunse
awo Aje
adifa fun Aje
o n tiikole orun bo waiye
won ni ebo ni ko ma se
ateewe,ataagba
ere Aje n la sa kiri
Eropo ero ofa
Erifa awo ki, Ifa nse
ase

Ofunse

THE HOLY ODU

The priest of Aje
cast divination for Aje
when she was coming from heaven to earth
she was ask to perform ebo
both the youth and elder
will look after getting wealth
Pilgrims of Opo, pilgrims of Opa
Come and see how Ifa's declarations come to pass
ase

NOTES:

ABOUT THE AUTHOR

Awo Fategbe Fatunmbi Fasola (Stuart "Dino" Soto) is a priest in the Ifa Tradition as well as a writer, teacher, metaphysician, college instructor, and anthropologist. Immersed in the sacred technologies of Africa and the diaspora from childhood, Awo Fategbe brings a world of knowledge and experience to those who have the pleasure of his guidance.

Born in Los Angeles to a father who was a healer and a mother who was a medium in the Puerto Rican manifestation of African Traditional Religion, he spent his early childhood in Guayama, a city on the southern coast of Puerto Rico known as "La Ciudad de los Brujos" or "the city of witchdoctors." As he moved to the United States, his knowledge was expanded by his exploration of comparative theology and other spiritual traditions along with a degree in Anthropology, giving him a well rounded approach.

His calling deepened at the age of 33 and around 2000. He had a spiritual experience that would lead him to become a devotee in traditional Ifa and was initiated in May 2011, five years after receiving his first hand of Ifa. His Oluwo is Baba Falokun Fatunmbi and he is a member of egbe Ifa Sango Ota and connected to the Fasola lineage in Ota, Nigeria

Over the years, Awo Fategbe has written a number of articles on the Ifa Tradition and administrates a fast growing group called the Odu Access Network where Odus in traditional Ifa are discussed and shared. He has written extensively over the years and his writings can be found online under the names Awo Fategbe and Awo Dino. He has been frequently featured on Blog Talk Radio in the show entitled, *Friday Nights with Awo Fategbe* where he delivers a unique blend of Ifa Wisdom and practical advice for beginners and practitioners alike. He currently lives in Los Angeles, California

Made in the USA
Monee, IL
07 July 2021